LOGIC:
ITS USE AND BASIS

H. G. Bohnert

Copyright © 1975 by

H. G. Bohnert

All rights reserved
Printed in the United States of America
ISBN: 0-8191-0265-2

PREFACE

Logic's use is ancient. Its basis is modern. It was in polished use by rhetoricians in Syracusan courts and by Sophists in Athens before any of its rules were more than craft secrets. Early formulations by the Greeks won it a central role in academic training in the middle ages. Yet its basis was examined in detail only after the great systems of symbolic logic arose, near the beginning of the twentieth century, dwarfing preexisting conceptions. The examination of logic's basis, made possible by the great systems, has been rewarded by a series of discoveries and insights of unexpected depth and significance. Understandably, this success has resulted in textbooks of an increasingly advanced character. Undergraduate logic courses increasingly must choose between smaller courses for more specialized students, and texts which teach little modern logic at all.

The present book is designed to lead the undergraduate reader into modern logic, as rapidly and simply as possible, yet without assuming specialized training or interest. Use is stressed over basis. That is, the methods made available by the great systems are stressed over metalinguistic superstructure. Basic metalinguistic concepts emerge and become increasingly clear, however.

Aids are offered in the form of an Answer Section for asterisked questions, and a more detailed table of contents following the Answers Section.

The book has drawn from many sources, not least from texts previously used in the author's undergraduate logic sequence at Michigan State University: the valuable books by W. Quine, G. Massey, P. Suppes, I. Copi, and R. Jeffrey.

The main innovation in presenting truth functional logic, beside a very fast, instructive variation on validity tests (the Loophole Method), and a fresh application of partial evaluation to contract clauses, lies in the order of presentation: familiar deductive patterns first (elimination), followed by truth value analysis as justifying basis.

The system of quantificational logic used is, at the outset, the natural deduction method in the form given it by Quine (<u>Methods of Logic</u>, second edition, 1950), with modifications drawn from Massey, Suppes, and Copi, and a small, new simplification (the crossout test, pp. 202-203). The natural deduction method is later extended, beginning with Chapter XV, to higher order, type-theoretic logic, replacing axiomatic deductive procedures, but otherwise retaining the form given it by Rudolf Carnap (<u>Introduction to Symbolic Logic and Its Applications</u>, English translation 1958), which makes use of a lambda abstraction operator derived from Alonzo Church.

Beside the indebtedness indicated, I am grateful to John Corcoran who first suggested to me the possibility of extending natural deduction to type-theoretic logic.

H.G.B.

East Lansing, Michigan
June 13, 1977

CONTENTS

Chapter   Page

I. <u>Preliminary Considerations</u>.

    1. Inference   1
    2. Deduction and Induction   2
    3. Truth and Falsity   5
    4. Relations Between Truth and Validity
       (of Inference)   7
    Optional Further Reading   12

II. <u>Stepwise Deduction</u>.

    1. Keeping Track   18
    2. Justifying Steps by Rules   22
    3. Reasoning from Suppositions   27
    4. Compounds and Their Logic   34

III. <u>Basing Validity on Meaning</u>.

    1. The Meanings of Connectives as Truth Functions   40
    2. Validity Based on Truth Table Relationships   48
    3. Logical Equivalence   53
    4. Logically Determinate Sentences   59
    Optional Further Reading   66

IV. <u>Using the Logic of Connectives</u>.

    1. Connectives in English Usage   77
    2. Partial Evaluation, Laws, and Contracts   87
    3. Testing Validity by the Loophole Method   92
    4. Simplification   96

V. <u>A Deductive System for Connective Logic</u>.

    1. Deductive Systems   103
    2. Rules of This System   104
    3. Discussion of the Rules   108
    Optional Further Reading   117

CONTENTS (continued)

Chapter		Page
VI.	Predication and Quantification.	
	1. Predication	122
	2. Quantification	127
	3. Quantifying Compounds	132
	4. Diagrams and Classes	
	Optional Further Reading	150
VII.	More Complex Quantification.	
	1. Relational Quantifications	152
	2. Combining Quantifiers and Connectives	154
	3. Syntax for Quantificational Symbolism	157
	Optional Further Reading	162
VIII.	Further Methods.	
	1. New Quantifier Rules: Hypothetical Individuals	166
	2. Quantifier Shifting	178
	3. Fission and Fusion of Quantifiers	183
	4. Prenex Form	187
	Optional Further Reading	190
IX.	Final Safeguards.	
	1. Variable Capture: Kinds of Instances	196
	2. Quantifier Order and Dependencies among Hypothetical Individuals	200
	3. Transitional Steps	209
X.	Theories.	
	1. Deductive Development from Axioms	219
	2. Broadening Deductive Methods	223
	3. Axioms on Relations	228
XI.	Definitions.	
	1. Definitions in Theory Development	233

CONTENTS (continued)

Chapter		Page
XII.	Identity and Number.	
	1. Identity	242
	2. QI Deduction	248
	3. Number	251
XIII.	QI Theories.	
	1. QI Axioms on Relations	256
	2. Order	259
	3. Partial Order	268
XIV.	Functions.	
	1. Functions and Functional Relations	272
	2. QIF Logic	274
	3. Defining Function Symbols	276
	4. The Problem of Partial Functions	279
XV.	Toward Higher Logic.	
	1. Quantifying Predicate Variables	282
	2. Abstraction	289
XVI.	Extensionality.	
	1. Extensions	297
	2. The Theory of Classes	302
XVII.	A System of Higher Logic.	
	1. The System	305
XVIII.	Logic and Set Theory.	
	1. Logic and Mathematics	319
	2. Russell's Paradox	320
	3. Set Theory	324

Answer Section. 331
Index. 380

I

PRELIMINARY CONCEPTIONS

1. _Inference_

The focal concept in logic is inference. A scientist infers from specimens of moon rock to possible volcanic activity. A detective infers from a phrase in an alleged suicide note to possible murder. A dog, seeing his master don galoshes, infers (apparently) that the front door will soon open. As a natural process, it is familiar, important, and not well understood. Logic's concern with inference, however, is not with thoughts, or with causal processes in the brain. Logic's concern is with what distinguishes good inferences from bad. Logic seeks rules to ensure the goodness of inference. And it seeks to understand the basis for their goodness.

For the purposes of logic, it suffices to confine attention to inference as expressed in language. After all, thoughts are typically expressed in sentences; and inferential transitions are indicated by such expressions as "so", "hence", "therefore", etc. Accordingly, an inference may be thought of as a transition from a group of sentences, called _premisses_, A, B, C,... to a sentence, G, called the _conclusion_. Whether a given transition ever occurred can be left aside, since logic must consider all possible inferences. Therefore, an _inference_ may be taken to be simply any pair consisting of (1) a group of premiss sentences, P, and (2) a single conclusion sentence, C.

In citing an inference, the premisses are typically separated by a line from the conclusion, thus:

2. Deduction and Induction

>The alleged suicide note speaks of "Elizabeth"
><u>If Phelps wrote the note, it would speak of "Beth"</u>
>Phelps did not write the note

Instead of writing the sentences out, single letters may be used instead. And it is often convenient to let the separating line slant. Thus, A,B/C will serve as A. However, the line is not meant, as in addition,
$$\frac{B}{C}$$
to suggest that an inference can have only one correct "answer". From the premisses above one could infer "Someone other than Phelps wrote the note" with equal reasonableness.

2. <u>Deduction and Induction</u>

Inferences are divided into two kinds: deductive and inductive. A deductive inference, when good, has a certain relative conclusiveness that inductive inferences typically lack, even when reasonable.

<u>Deduction</u>. Suppose a child is told that all red raspberries are sweet, and that, on finding some red raspberries, he infers that they are sweet. This is a <u>deductive</u> inference.

>All red raspberries are sweet
><u>These are red raspberries</u>
>These are sweet

The inference is conclusive, assuming both premisses true, because what the conclusion says about certain red raspberries is simply part of what the premiss (about <u>all</u> red raspberries) already says. The conclusion does not go beyond the information already in the premisses, but simply makes part of it explicit.

An inference which has this sort of conclusiveness is said to be <u>valid</u>. Equivalently, we can say that the premisses <u>logically imply</u> the conclusion.

2. Deduction and Induction

<u>Induction</u>. Now suppose that a child (with no prior information on berries) infers from his sampling of certain red berries, that all red berries are sweet. This would be a typical <u>inductive</u> inference.

<u>These red berries are sweet</u>
All red berries are sweet

It would not be especially unreasonable, but it could lead to stomach aches. The conclusion clearly says more than the particular premisses do. The general conclusion could be false even though the premisses, about the particular berries, were all true. Despite the lack of conclusiveness of inductions, and occasional stomach aches, we use them. Indeed, only by using them can we get to any generalizations at all, whether about raspberries or viruses.

An old characterization of deductive and inductive inference was that 'Deduction goes from general to particulars' (e.g., from something about <u>all</u> red raspberries to some particular red raspberries). 'Induction goes from particulars to general' (e.g., from what holds for particular red raspberries to all of them). However, although the old characterization fits the examples above, it fails to cover many others. For example, a child might reason from his particular experiences with red berries, only to another particular, namely that a newly spied red berry is sweet, (a particular-to-particular inference!) Such a particular-to-particular inference would also be classed as inductive by modern logicians. Similarly, a general-to-general inference, such as "All red raspberries are sweet" to "All red berries are sweet" would also be inductive. And so would be a general-to-particular inference such as from "All red raspberries are sweet" to "This red berry is sweet". What makes an

2. Deduction and Induction

inference inductive is simply that what the conclusion says is <u>not</u> already fully contained in the premisses. The conclusion of an inductive inference typically contains genuinely new information. It goes beyond the premisses.

For the foregoing reasons, the goodness of inductive inference is a matter of degree — the degree of probability of the 'conclusion' relative to the 'premisses'.

<u>Scientific Inference</u>. A special, very important kind of inference, with both deductive and inductive aspects, involves the use of new, theoretical concepts. When scientists tentatively adopt general laws about intra-nuclear forces, they are not just generalizing from observed facts about observed particulars. But neither are they <u>deducing</u> what was implicit in already established laws. Such inference is inductive in that the (tentative) conclusion is not implicit in what was inferred from. Yet, the type of reasoning that is most prominently used is deductive. The overall method of science, in such complex inference, is called the <u>hypothetico-deductive method</u>. Roughly speaking, this method is to seek a hypothesis (possibly containing new concepts) from which observed puzzling phenomena can be <u>deduced</u>. But the hypothesis itself will not be deduced, or induced (in any now clearly understood) way.

It is with deductive logic that this book will principally be concerned. Not only is deduction a crucial tool in theoretical inductive science, but it is basic to an understanding of inductive logic (what little we know about it.)

3. Truth and Falsity

Truth, as spoken of in logic, is a natural, straightforward concept. A (declarative) sentence is true when in conformity with the facts, otherwise false. "The facts" here does not mean just pieces of information acquired by various humans. It refers to the way things actually are, whether anyone knows or not. When one seeks "the facts of the matter" one seeks more than previously believed information. It is sometimes supposed that to say that a sentence is true means only to say that all available evidence is in its favor. But if a detective, thinking about a suspect's unlikely story, says "Suppose it is true!" he does not mean "Suppose all available evidence is in its favor". He means "Suppose events actually were as the suspect says" (whatever evidence there may be to the contrary). This is precisely logic's usage.

To be sure, each person's own beliefs as to what is true can be guided only by the evidence which is available to him. No one has direct access to "the facts". No one can ever be quite sure that any given sentence is true. Our beliefs are almost all obtained by use of inductive inference at some point. But it is truth that is sought, not just evidence-of-truth.

Evidence and Shades of Gray

Because truth in the logician's sense tends to be confused with available evidence of truth, it is sometimes supposed that there are "shades of gray" between truth and falsity. But the shades belong to the available evidence -- all the way from extremely favorable to extremely against (with a neutral point in between where evidence is either lacking

3. Truth and Falsity

or in conflicting balance). Rational belief should also exhibit degrees. But truth has no degrees. No shades of gray between truth and falsity are called for -- only between certainty of truth and certainty of falsity.

Negation

Logic's treatment of negation is closely tied to its treatment of falsity and truth. Just as there are no middle values between truth and falsity, there are no middle possibilities between a sentence and its negation. The negation of a negative sentence "not A", i.e. "not (not A)" yields A again.

It may help in understanding logic's treatment of negation to consider a differing usage in English. It concerns the double negative which arises from using "not" in connection with a word having "negative" prefix, as in the phrase "not unintelligent". That phrase seems not quite as strong an assessment of intelligence as "intelligent" would be. The reason for this is that the effect of a negative prefix is often stronger than simple logical negation. Supposing intelligence represented on a scale from "high" to "low", we feel a gap between "intelligent" and "unintelligent".

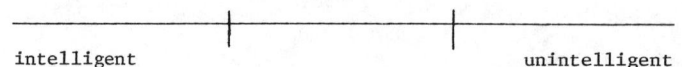

  intelligent   unintelligent

In view of the gap it would be possible to be neither intelligent nor unintelligent. But in the logical sense of "not" it would not be possible to be neither intelligent nor not-intelligent. The meanings of the various phrases may be pictured as shown below.

4. Truth and Validity

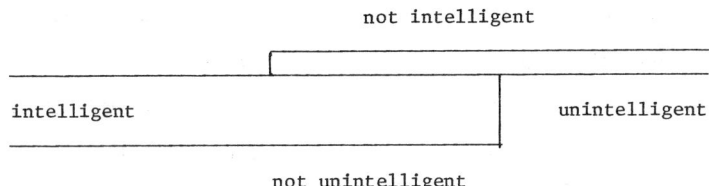

Other usages, different from the one used in logic, arise from understanding negation as lack of proof, as rescindment of a claim, or as opposing force. Other opportunities for confusion are noted in the Optional Further Reading Section at the end of the chapter, for example in the section on Accuracy (and inaccuracy).

4. Relations Between Truth and Validity (of Inference)

Earlier, an inference having a certain relative conclusiveness was said to be valid. That is, a valid inference is one which assures the truth of the conclusion provided all premisses are true. We shall presently see more clearly how an inference can provide such assurance, but we may glimpse some of the value of valid inference, and guard against confusion, by taking note of certain relations between validity and truth.

Confusion threatens right at the beginning since "valid" is sometimes used to mean true (as well as pertinent, relevant, currently in effect officially, genuine, etc.). However, "valid" as applied to inference, does not apply to single sentences, as "true" does, but only to a premiss-conclusion pair, asserting a certain connection between them.[1]

---

[1] Although logicians have traditionally used "valid" as it is used in this book, they have sometimes introduced variations. Sometimes "valid" has been used to apply to single sentences, meaning, e.g., deducible from a given theory. Sometimes it has been used to apply to "good" inductive inferences. Neither of these variations are used in this book.

4. Truth and Validity

It may help to remember this if we represent the situation $P \Rightarrow C$, which may be read "P logically implies C", or "The inference P/C is valid".

Not only is validity not the same thing as truth, but validity alone does not assure the truth of an inference's conclusion. It does so only on the proviso that all premisses are true. Thus, to make an <u>argument</u> one must assert not only the validity of the inference but also the (truth of the) premisses. In other words, when someone says A and B <u>therefore</u> C, he means A and B <u>and</u> A,B $\Rightarrow$ C. To attack an argument one may attack the truth of any premiss, or one may attack the validity of the inference, whether the truth of any premiss is questioned or not.

We see that validity is not the same thing as truth, and does not, of itself, assure truth in a conclusion. Nevertheless, there is a significant connection between validity and truth. It may best be seen by comparing a valid to an invalid inference, which establishes no connection at all between premisses and conclusion. Premisses and conclusion of an invalid inference may exhibit any combination of truth and falsity. But a valid inference rules one combination out, as pictured in the diagram.

Possible combinations of truth (T) and falsity (F) for premisses (P), taken together, and conclusion (C).

<u>Invalid</u>			<u>Valid</u>	
<u>P</u>	<u>C</u>		<u>P</u>	<u>C</u>
T	T		T	T
F	T		F	T
T	F			
F	F		F	F

4. Truth and Validity

By ruling out the TF combination, valid inference leaves only the TT combination, when premisses are true. It thereby assures the truth of the conclusion when premisses are true. Similarly, valid inference leaves only the FF combination when the conclusion is false. This means that if someone validly infers a false conclusion, he can be sure that not all his premisses are true. Thus a child who finds red berries which are not sweet (nightshade for example) he can be sure that it is false that all red berries are sweet. The reasoning is as follows.

FF combination for valid inference

All red berries are sweet
These berries are red
These berries are sweet

This inference is valid. The conclusion is found to be false. So not all premisses can be true. But the second premiss is true. So it is the first premiss that is at fault.

Looking over the two columns of combinations, one can further see that validly inferring a true conclusion does not prove all premisses to be true, since the FT combination is not ruled out by valid, any more than invalid, inference. One can validly infer a true conclusion from false (not all true) premisses, as in the following example.

FT combination for valid inference

Raspberries are made of sugar
Things made of sugar are sweet
Raspberries are sweet

Valid inference is not fully characterized by the truth combinations it allows. We should not, for example, suppose that merely because TT appears in the column of valid inference that the truth of both premisses and conclusion shows the inference to be valid. TT also occurs in the

4. Truth and Validity

invalid inference column. Consider the following two examples.

<u>TT combination for invalid inference</u>

Some red berries are poisonous
<u>Some red berries are not raspberries</u>
Some raspberries are not poisonous

<u>TF combination for invalid inference</u>

Some red berries are poisonous
<u>Some red berries are not nightshade berries</u>
Some nightshade berries are not poisonous

In the first example, premisses and conclusion are all true. Yet the inference is invalid, as can be appreciated by study of the second example, in which the conclusion is false despite the truth of both premisses, and which differs from the first only in referring to nightshade berries where the first refers to raspberries. (The invalidity of the first inference might be informally conveyed by "You might as well say" followed by the second inference.)

EXERCISES I 1

In the exercises, some of the examples (marked by asterisks) are for self-testing. After giving your own answers, they may be checked against answers provided in the Answers Section at the end of the book. If they do not check, reread the pertinent part(s) of the text mentioned there.

1. Mark T or F.

   *a. Logic is based on the psychology of human thought.

   *b. Any deductive inference whose premisses and conclusions are all true is valid.

   *c. A deductive inference can not be said to be true or false but only valid or invalid.

   *d. A deductive inference whose conclusion is false and whose premisses are all true may nevertheless be valid.

   *e. Logic overlooks shades of gray between true and false, and so, strictly, should be replaced by probability theory.

   *f. According to logic, a sentence for which there is no known evidence for or against is neither true nor false.

   g. If a premiss adopted, just for sake of argument has, by itself, a valid conclusion, and the premiss happens to be true, its conclusion has to be true also.

   h. An inference can not be valid unless its premisses are true.

   i. If an inductive inference leads to a sentence which proves to be false, the inference is thereby proved to have been unreasonable.

   j. If a deductive inference leads to a sentence which proves to be false, the inference is thereby proved to have been invalid.

   k. From false premisses only false conclusions can validly follow.

   l. A set of premisses can have only one valid conclusion.

OPTIONAL FURTHER READING

Complete Sentences and Relative Truth

Strictly speaking, when logic takes the truth of a sentence to be its conformity to fact, and rules out shades of gray between truth and falsity, it is tacitly assuming that the sentence is a complete sentence -- a sentence which does not depend on circumstances of utterance for an understanding of what it would mean for the sentence to be true. The sentence "It is ill" would not **qualify**. It would communicate well enough in various circumstances, e.g., in the presence of an inert dog. But it would communicate different things in different circumstances. And if found by itself on a scrap of paper it would hardly communicate at all. It would be meaningless to say it was true, or false. In practice, of course, logic is applied to context-dependent sentences, but with the understanding that they are dealt with as representatives of longer, complete sentences that could be produced if necessary. After all, it is only natural to depend as much as possible on circumstances to convey meanings, so that sentences can be brief and take no more effort than necessary to read or write. The complete sentence corresponding to "It is ill", said in the presence of an inert dog, might be something like "The Airedale at 22 Bingham Place, Larchmont, N.Y., is ill on the evening of April 21, 1895".

Because understood specifications are commonly omitted, truth is sometimes said to be <u>relative</u> in various ways. It is not unreasonable, indeed, to speak informally of a certain sentence being true at one time or under one set of circumstances and false at another time or another set of circumstances. But complete sentences, as assumed in logic, specify time and circumstances, as needed, so that their truth or falsity are not relative (to time or anything else).

Vagueness and Ambiguity

Sentences may vary in degrees of vagueness and ambiguity so that it may be hard to say whether it is true or false, no matter how much is known about the facts. In the case of such a sentence, logic need not suppose it to be "vaguely true", or have an intermediate degree of truth, or to be neither true nor false. Instead, logic need merely assume that in any one of its possible senses it is either true or false (though its meaning may be doubtful). There are times, to be sure, when a sentence seems to be true in many or most of its possible meanings and we are inclined to say "That is largely true" or "There is a lot of truth in that". Such usages are harmless, and sometimes convenient, if we understand what we are doing and do not suppose that a sentence in any one clear meaning is other than simply true or false. With the assumption that a sentence in any one clear meaning is either true or false, the application of logic can often be used to clarify meanings. Indeed, everyone makes use of this fact in reading an obscure book. At first one may be very puzzled, but as one reads further one finds oneself thinking "He can't mean this word to mean so-and-so because if it did, this sentence would imply the falsity of what he said in the preceding paragraph". And by repeated parings away of possible meanings one may converge on meanings that make the whole more intelligible than at first appeared. Indeed, one refines vague ideas in one's own thinking, by a not dissimilar process.

I 14
Accuracy, Truth

Accuracy and Truth

A sentence can have <u>degrees of accuracy</u> in various senses without implying degrees of truth. For example, suppose a certain distance is in fact 1.11 miles, and sentences A-E give its mileage as

A	B	C	D	E
1	1.1	Between 1 and 1.2	Between 1.1 and 1.13	Over 1

B might be said to be more accurate than A, but both are false.

D might be said to be more precise than C. Both are true, but D is not more <u>true</u> than C, nor more true than E, which is also true.

Each of A, B, C, D, E might be thought the most valuable information under varying conditions, depending on needs. But such variations are not variations in truth.

Evidence and Belief

The Weight of Evidence and Rational Belief

As was earlier explained, logic's assumption that a complete, declarative statement is true or false, without shades of gray between, does not mean that each sentence should be either believed or disbelieved without shades of gray between. Belief is guided by reason, and reason is necessarily inductive as well as deductive. The force of an inductive inference from P to C is a matter of degree. Instead of speaking of P/C as deductively valid (or not), we might represent its inductive force on a scale, say, from 0 to 1, with .5 as a neutral midpoint. Like deductive inference, the force of inductive inference is independent of the truth of P. But its value needs truth.

Since a person can never be sure that any given P is true, except possibly his own direct experiences, a rational person must build up his beliefs tentatively, with many reevaluations. At any given moment we may picture a certain core body of beliefs (represented as sentences) as constituting the _evidence_, E, tentatively accepted by a given person at a certain time. All other sentences could be given an inductive probability relative to E. In these terms, a rule of rational belief might be expressed:

> One's degree of belief in a sentence, S, ought, rationally, to be no more or less than the degree of probability of S relative to one's evidence at a given time.

Or, in terms of the popular metaphor "weight of evidence", it could be expressed:

> One ought, rationally, to believe a sentence in proportion to one's weight of evidence for it.

Such a prudent policy of belief is in no way at odds with logic's two-valued treatment of truth and falsity.

I 16
Evidence and Belief

Suppose that degree of belief and weight of evidence both vary from 0 to 1, with a neutral point at .5. Then relations between belief and evidence could be indicated on a square diagram, below at left. For example, an extreme black-or-white policy, such as logic is sometimes supposed to foster, is shown on the right.

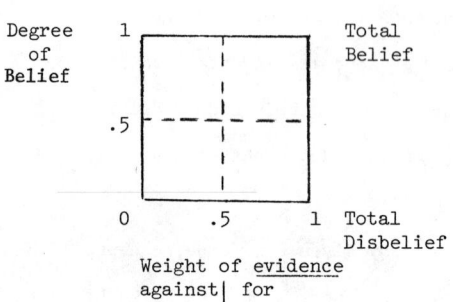
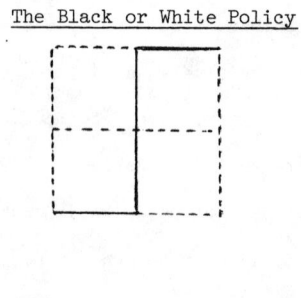

The black-or-white policy shows a sharp jump from total disbelief, (0), to total belief, (1), in a sentence, the moment the weight of evidence tips in its favor. Such an extreme policy is probably followed by no one, certainly not by logicians. But something like it is exhibited by people who "jump to conclusions", and believe something more than evidence warrants (or disbelieves more than is warranted by evidence against). And, of course, by contrast, we find over-cautious people who remain more neutral than their evidence warrants, believing only when evidence is overwhelmingly strong:

The Opinionated
Conclusion Jumper

The Skeptical
Fence-Sitter

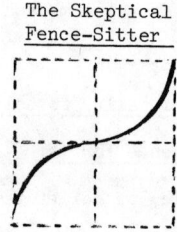

I 17
Evidence and Belief

All three of the foregoing policies are marginally rational in the sense that belief agrees with evidence at least in <u>direction</u>. Some people seem perversely attracted to beliefs precisely because evidence is against them; while for others belief may bear no relation to evidence at all. But the greatest rationality, according to the rule mentioned, is to have belief varying exactly in proportion to evidence:

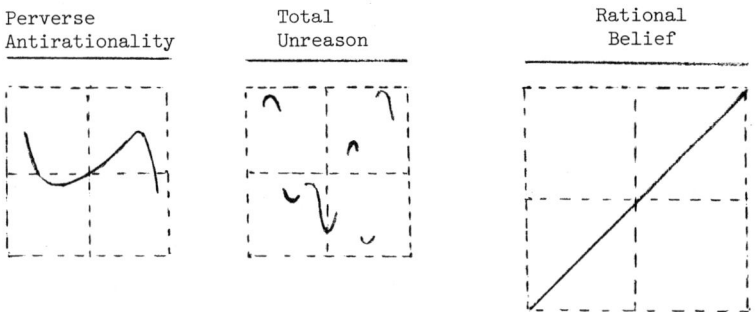

The purpose of these somewhat imprecise remarks, concluding this Preliminary Conceptions chapter, is simply to guard against any reader supposing that logic is overly dogmatic, or, at the other extreme, that logic offers a special road to certainty about matters of fact.

II
STEPWISE DEDUCTION

1. <u>Keeping Track</u>

Inferences and their validity often seem immediate, especially one's own. But others require steps. Sometimes the steps are perfectly straightforward, at other times complex. To make perfectly clear that an inference, A,B,C /G, is valid (or that A,B,C logically imply G, as we shall also say) one may seek to interpose other sentences, step by step, in such a way that the validity of each is obvious from the foregoing, with the conclusion, G, being reached as the last, equally obvious step.

When the step relationships become at all complex, it is helpful to have a method of record-keeping to keep track of where each step comes from. For example, suppose you want to convince someone that three premisses, A, B, and C logically imply G (i.e., that A,B,C/G is valid, or A,B,C $\Rightarrow$ G). And suppose you convince him that A and B together imply D, that B and D imply E, that A and C imply F, and that E and F imply G. The structure of your reasoning would look something like this:

$$\begin{array}{ccc} A & B & C \\ \downarrow\searrow\swarrow & & \downarrow \\ D & & \\ \searrow\swarrow & \searrow\swarrow & \\ E & F & \\ & \searrow\swarrow & \\ & G & \end{array}$$

The steps can be arranged in an orderly column without loss of information by the following procedure:

1. Stepwise Deduction

(1) Number all sentences successively (premisses, intermediate steps, and conclusion) by writing a <u>line number</u> to the left of each sentence (one sentence per line);

(2) Indicate for each line (other than a premiss) the preceding line(s) it came from by writing their line number(s) to the right of the line. There they will be called the <u>citation numbers</u> of that line.

For the example described above, the result would be as follows:

Line Numbers	Sentences	Citation Numbers
1	A	(Premiss)
2	B	(Premiss)
3	C	(Premiss)
4	D	1,2
5	E	2,4
6	F	1,3
7	G	5,6

This columnar method has obvious advantages when the sentences are written out and the step structures are more complicated.

An additional aid to "bookkeeping" during a stepwise inference (illustrated below), is to keep a record of exactly which of the original premisses a given step ultimately stems from. This is done by listing the (line numbers of the) premisses from which the "current" line stems to the left of the current number. Such numbers are the <u>premiss numbers</u> of that line. The premiss numbers can be kept in a separate <u>premiss number column</u>, separated from the line numbers by a vertical line. The column can be conveniently started by copying the line number of each premiss into the premiss number column (i.e., as its own premiss number). Then the original premisses of later lines can be obtained simply by merging the premiss numbers of the preceding lines from which the current

1. Stepwise Deduction

line is immediately obtained (as given in the citation of the current line). In other words, the premiss numbers of later lines are simply "inherited" from the lines they directly come from. With premiss numbers added our example would appear as follows:

Premiss Nos.	Line Numbers	Sentences	Citation Nos.
1	1	A	P (for Premiss)
2	2	B	P
3	3	C	P
1,2	4	D	1,2
1,2	5	E	2,4
1,3	6	F	1,3
1,2,3	7	G	5,6

Keeping track of the premiss numbers will have several uses. One of them may be suggested by imagining that your friend agrees with your reasoning but points out a reason to doubt the truth of your premiss C, as stated, but that he might accept some modification of it. From your record of premiss numbers you will easily see what parts of your argument will not need to be revised. For example, your steps 4 and 5 will be unaffected by any change you make in C. Neither one depends on C, as you can see from the fact that 3, the line number of C, does not appear among the premiss numbers of either line 4 or line 5. Only modifications of F will need to be considered. (This general method of bookkeeping can also be of use when inductive steps also occur, as in preparing and defending a complicated legal brief. But caution is necessary. Altering an inductive "premiss" may have "side effects" on points apparently resting only on other premisses.)

We shall take up specific rules and concrete examples in a moment. But the simple bookkeeping technique just described can be practiced immediately on the following abstract exercises.

EXERCISES II **1**

Suppose each of the diagrams below represents the structure of a stepwise inference. The premisses are numbered in the top line. The conclusion is numbered at the bottom. Construct the corresponding columns of premiss numbers, line numbers, and citations. (Suggestion: Begin by writing the line numbers in order, labelling the premisses P in the citation column and copying their line numbers into the premiss number column.)

*<u>1</u>. 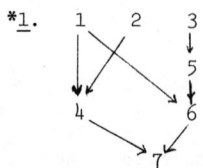   *<u>2</u>.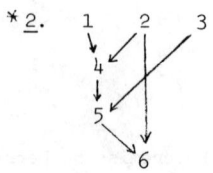

<u>3</u>. 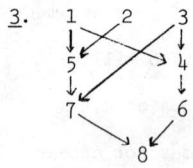   <u>4</u>.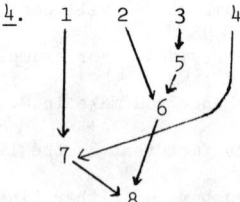

2. Justifying Steps by Rules

Breaking down an inference into more obvious steps (inserted between premisses and conclusion) can be made more convincing if a set of rules can be agreed upon as valid. Every step can then cite not only previous lines but also the rule used.

In this chapter a number of rules will be pointed out which have long been recognized as valid. Other rules will be needed, but these will provide initial practice with the stepwise method.

<u>Elimination</u>. One of the oldest and most familiar steps is that of eliminating one of a set of alternatives, when that one has been found false. A simple example would be:

    Adams, Beeman, or Clark stole the brooch
    <u>Adams did not steal it</u>
    Beeman or Clark stole it

For convenience, we will symbolize "not" and "or" as follows:

    $A \vee B$ (Either) A or B

    $\sim A$ It is not the case that A (or simply not A)

The above inference in symbols, and with citation of the rule added:

```
  1  | 1    A v B v C        P
  2  | 2    ~ A              P
 1,2 | 3    B v C            1,2 Elim
```

<u>Modus Ponens</u>. Another basic step is one which is made from an if-then sentence when the if-part is found to be true. Example:

    If the Ackroyd test proves positive, Burns is cured
    <u>The Ackroyd test proves positive</u>
    Burns is cured

2. Rules

Our symbol for if-then will be:

    $A \supset B$ If A then B

The above inference in symbols:

```
1    | 1   A ⊃ B      P
2    | 2   A          P
1,2  | 3   B          1,2 MP
```

The phrase "modus ponens" (abbreviated MP in the citation of line 3) is shortened from the longer Latin, "modus ponendo ponens", which meant "the method of establishing the <u>consequent</u> (or second part) by establishing the <u>antecedent</u> (or first [if] part)". The inference is so obvious that it has not even acquired an English name, but is still referred to, in most logic texts, by the Latin. Though obvious, it can, like all inferences, carry important weight. It may help proper assessment of these simple rules to give a slightly more extended example of this one, in use. Suppose a high government official is being shown through a top secret military installation by the commanding officer and is left alone by his guide for a few moments. The officer returns and continues the tour by saying "Now this red button, if pushed, launches all siloed missiles toward their current contingency targets". The visitor, suddenly pale, says "I just pushed it". A moment before, the two men had each been in possession of separate pieces of information. The visitor, hearing the officer's information, "puts one and one together" and gives the officer his own information. Neither man needs to mention what both have then inferred.

<u>Modus Tollens</u>. A related step is used when the consequent of an if-sentence is found to be false. Example:

```
If Arndt crossed the fen, his boots are muddy    1   | 1   A ⊃ B     P
Arndt's boots are not muddy                      2   | 2   ∼B        P
Arndt did not cross the fen                      1,2 | 3   ∼A        1,2 MT
```

2. Rules

"Modus Tollens" is a shortening of "modus tollendo tollens" which meant "the method of destroying the antecedent by destroying the consequent ".

In symbolizing the preceding kinds of steps, the letters, A,B,C, etc., stand for <u>any</u> sentences. In particular, they may stand for sentences which themselves contain <u>not</u>, <u>or</u>, <u>if</u> (or, if symbolized, $\sim$, v, $\supset$). Thus, examples of elimination steps could be:

```
1|1   A v (~B ⊃ C)     P                1|1   ~A v ~B      P
2|2   ~(~B ⊃ C)        P                2|2   ~ ~B         P
1,2|3  A              1,2 Elim          1,2|3  ~A          1,2 Elim
```

Both examples are of the form
```
1|1   A v B      P
2|2   ~B         P
1,2|3  A         1,2 Elim
```

In the first example, the B in the form stands for $(\sim B \supset C)$. In the second example, the B in the form stands for $\sim B$ and the A in the form stands for the $\sim A$.

<u>Double Negation</u>. As remarked in Chapter I, not (not A) is understood as logically equivalent with A. We will adopt the general rule that all or any part of a sentence may be replaced by something logically equivalent to it. "N" will be used as a citation of the double negation rule. The following would be examples of permissible double negation steps:

```
|8   ~ ~A           |6   A                |3   A ⊃ ~B
|9   A      8N      |7   ~ ~A    6N       |4   ~ ~A ⊃ ~B    3N
```

For convenience, we will often shorten a stepwise deduction by combining a double negation step with another, adding "(N)" to the citation of the combined step. For example, the inference $\dfrac{A \supset \sim B}{\sim A}$ is valid for much the same reason as Modus Tollens. But is is not strictly of the Modus Tollens form, which requires a premiss to be the negation of the consequent of the if-sentence. To

2. Rules

obtain the proper MT form, one would have to insert a double negation step:

```
1 |1   A ⊃ ~B       P
2 |2   B            P
2 |3   ~ ~B         2N
1,2|4  ~A           1,3 MT
```

Combining the N step with the MT step, as suggested, we would merely write

```
1 |1   A ⊃ ~B       P
2 |2   B            P
1,2|3  ~A           1,2 MT(N)
```

Other inferences may be shortened by combining N steps with others, for example:

<u>Shortened</u>

```
1 |1   A v ~B       P           1 |1   A v ~B      P
2 |2   B            P           2 |2   B           P
2 |3   ~ ~B         2N          1,2|3  A           1,2 Elim (N)
1,2|4  A            1,3 Elim
```

EXERCISES II 2

The following exercises applying the foregoing rules to construct simple stepwise deductions are all asterisked, so that answers may be found in the answers section. But seek as little help as you can. Symbolizations are given for each inference. Study carefully the relation between the English and its symbolizations. The capitals used as memory aids are indicated by underlines in the English.

*1. If Ankara does not agree, Boyd will bow out
Either the embargo does not continue or Ankara will not agree
The embargo will continue
Boyd will bow out

$$\sim A \supset B$$
$$\sim C \ v \sim A$$
$$\underline{C}$$
$$B$$

*2. Either Alf was involved or Bill is not levelling or Cook is covering up
Cook is not covering up
Bill is levelling
Alf was involved

$$A \ v \sim B \ v \ C$$
$$\sim C$$
$$\underline{B}$$
$$A$$

*3. If Brooks were blackballed, then Art would not join
If Cowles attended then Digby would not complain
If Brooks were not blackballed, then Cowles would attend
Art joined
Digby did not complain

$$B \supset \sim A$$
$$C \supset \sim D$$
$$\sim B \supset C$$
$$\underline{A}$$
$$\sim D$$

3. Suppositions

3. Reasoning From Suppositions

It is when we are confronted with a set of alternatives that we become most aware of making inferences. Conscious deliberation is typically called for. It is then that we are most typically prompted to hypothetical reasoning. In seeking a lead as to which of a set of alternatives, A v B v C v ... is the right course of action, the right explanation, the right fact, etc., the most natural procedure is to suppose a particular one to be true and see what can be inferred. It may lead to something that will allow us to rule out that alternative by elimination. Even if it does not, the situation is usually clarified to some extent. If we had supposed A and had inferred G, we could "store" the result by writing "If A then G", and proceed to suppose B, the next alternative, and so on. For example, imagine that a student is faced with a choice, for the coming term, between a certain course in chemistry, in history, in economics, or in art. He begins: "Suppose I take chemistry", and infers, on that supposition and other things he has heard, that he will be spending long hours in the laboratory. He could store this result by writing "Chem $\supset$ long hours" (as we may abbreviate it). Dropping the first supposition, he makes another: that he takes history, and infers he will be bored (History $\supset$ bored). The supposition that he takes economics, leads to the conclusion that he is forced to miss chorus practice. He is already committed to the chorus. So that alternative is eliminated.

We need not continue. The process is familiar. It occurs in both deductive and inductive reasoning. It is used in matters of decision and in matters of fact. For purposes of stepwise deduction, we can embody it in specific rules for suppositional reasoning.

3. Suppositions

Supposing that we are writing a deduction from a group of premisses, P, to a conclusion C, we can lay down the following rules:

<u>The Rule of Supposition</u> (S). Any sentence (supposition) may be written at any line, receiving its line number, in order. Its citation will contain no line numbers of earlier lines, but only the letter "S" (just as premiss receives a "P"). Like a premiss, its premiss number is simply a copy of its line number. For later lines the supposition will be treated exactly as if it were an additional premiss, <u>except</u> that the conclusion can not have any supposition's line number among its (the conclusion's) premiss numbers. (Otherwise, the conclusion would only be shown to follow from the premisses <u>together with the supposition</u>, not from the premisses alone.)

For the conclusion to be arrived at without the supposition being listed among its premiss numbers, we add two rules. (Both rules have been informally illustrated in our example of choosing courses.)

<u>Discharging a Supposition as Qualification</u> (SQ). If a certain sentence B has been inferred with the help of a supposition A (i.e., so that A's line number is among B's premiss numbers), then the result can be "stored", by writing, as a new line: $A \supset B$. In other words, supposition A is written as an explicit <u>qualification</u> of B (<u>If</u> A, then B). The citation of the new line will consist of two citation numbers, first for the supposition A, then for the provisional result, B, and the letter "SQ" (for <u>supposition discharged as qualification</u>). Furthermore, the premiss number of the supposition is omitted from the premiss numbers of the new line (or <u>discharged</u> as we shall say).

3. Suppositions

Thus, part of one's class-choosing reasoning might be represented as follows.

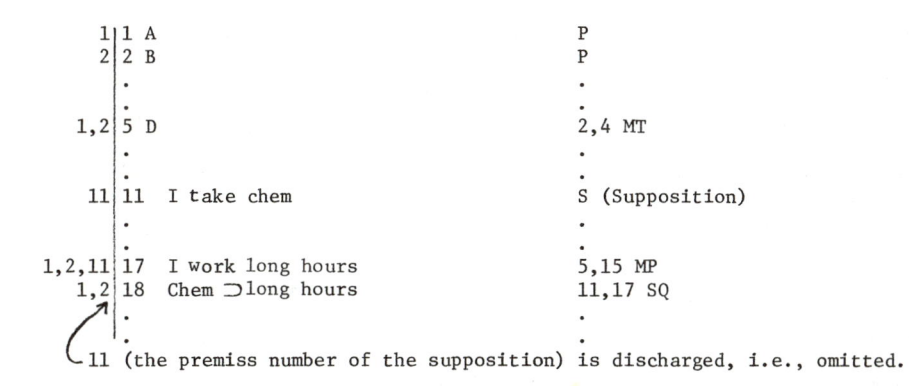

```
  1 |1  A                          P
  2 |2  B                          P
    |   .
    |   .
1,2 |5  D                          2,4 MT
    |   .
    |   .
 11 |11  I take chem               S (Supposition)
    |   .
1,2,11|17  I work long hours       5,15 MP
  1,2 |18  Chem ⊃ long hours       11,17 SQ
  ↗ |   .
  11 (the premiss number of the supposition) is discharged, i.e., omitted.
```

The second way of disposing of a supposition was illustrated in the example of course-choosing, where economics was eliminated because something was inferred from it (missing chorus practice) that collided with something already taken as fixed. The principle is the same as that of a famous strategy called <u>reductio ad absurdum</u> (reduction to absurdity) which was expertly used well before Aristotle. The idea is to "grant for the sake of argument" some sentence and then "reduce it to absurdity" by showing that it logically leads to collision with granted facts, with logic, or even with itself. (The possibility of the maneuver is inherent in the independent force of valid inference even from false premisses, as noted in Chapter I.)

3. Suppositions

The method has many applications. Not only is it a strategy for attacking an opposing view, but it can rule out alternatives in an elimination inference, it can facilitate a modus tollens by yielding the negation of the consequent of an if-sentence (supposed for sake of argument), or it can yield a so-called <u>indirect inference</u> to a conclusion, by supposing the negation of the conclusion and reducing it to absurdity. Once the supposition has served its purpose, it may be <u>discharged</u>. The rule is as follows:

<u>Discharging a Supposition as Absurd</u> (SA). If, by using a supposition A, one infers a line ~B (i.e., A's line number is among the premiss numbers of ~B), while B is among the previous lines (whether as premiss, or inferred with or without A's help), then one may write ~A as a new line.

The <u>citation numbers</u> will be, first, that of A, and then those of the two mutually contradictory lines.

The <u>premiss numbers</u> will be the merged premiss numbers of the two contradictory lines, but with (supposition) A's line number omitted (discharged). The <u>rule abbreviation</u> is SA.

Another part of one's class-choosing reasoning is shown, using SA, as follows:

```
1| 1  P                              P
2| 2  Q                              P
3| 3     I take chorus practice      P
 | .                                 .
 | .                                 .
9| 9     I take econ.                S (Supposition)
 | .                                 .
 | .                                 .
2,3,9| 13   ~(I take chorus practice)   7,11 MP
2,3  | 14   ~(I take econ.)              9,3,13 SA (Supposition eliminated
                                                              as absurd.)
                                         contradictory lines
```

3. Suppositions

As remarked, the absurdity strategy is used also for <u>indirect proof</u>. Here, one supposes the negation of the desired conclusion, and infers until two contradictory lines are obtained. SA then yields the negation of the negation of the desired conclusion. In this case, we will ordinarily omit the negations, and combine a double negation step with SA, writing SA(N).

<u>Dilemmas</u>. Among the ways in which reasoning from suppositions helps, when faced with a set of alternatives, are several inference patterns which are still known technically as <u>dilemma</u> inferences (though everyday usage, speaks more broadly of every confrontation with alternatives as being "in a dilemma"). One sort of dilemma inference is used when more than one alternative leads to the same result.

The Simple Dilemma:

$A \supset B$	If Anne diets she repels boys (by crossness)
$\sim A \supset B$	If Anne does not diet she repels boys (by appearance)
B	Anne repels boys (diet or no)

Here, the or-sentence $A \vee \sim A$ is left implicit. (Recall what was said about truth and negation.)

The Compound Dilemma:

$A \vee B$	I must take art or botany
$A \supset C$	If I take art, I must cut lunch short
$B \supset C$	If I take botany, I must cut lunch short
C	I must cut lunch short

A complex dilemma is called for when each alternative leads to different things, as follows.

3. Suppositions

The Complex Dilemma:

    A v B   I must take art or botany
    A ⊃ C   If I take art, I must cut lunch
    B ⊃ D   If I take botany, I must delay lunch
    C v D   I must cut lunch or delay it

(Note that in the dilemma forms themselves, the if-sentences are simply stated as such. They need not be the result of inferring from suppositions. I.e., A ⊃ C may be simply a premiss, it need not be obtained by inferring C with the help of A.)

The citation abbreviations for the simple, compound, and complex dilemma forms are:

```
   1|1 A ⊃ B          P                     1|1 A v B          P
   2|2 ~A ⊃ B         P                     2|2 A ⊃ C          P
 1,2|3 B              1,2 Dsimp             3|3 B ⊃ C          P
                                        1,2,3|4 C              1,2,3 Dcomp


   1|1 A v B          P
   2|2 A ⊃ C          P
   3|3 B ⊃ D          P
 1,2,3|4 C v D        1,2,3 Dplex
```

EXERCISES II 3

Write out the deductions (stepwise inferences) for the following inferences.

Strategy suggestions:

If the desired conclusion is an if-sentence, suppose the antecedent.

If a premiss is an or-sentence, use elimination, possibly aided by supposing an alternative and showing it absurd, or use a dilemma, possibly aided by supposing some or all of the alternatives, discharging them by qualification.

When in doubt, suppose the negation of the desired conclusion and use absurdity.

The first few provide an English reading, but the basic task is always abstract.

*1. If Argentina refuses, Brazil will refuse $A \supset B$
If Brazil refuses, Colombia will refuse $B \supset C$
If Argentina refuses, Colombia will refuse $A \supset C$

*2. If Alexius held, Bohemund retreated $A \supset B$
Bohemund did not retreat or else Claudius reached Corinth $\sim B \vee C$
If Claudius did not reach Corinth, Alexius did not hold $\sim C \supset \sim A$

*3 If the suspect reaches Alberta, he did not backtrack $A \supset \sim B$
If the suspect reaches Alberta, he did not camp out $A \supset \sim C$
But he did backtrack or camp out $B \vee C$
The suspect does not reach Alberta $\sim A$

4. If Ames knows, then either there has been a break-in or Cain talked $A \supset (B \vee C)$
There has been no break-in $\sim B$
If Ames knows then Cain talked $A \supset C$

5. $A \supset B$, $A \vee C$ / $\sim B \supset C$

6. $A \vee B \vee C$, $\sim B$ / $\sim C \supset A$

7. $A \supset \sim B$, $C \supset A$, $D \vee B \vee \sim E$, $\sim D / C \supset \sim E$

4. Compounds and Their Logic

The rules and examples which have been given so far have all hinged upon such expressions as "not", "either...or", and "if...then...". Such expressions form compound sentences from others. Logicians call them <u>connectives</u>. ("Not" is counted as a connective, though it does not connect sentences; it does form sentences from others — by negating them.) As you may expect, the logic of connectives is only part of logic. But it is a very basic part. It can be developed on its own, whereas other parts must presuppose it. We shall round off this chapter on stepwise deduction with a summary of the notation needed for the logic of connectives, and a mention of a few more rules.

Taking A,B,C,... as any sentences, we shall be concerned principally with compounds formed as follows:

```
∼A          It is not the case that A
(A.B)       (Both) A and B
(A v B)     (Either) A or B
(A ⊃ B)     If A (then) B
```

In previous examples, parentheses have been left off. But parentheses are shown here along with the connectives to avoid ambiguity when compounds are built from compounds. No ambiguity arises when only one connective is used. But ambiguity can arise when compounding goes further.

<u>Ambiguous</u>:

Adams is on duty and Burk is off or Cobb is on   A.B v C

<u>Unambiguous</u>:

Adams is on and either Burk is off or Cobb is on   A.(B v C)
Either Adams is on and Burk is off or else Cobb is on   (A.B) v C

4. Compounds

English has various ways of indicating the grouping intended. It can insert a grouping word like "either"; it can insert a spacer word like "or <u>else</u>"; or it can employ other ways. Logical symbolism uses only parentheses.

However, it is customary to:
(1) omit outermost parentheses, e.g., to write (A.B) v C instead of ((A.B) v C).
(2) omit parentheses that separate members of an or-sentence, e.g., to write A v B v (C.D) instead of ((A v (B v (C.D))). Similarly for conjunction.

Notice that parentheses are not provided for "∼". Those that accompany the other connectives suffice. For example, with previous readings for B and C, then

∼(B v C)   means: It is not the case that either Burk or Cobb is on.
(∼B v C)   means: Either Burk is not on or Cobb is.

Other combinations with "∼":

∼∼B   It is not the case that it is not the case that Burk is on.
           (or It is not so that Burk is not on.) Same as ∼(∼B).

∼B ⊃ C   If Burk is not on, then Cobb is. Same as (∼B ⊃ C).

∼(B ⊃ C)   It is not the case that if Burk is on, then Cobb is.

It is often useful to read the left-hand parenthesis as the corresponding English grouper (both, either, or if). (Even when outermost parentheses have been omitted, as in the next to last example above, the if corresponds to the <u>omitted</u> left parenthesis.)

4. Compounds

So far, we have given examples of four kinds of rules:

(1) Stipulation rules, that require no reference to preceding lines; namely: P and S, for premises and suppositions;

(2) Implication rules, that come from two previous, complete lines, such as elimination, modus ponens, modus tollens, and the dilemmas; (Some single line implication rules are given below.)

(3) Equivalence rules, that come from a single, previous line by replacing all or part of the earlier line by a logical equivalent. Our only example so far has been double negation;

(4) Discharge rules, that yield lines which discharge an earlier supposition: namely, SQ and SA, which discharge the supposition by incorporating it as a qualification, or eliminate is as absurd.

We will not need to add to the first and fourth kind, even when we progress beyond the logic of connectives. We shall find it convenient to add extensively to kinds (2) and (3) presently. But for the present we shall add only three simple rules of kind (2).

<u>Drop</u>. One may infer either member of an and-sentence which makes up an entire preceding line, and Drop the other member. Examples:

```
|  .                    |  .                    |  .
|  .                    |  .                    |  .
| 7 A.B                 | 5 C.D                 | 8 (A ⊃B).(∼B v C)
|  .                    |  .                    |  .
|  .                    |  .                    |  .
|11 A      7 Drop       | 9 D      5 Drop       |12 ∼B v C      8 Drop
```

Example of an incorrect Drop:

```
| 1 (A.B) ⊃ C            If Al and Bob push, the car will move
| 2 A ⊃ C     1Drop      If Al pushes, the car will move
```

Drop is an implication rule, (kind (2)). It can not lead to replacing merely a <u>part</u> of an earlier sentence. (A.B is not logically equivalent to A!)

4. Compounds

Join. One may Join the sentences of previous lines.

Examples:

```
 .                          .
 .                          .
 2 A                        2 A
 .                          .
 .                          .
 5 B                        4 (B v C)
 .                          .
 .                          .
 7 A.B    2,5 Join          8 D
                            9 D.A.(B v C)    2,4,8 Join
```

Add. From any sentence A one may infer an or-sentence of which A is a member. Examples:

```
 7 A            6 A              5 A
 .              .                .
 .              .                .
 12 A v B  7 Add   7 B v A  6 Add   9 (C.D) v A v B   5 Add
```

Add may appear odd as an inferential step — to infer A or B from A. But if A is true then it is surely true that A is true or B is true. A typical use of this move is in an inference like the following:

If the student has taken 321 or has the instructor's
    permission, he may take business law   (H v P) ⊃ B
The student has taken 321   H
The student may take business law   B

The inference is so obvious we do not notice the Add step, but it is needed here for the MP.

```
1  |1  (H v P) ⊃ B      P
2  |2  H                P
2  |3  H v P            2 Add
1,2|4  B                1,3 MP
```

II 38

Overview of Chapter II Rules

(i,j,k..are used as dummy line numbers. Premiss numbers are omitted.
Letters A,B,C, etc., stand for sentences of any complexity.)

Stipulation Rules: Premiss (P), Supposition (S)

Implication Rules:

Elimination (Elim)
i (Any disjunction)
j (Negation of a member)
k (The disjunction without
  the negated member) i,j Elim

Modus Ponens (MP)
i $A \supset B$
j A
k B   i,j MP

Modus Tollens (MT)
i $A \supset B$
j $\sim B$
k $\sim A$ i,j MT

Simple Dilemma
i $A \supset B$
j $\sim A \supset B$
k B   i,j Dsimp

Compound Dilemma
i A v B
j $A \supset C$
k $B \supset C$
l C   i,j,k Dcomp

Complex Dilemma
i A v B
j $A \supset C$
k $B \supset D$
l C v D   i,j,k Dplex

Drop (a conjunct)
i (Any conunction)
j (Any member)   i Drop

Join
i A
j B
k C
.
.
m (conjunction of any   i,j...Join
  preceding lines in any order)

Add (a disjunct)
i A
j (Any disjunction of which
  A is a member)   i Add

Equivalence Rules: Double negation (N): A, $\sim\sim$A mutually replaceable.

Discharge Rules:

Qualification (SQ)
A   S
.
.
.
B
─────
$A \supset B$ SQ

Absurdity (SA)
B
A   S
.
.
.
$\sim B$
─────
$\sim A$ SA

The rules above have been used for centuries, simply on the basis of their felt validity. In the next chapter we shall see how their validity can be given a more explicit basis. But skill at applying the rules still rests on a natural feel for their validity. This chapter has simply pointed to these new forms as valid, for the reader to "feel".

Exercises II 4

Provide stepwise deduction for the valid inferences shown:

*1. (B v C) ⊃ A
    B   /A

2. A.B
    B ⊃ C   /C

3. A.~C
    B ⊃ C   /~B

*4. A.B
    ~C
    (~C.A) ⊃ D   /D

*5. A ⊃ (B.C)
    C ⊃ D   /A ⊃ D

6. A ⊃ B
    (B.C) ⊃ D
    A ⊃ C
    ~E.A   /D

7. (A.B) ⊃ (C.D)
    E ⊃ (A.G)
    E ⊃ (H.B)
    (J v D) ⊃ K   /E ⊃ K

8. A v (B.C)
    A ⊃ D
    ~D
    (E v B) ⊃ (G.~H)   /~H

III

BASING VALIDITY ON MEANING

1. The Meanings of Connectives as Truth Functions.

Although the rules of the preceding chapter have long been accepted as "standing to reason", it was not until this century that the basis of their validity was analyzed more deeply. This analysis suggested that the meaning of the connectives lay in their relationship to truth and falsity. More exactly, the meaning of each connective seemed to consist in the way it determined the truth value (truth or falsity) of a compound formed by that connective as a function of (i.e., depending upon) the truth value of the component sentences. For example, if A were true and B were false, then A and B would be false, but A or B would be true, and so would A and not B. The different truth values of the compounds results from the meanings of "and", "or", and "not". In fact, it was found that if the meanings of the connectives were taken to consist of nothing more than their truth-value indicating function, the validity of the long established patterns, and many others, was established in a very obvious way. This chapter examines, for each connective in turn, the way in which such truth-functional meanings were assigned, and how this provided a widely useful basis for the logic of connectives.

Negation.

The relations between the concepts of truth, falsity, and negation, already discussed in I, can be displayed by writing the two values, T (for true) F (for false) beneath A, and contrasting them with the corresponding values for $\sim A$.

$$\begin{array}{c|c} A & \sim A \\ T & F \\ F & T \end{array}$$

III 41
1. Meanings of Connectives

The displayed relationship tells all there is to know about the <u>meaning</u> of "not". It is simply a <u>truth value inverter</u>. In forming the negation of a sentence A, one obtains the assertion which is true if A is false (and false if A is true).

<u>Conjunction</u>.

In joining two sentences A, B by <u>and</u>, one obtains a sentence (called the <u>conjunction</u> of A, B) which is true just in case both <u>conjuncts</u>, A and B, are true, and false otherwise. As in the case of negation, the truth-functional relation can be displayed in a truth-table, giving the truth value of the conjunction for each combination of truth-values of the conjuncts.

A B	A.B
T T	T
F T	F
T F	F
F F	F

If a conjunction is formed of sentences which themselves contain truth-functional connectives, the truth-functional rule of conjunction yields a characteristic column for each. Consider the following combinations involving negation:

A B	~A	~B	A.B	~(A.B)	A.~B	~A.B	~A.~B	~(~A.~B)
T T	F	F	T	F	F	F	F	T
F T	T	F	F	T	F	T	F	T
T F	F	T	F	T	T	F	F	T
F F	T	T	F	T	F	F	T	F

Such characteristic columns are easily constructed by applying the rule "true just in case both are true" to the truth-value columns of the conjuncts. E.g., the column for A.~B is found by comparing the A column with the ~B column. Two of the tables shown are not conjunctions, but negations (of conjunctions). Their truth tables must employ the rule of negation rather than conjunction. For example, the last truth table (for ~(~A.~B))

1. Meanings of Connectives

is found by negating (interchanging) the truth values of its neighbor.

Disjunction.

In considering the truth-functional meaning of "or", we are confronted with an ambiguity in its English usage. Originally, "or" was used to express exclusive alternatives (stemming, etymologically, from the same root as "other"). It is often used, however, to assert that at least one of the alternatives is the case, possibly both. For example, a person who said "Alex is a poet or a playwright" would be considered to have told the truth if Alex proved to be both. This inclusive use of "or" is also extended to more than two alternatives, as in: "Prerequisites: Psych 313, or 12 credits in Psychology, or approval of the Department". Obviously, one, two, or all three of the alternatives, would meet the requirement.

For precision in English, one must use an extra phrase:

Exclusive: A or B, but not both

Inclusive: A or B, or both

In logic, we assign a separate symbol to each meaning. Our "v" symbol, earlier specified only as "or", is given the inclusive meaning. The exclusive meaning will be expressed by "$\not\equiv$". Compare the tables below:

A B	A v B	A $\not\equiv$ B
T T	T	F
F T	T	T
T F	T	T
F F	F	F

As in the case of conjunction, the basic tables above express rules which can be used to yield characteristic truth tables for sentences containing other truth-functional connectives.

1. Meanings of Connectives

The rule for inclusive disjunction can be summarized as: False just in case <u>both</u> <u>disjuncts</u> are false (true, otherwise).

Use the rule to check the tables below.

A	B	~A	~B	A v B	~A v B	A v ~B	~A v ~B	~(~A v ~B)
T	T	F	F	T	T	T	F	T
F	T	T	F	T	T	F	T	F
T	F	F	T	T	F	T	T	F
F	F	T	T	F	T	T	T	F

<u>Implication</u>.

"If" has an ambiguity problem even more acute than "or". Not only is it used in two truth-functional ways, but in other ways also. For example, if used with the subjunctive, e.g., If A <u>were</u> so, than B <u>would</u> be. The possibility that A is true and B is false is clearly ruled out, (i.e., an F case), but no combination of truth values, by itself, suffices for its truth. The situation has an analogy in logical implication (A $\Rightarrow$ B) in that although logical implication could not hold in case A were true and B were false, it would not be <u>made</u> true merely by one of the other combinations of truth values. For logical implication, truth would require that the meaning of B be "contained" in the meaning of A, in the informal sense earlier mentioned. But no such meaning containment is involved in the subjunctive if-sentence "If supersonic flights were to exceed five hundred a year, the incidence of skin cancer (from increased ultra-violet radiation) would increase significantly".

A truth-functional meaning can be given to our if-then symbol ("$\supset$"), however, which will make A $\supset$ B true whenever any of the more demanding "ifs" hold true, simply by ruling all cases but that in which A is true and B is false to be T cases. That is, we can take the meaning of "$\supset$" to be the

III 44
1. Meanings of Connectives

truth function whose values, as a function of the truth values of A and B, are shown in the table below:

A	B	A ⊃ B
T	T	T
F	T	T
T	F	F
F	F	T

Because of the relationship with logical implication, all if-sentences are called <u>implications</u>. They are distinguished from one another by various adjectives: <u>logical</u> implication, <u>causal</u> implication, <u>subjunctive</u> implication, etc. The truth-functional meaning above has been distinguished from the others by the not especially appropriate phrase <u>material</u> implication.

> Terminological note: Because of the possibilities of confusion, many logicians (following Quine) have dropped "material implication" for "conditional" and have reserved "implication" for logical implication. But this is hardly an improvement since, although avoiding confusion with logical implication, it invites the misapprehension that the antecedent must be a causal, legal, or other non-truth-functional <u>condition</u> for the truth of the consequent. Furthermore, it prevents convenient comparison of the various implications unless the same system of <u>adjectives</u> is reintroduced for conditionals: subjunctive, causal, logical, material,..., etc. If word-coining were not so despised, one might venture to suggest something like "ification". It would still call for qualifying adjectives, but would be a more neutral generic term for all.

<u>Equivalence.</u>

"If" is often used in English in the stronger sense of "if and only if". For example "If you show your pass, you will be admitted" is ordinarily meant in a sense which could be paraphrased "You will be admitted if and only if you show your pass". As in the "or" ambiguity, logic uses distinct symbols for distinct meanings. We have already introduced "≡" (in II) as a symbol for if and only if, and will use it often to symbolize English "if", where the stronger sense is clearly meant. The truth-functional meaning of "≡"

1. Meanings of Connectives

is displayed in the truth table below.

A B	A ≡ B
T T	T
F T	F
T F	F
F F	T

Terminological note: Remarks exactly paralleling those for implication can be made about equivalence. Those who prefer the "conditional" usage call equivalence <u>biconditionals</u>. Mathematicians (following Halmos) have begun to abbreviate "if and only if" as "iff". Considered as a coined <u>word</u>, "iff" is not distinctive to the ear. Equally short, and more audible would be "fif". A corresponding neutral coinage for equivalence might be "fifalence".

Summary of Truth Rules

In summary, the truth-functional meanings of the connectives we have examined are gathered together below:

Kind	Connective	Compound			Component(s)
Negation	Not (~)	True	just in case		False
Conjunction	And (.)	True	"	"	All true
Disjunction	Or (v)	False	"	"	All false
Implication	If (⊃)	False	"	"	Ant. True, cons. false
Equivalence	Fif (≡)	True	"	"	Match in truth-value
Ex. Disjunct.	Or (≢)	True	"	"	Differ in truth-value

The rules give rise to the "defining" truth value columns below:

A	~A	AB	A.B	A v B	A ⊃ B	A ≡ B	A ≢ B
T	F	TT	T	T	T	T	F
F	T	FT	F	T	T	F	T
		TF	F	T	F	F	T
		FF	F	F	T	T	F

(But the reader must be on guard against supposing that a connective's defining truth value column appears wherever the connective does. For example, with the usual display of truth combinations, the truth column for A v ~B is not <u>A v ~B</u> but <u>A v ~B</u>)

T	T
T	F
T	T
F	T

1. Meanings of Connectives

An even more condensed summary:

Compound	Value	Case
~A	T	F
(A.B)	T	TT
(A v B)	F	FF

Compound	Value	Case(s)
A ⊃ B	F	TF
A ≡ B	T	Match
A ≢ B	T	Differ

Practice in applying the above rules is offered in the following exercise section (III 1), where the rules are to be applied in finding the truth value of given compounds when the value of the basic components is given. The basic values will be given at the left and the compound to be evaluated at the right.

Example with method displayed:

$$\frac{A\ B\ C}{F\ T\ T} \qquad \begin{array}{c} B \supset (A \supset C) \\ T \quad F \quad T \\ T \\ T \end{array}$$

As shown, the components in the compound are first tagged with their values. Then the "inmost" part, A ⊃ C, is evaluated. It is T, since "if" (⊃) yields F only for the TF case for the compounds. Then the value of the whole is found. It is T, since TT is one of the T cases for ⊃.

The initial tagging step may be omitted, if desired, e.g.:

$$\frac{A\ B\ C}{T\ F\ T} \qquad \frac{A\ v\ B}{T} \qquad \begin{array}{c} \sim(B \equiv C) \\ F \\ T \end{array} \qquad \begin{array}{c} (A\ v\ B) \\ T \end{array} \qquad \begin{array}{c} (B . (B \supset C)) \\ T \\ F \\ F \end{array}$$

It is usually an aid to clarity if the value of a compound is placed directly below the main connective of that compound, as shown above.

EXERCISES III 1

1. Evaluate for

   $\dfrac{A\ B}{F\ T}$ a. A v B   b. A ⊃ B   c. B ⊃ A   *d. ~A.B   *e. ~(A.B)

   *f. ~A v ~B   *g. ~(A v B)   *h. ~B ⊃ A   *i. ~(B ⊃ A)

*2. Evaluate for

   $\dfrac{A\ B\ C}{T\ F\ T}$ a. (A.C) ⊃ B   b. (A v B) ⊃ (B ≡ ~C)

   c. (~B v ~C) ⊃ (A.~C)

3. Letting your own knowledge provide the values of the components, evaluate:

   a. New Orleans is in Mississippi or Louisiana.   M v L

   b. If Alaska is a state, so is Bermuda.   A ⊃ B

   c. If Benjamin Franklin was ever U.S. President so was Charlie Chaplin.   B ⊃ C

   d. It is not the case that both Bucharest and Ankara are in Europe.   ~(B.A)

   e. If both Bucharest and Athens are in Greece then Romanian is spoken in Athens.   (B.A) ⊃ R

2. Validity Based on Truth Table Relationships.

The forms of inference discussed in II, and studied explicitly for over two thousand years, may now be seen to be based on truth table relationships.

Recall the elimination form $\dfrac{A \lor B}{\sim A}$ and consider the truth-value columns of the sentences involved.

A B	∼A	A v B / B
T T	F	T T
F T	T	T T
T F	F	T F
F F	T	F F

— cases where conclusion is true.
— case where both premisses are true.

As indicated, the only case in which both premisses are true, is one of the cases in which the conclusion is true. Since the four rows of the truth tables cover all possibilities, the way in which the truth of the premisses guarantees the truth of the conclusion is obvious. It is impossible for the conclusion to be false if both premisses are true, by virtue of the truth-functional meanings of the connectives. There is no possible case in which the conclusion can be false while both premisses are true.

Just as the truth table method establishes the validity and the elimination inference, so it does for the other implication rules of Chapter II, as the reader will have the opportunity to verify in the next exercise section. The method validates many more. By the same token, it can show that other inference forms are not valid. If the conclusion of a given inference can be false while all premisses are true, it is not a valid deductive inference. (It has, so to speak, a loophole.) In short, inferences can be tested for validity by truth table.

2. Validity by Truth-Table

The method of testing is simple:

(1) Display all truth value combinations of the component sentences represented by single letters.

(2) Construct a characteristic truth value column for each of the premisses and also for the conclusion.

(3) Locate the rows in which <u>every</u> premiss has a T (the cases where all are true).

(4) For each such row, check whether the conclusion has a T in that same row. The inference is shown <u>invalid</u> by the first conclusion F encountered, and the checking need go no further.

(5) If the conclusion has a T in all rows in which the premisses <u>all</u> have T, the inference is <u>valid</u>.

<u>Displaying the Basic Truth-Value Combinations</u>.

If there is just one basic letter component, as in $(\sim A \supset A)$ v A, the basic truth combinations are just two:

A
T
F

If there are two basic letter components, as in A v (B $\supset \sim$A), there are four combinations:

A	B
T	T
F	T
T	F
F	F

Three letters as in the compound dilemma give rise to eight possible cases:

A	B	C
T	T	T
F	T	T
T	F	T
F	F	T
T	T	F
F	T	F
T	F	F
F	F	F

It will be seen that adding a new sentence letter always doubles the number of possibilities. With any of the previous combinations the new sentence could be true; or it could be false. In short, if the number of letters involved is n, the number of cases to be displayed will be 2^n.

2. Validity by Truth-Table

Construction of the Characteristic Truth Column of a Sentence.

The principle is already clear. The column of a given sentence is constructed by beginning with "inmost" parts first, as in the case of evaluating a compound for a single case. Except that we now proceed vertically downward, finding the value for each case. Then columns of inner parts may be combined in turn, until the column for the whole compound is obtained. A long, but clear, way is to construct the columns for the subsentences separately, e.g., to find the column for $(A \lor B) \supset \sim(\sim A.B)$ we could proceed as follows:

Display

A B	A v B	~A	~A.B	~(~A.B)	(A v B) ⊃ ~(~A.B)
T T	T	F	F	T	T
F T	T	T	F	T	F
T F	T	F	F	T	T
F F	F	T	F	T	T

A more condensed way is to write the column of each subsentence directly under the main connective of the subsentence. With the same example, the result would appear:

A B	(A v B) ⊃ ~ (~A.B)
T T	T T T F F
F T	T F F T T
T F	T T T F F
F F	F T T T F
	1 5 4 2 3

The numbers under the columns are simply to indicate the order in which they were formed.

Even more condensation is obtained by writing the original display values under the first occurrences of the letters themselves. (Great care is required to remember which column is being compared with which, and in which order.)

2. Validity by Truth-Table

Remember that only as many truth combinations are needed as required by the number of component letters in the inference as a whole. E.g. For the inference $\sim A \lor (A \supset \sim A)$ / $(A \supset A) \supset \sim A$ we need only two:

A	$\sim A \lor (A \supset \sim A)$	/ $(A \supset A) \supset \sim A$	
T	F F F F	T F F	
F	T T T T	T T T	(Valid)

While for $\sim B$, $A \lor B \lor C$ / $\sim A \supset C$, 8 combinations are required, and the column for $\sim B$ must be 8 rows deep:

A B C	$\sim B$	A v B v C	/ $\sim A \supset C$	
T T T	F	T	T	
F T T	F	T	T	
T F T	T	T	T	
F F T	T	T	T	(Valid)
T T F	F	T	T	
F T F	F	T	F	
T F F	T	T	T	
F F F	T	F	F	

In constructing the column for A v B v C above, one needed only to look for the false cases (in which all <u>three</u> components were false). But strictly speaking, since we are regarding each connective as binary (connecting just two sentences), A v B v C could be regarded as (A v (B v C)). Combining the columns two by two would lead to the same result.

EXERCISES III 2

1. Prove the following valid by the truth table method:

    a. Modus Ponens: A, A ⊃ B /B

    b. Modus Tollens: ~B, A ⊃ B /~A

    *c. Simple Dilemma: A ⊃ B, ~A ⊃ B /B

    d. Add: A /B v A

2. Test the following for validity:

    a. A ⊃ B, B /A   b. A ⊃ ~A /~A

    c. A ⊃ B /B ⊃ A   *d. A ⊃ ~B /B ⊃ ~A

    *e. A, A v B /~B   f. A, A ≢ B /~B

3. Prove the validity of:

    a. Compound Dilemma: A v B, A ⊃ C, B ⊃ C /C

    *b. Complex Dilemma: A v B, A ⊃ C, B ⊃ D /C v D

4. Test the following for validity:

    a. (A v B) ⊃ C /B ⊃ C   b. (A.B) ⊃ C / B ⊃ C

    c. (A.~B) v (A.C) /A.(B ⊃ C) d. A ⊃ B, B ⊃ C /A ⊃ C

    e. ~C v ~D, A ⊃ C, B ⊃ D /~A v ~B

3. Logical Equivalence.

One of the four kinds of rules mentioned in Chapter II allowed replacement of any part of a previous sentence by a logical equivalent. A sentence A is <u>logically equivalent</u> with a sentence B when inferences in both directions are valid, i.e., when $A \Rightarrow B$ and $B \Rightarrow A$. This relationship will be represented as $A \Leftrightarrow B$. Logical equivalence (in virtue of connectives) between two sentences is indicated by their having the same characteristic truth-column. Sameness of truth-column ensures that when either one is true, the other is also, and vice-versa. Though only one example was cited (Double Negation: $A \Leftrightarrow \sim\sim A$), there are a large number of them. We tend to use them without being aware of it. They appear usually as matters of language rather than of logic - rephrasings, not inferences. In a way they are. It is the meaning of the connectives that determines the equivalence.

A moment's thought suffices to see that A.B will have the same truth-value column as B.A. Nevertheless, other equivalences may not be quite so automatic. Consider the four sentences below. The first is logically equivalent to which one(s) of the other three:

If crime does not pay, then laws are in force.	$\sim P \supset L$
If crime pays, then laws are not in force.	$P \supset \sim L$
If laws are not in force, then crime pays.	$\sim L \supset P$
If laws are in force, then crime does not pay.	$L \supset \sim P$

Truth tables give the answer:

P L	$\sim P$	$\sim L$	$\sim P \supset L$	$P \supset \sim L$	$\sim L \supset P$	$L \supset \sim P$
T T	F	F	T	F	T	F
F T	T	F	T	T	T	T
T F	F	T	T	T	T	T
F F	T	T	F	T	F	T

The first has the same truth column as the third; the second is logically equivalent to the fourth.

III 54
3. Logical Equivalence

The difficulty that one feels in the preceding question is related to the ambiguity of "if". Some times we use "if" in the strong sense we have symbolized by $\equiv$. $A \equiv B$ is logically equivalent to $B \equiv A$. And because of the ambiguity we are often led into the <u>fallacy of simple conversion</u> for weak if.

<u>If the dam has broken, the phones are out</u> $D \supset P$
If the phones are out, the dam has broken $P \supset D$

D P	$D \supset P$	/ $P \supset D$
T T	T	T
F T	T	F
T F	F	T
F F	T	T

⎫ The dam's not being broken but
⎬ with the phones out anyway is a
⎪ true case for the premiss, but
⎭ not for the conclusion.

In other words, although ., v, and $\equiv$ are all commutative, like + and x in algebra, $\supset$ is not. Instead, $\supset$ obeys the following rule.

Contraposition.

A long known principle, now validated by truth table, is that of contraposition: $A \supset B \iff \sim B \supset \sim A$. The equivalence of the pair:

If crime does not pay, then laws are in force. $\sim P \supset L$
If laws are not in force, then crime pays. $\sim L \supset P$

can be viewed as contraposition with double negation:

1 $\sim P \supset L$	P
2 $\sim L \supset \sim \sim P$	1 Contra.
3 $\sim L \supset P$	2 N

1 $\sim L \supset P$	P
2 $\sim P \supset \sim \sim L$	1 Contra.
3 $\sim P \supset L$	2 N

The De Morgan Laws (Nor and Nand)

The use of symbols sometimes prompts analogies with mathematics. Sometimes the analogies work and sometimes not. For example, it is tempting to suppose that $\sim(A \lor B)$ is equivalent to $\sim A \lor \sim B$ in analogy with $-(x+y) = -x + (-y)$. But to deny that <u>either</u> A or B is true is to assert that <u>neither</u> A nor B is true, i.e., that A is not true <u>and</u> B is not true. The correct equivalence is $\sim(A \lor B) \iff \sim A . \sim B$. Similarly, to deny that <u>both</u> A and B are true is to assert that either A is not true **or** B is not true (or neither). These two relationships, now known as the De Morgan Laws,

3. Logical Equivalence

and which we may distinguish as <u>Nor</u> and <u>Nand</u>, then, are:

$\sim(A \vee B) \Longleftrightarrow \sim A \cdot \sim B$ Nor

$\sim(A \cdot B) \Longleftrightarrow \sim A \vee \sim B$ Nand

Material If (Mif)

Because of the truth-functional meaning imposed on "$\supset$", it sustains a relation to "not" and "or" which we will refer to as the <u>Material-if law</u> (Mif):

$A \supset B \Longleftrightarrow \sim A \vee B$ **Mif**

Although not always in accord with the varieties of implication, the Mif equivalence is often used, e.g., in paraphrasing "If the car has gas, it will start" ($G \supset S$) as "Either the car is out of gas or it will start" ($\sim G \vee S$). It happens, moreover, that the ambiguity in both <u>or</u> and <u>if</u> has the effect that a mif-like equivalence also holds for strong if ($\equiv$) and strong or ($\not\equiv$):

If you misbehave, you'll be sent to bed   ($M \equiv B$)

Either you don't misbehave or you'll be sent to bed   ($\sim M \not\equiv B$)

Negation of Material If. (Not If: <u>Nif</u>).

Recalling that the one false case for $A \supset B$ is when A is true and B is false, we readily see the equivalence:

$\sim(A \supset B) \Longleftrightarrow A \cdot \sim B$ **Nif**

Even though we would not ordinarily take the denial of the statement "If it rains, the party's off" as equivalent to "It will in fact rain and the party will be called off", the Nif equivalence proves to have many, more natural uses, and it will come to figure in our reasonings as prominently as the equivalences for the negations of <u>or</u> and <u>and</u> (the Nor and Nand rules).

3. Logical Equivalence

<u>Equivalence Rules for $\equiv$</u>.

Logicians seldom have need for exclusive-or, since it is easily expressible in other terms. In particular the following pairwise, logical equivalences are revealed by sameness of truth-columns:

$A \not\equiv B \iff \sim(A \equiv B) \iff \sim A \equiv B \iff A \equiv \sim B.$

Furthermore, the following two rules will be of special importance.

<u>Equivalence as Two-Way If (Eqi)</u>
$A \equiv B \iff (A \supset B).(B \supset A)$

<u>Equivalence as Both Or Neither (Eqo)</u>
$A \equiv B \iff (A.B) \vee (\sim A . \sim B)$

The last logical equivalence, together with Mif, permits any sentence to be expressed in terms of negation, conjunction, and disjunction, only. Every occurrence of "$\supset$" or "$\equiv$" can be eliminated by replacing "$\supset$" using Mif, and "$\equiv$" using Eqi. This has many uses. For example, contraposition may be seen to be just the commutativity of v in disguise:

$A \supset B \iff \sim A \vee B \iff B \vee \sim A \iff \sim\sim B \vee \sim A \iff \sim B \supset \sim A$

Similarly, Modus Ponens and Modus Tollens may be seen to be closely related to Elimination:

```
Modus Ponens (=) Elimination       Modus Tollens (=) Elimination
    A ⊃ B         ~A v B               A ⊃ B         ~A v B
    A             (~~)A                 ~B            ~B
    ─────         ──────                ─────         ──────
    B             B                     ~A            ~A
```

EXERCISES III 3

1. Validate by comparing truth columns to logical equivalences:

   a. $A \supset B \iff \sim B \supset \sim A$ (Contra.) b. $A \supset B \iff \sim A \vee B$ (Mif)

   c. $A \vee B \iff \sim(\sim A \cdot \sim B)$ d. $A \cdot B \iff \sim(\sim A \vee \sim B)$
   ("Definitions" of $\vee$ and $\cdot$, each in terms of the other.)

   e. $A \cdot (B \vee C) \iff (A \cdot B) \vee (A \cdot C)$ *f. $A \vee (B \cdot C) \iff (A \vee B) \cdot (A \vee C)$
   (Distribution Equivalences)

2. Test each of the following pairs of sentence forms for logical equivalence.

   *a. $A \supset (B \supset C)$ $(A \supset B) \supset C$

   *b. $A \supset (B \supset C)$ $B \supset (A \supset C)$

   c. $A \supset (B \supset C)$ $B \supset (A \supset C)$

   d. $(A \cdot B) \supset C$ $(A \supset C) \cdot (B \supset C)$

   e. $(A \vee B) \supset C$ $(A \supset C) \cdot (B \supset C)$

   f. $(A \cdot B) \supset C$ $A \supset (B \supset C)$

3. In each of the following pairs, decide by truth table whether the left hand sentence logically implies the right ($\Rightarrow$), right implies left ($\Leftarrow$), both ($\iff$), or neither (write N).

   *a. $(A \cdot B) \supset C$ $(A \vee B) \supset C$

   b. $A \cdot (B \supset C)$ $(A \cdot B) \supset C$

   c. $A \supset (B \equiv C)$ $(A \supset B) \equiv C$

   d. $A \equiv (B \equiv C)$ $(A \equiv B) \equiv C$

4. Use Nor, Nand, and Nif to put each sentence form below in a logically equivalent form in which no negation sign applies to anything but a letter. Successive transformations may be written simply in a series. More than one of the rules may be used at a time, if obvious. (This process will be called <u>internalizing negations</u>.)

   *a. $\sim(A \vee \sim B)$ *b. $\sim((A.B) \supset C)$

   c. $\sim((A.B) \vee C)$ d. $\sim((A \supset B) \supset \sim C)$

5. Using Mif, Eqi, give a logical equivalent to each of the sentence forms below using only $\sim$, ., $\vee$.

   *a. $(A.B) \supset C$ *b. $A \supset (B \equiv C)$

   c. $(A \equiv B) \supset C$ d. $(A \equiv \sim A) \supset A$

4. Logically Determinate Sentences

In a language which was so primitive as to have no connectives, one sentence could conflict with another only through the meanings of the words. E.g., "Those are moose tracks!", "Those are ox tracks!". Adding connectives dramatically increases articulateness. It also makes grammatically possible sentences which can not possibly be true: "Those are moose tracks <u>and</u> they are not moose tracks", and sentences which can not possibly be false: "Those are moose tracks, unless (or) they aren't". Sentences of the first kind (which can not be true because of the arrangements of their connectives) are called (self-) <u>contradictions</u>. Sentences of the second kind (which can not be false because of their connectives) are called <u>tautologies</u>. The existence of such sentences is not really peculiar. They arise naturally from the essential functioning of connectives, coupled with the fact that a sentence may have multiple occurrences within a single compound sentence. In fact, in both examples above, the compounds in question each involve a single sentence, with two occurrences of "These are moose tracks":

M	∼M	M . ∼M	M v ∼M
T	F	F	T
F	T	F	T

In the language of truth tables:

A <u>tautology</u> is a compound sentence whose characteristic column contains only Ts.

A <u>contradiction</u> is a compound sentence whose characteristic column contains only Fs.

4. Principles

Tautologies and contradictions are called <u>logically determinate</u> because their truth value is determined from logic alone, as opposed to more familiar sentences whose truth value depends on logic and <u>facts</u>. Tautologies are said to be <u>logically true</u>, and contradictions <u>logically false</u>. (All three of these underlined terms go beyond the logic of connectives. E.g., not all logical truths are tautologies, we shall see.)

Logically determinate sentences may seem of interest only as oddities, at first. They are not the sort of sentence we think of using to <u>communicate</u> with. If we asked someone (pointing at some marks) "What are those?" and the reply was "Those are moose tracks, unless they aren't", we might shrug off the reply as an empty pretense of knowledge. If the reply was, "Those are, and are not, moose tracks", we might take the reply as indicating something serious, but not as ordinarily communicative.

Such impressions notwithstanding, tautologies and contradictions have important roles in logic. Consider the familiar elimination inference: A v B, ~A/B. Proving its validity by truth table involved examining cases where both premisses were true. Such cases may be exhibited in a single column by making the two premisses into one conjunction.

```
A B     (A v B) . ~A    /   B
T T        T     F F         T
F T        T     T T         T
T F        T     F F         F
F F        F     F T         F
              ↑compare↩
```

Validity is then checkable by comparing just two columns, one for the conjoined premisses and one for the conclusion.

4. Principles

If we form an if-sentence with the conjunction of premisses as antecedent, and the conclusion as consequent, we obtain a tautology!

A B	((A v B) . ~A) ⊃ B
T T	F T T
F T	T T T
T F	F T F
F F	F T F
	∧

Indeed, if any inference of connective logic did <u>not</u> yield a tautology, when so transformed, it would be invalid. Every F in the column of the resulting if-sentence would represent a loophole - a case where all premisses (and hence their conjunction) was true and the conclusion was false. Conversely, <u>no</u> loopholes would mean validity.

<u>Inferences and Their Principles</u>.

The relationship which has been summarized above between (valid) <u>inferences</u> and (logically true) <u>sentences</u> suggests a very useful bit of terminology. We will associate with every <u>inference</u>, P/C, valid or not, the sentence P ⊃ C (where we take P to be the conjunction of the premisses (assuming them to be finite in number)). The sentence P ⊃ C will be called the <u>principle</u> of the inference P/C. More explicitly, we define:

The <u>principle</u> of an inference P/C is the if-sentence whose antecedent is the conjunction of the premisses P, and whose consequent is the conclusion C.

For the logic of (truth-functional) connectives we can now express the relation as follows:

<u>An inference is (truth-functionally) valid if and only if its principle is a tautology.</u>

4. Principles

(More generally, we may anticipate the more powerful logic, of which the logic of connectives is a part, by saying with no restriction that an inference is valid if and only if its principle is logically true.)

All logically true sentences share the tautology's complete uninformativeness about the facts of reality. Thus we see a striking contrast between the enormous human importance of inference, and the factual emptiness of logical truth. We may recall (from Chapter II) the momentous inference:

If the red button is pushed, the missiles are launched.
<u>The red button is pushed</u>!
The missiles are launched!

The <u>principle</u> of that inference is the single sentence "If it is the case that if the red button is pushed, the missiles are launched, and that furthermore, the bed button <u>is</u> pushed, then the missiles are launched". The <u>principle</u> is completely unmomentous. No one would grow pale on hearing it. And it is undeniably true. (Even if the electronic arrangements are out of order!) Abbreviating "The red button is pushed" by P, and "The missiles are launched" by M, the principle may be symbolized as a single compound sentence and its characteristic truth value column may be examined:

P M	P ⊃ M	(P ⊃ M) . P	((P ⊃ M) . P) ⊃ M
T T	T	T	T T T
F T	T	F	F T T
T F	F	F	F T F
F F	T	F	F T F

It is a tautology.

This general fact about logic - the factual contentless of the principles of valid inference - is a major reassurance in our reliance on logic: In drawing a logical inference from premisses, we can be sure that

4. Principles

the use of logic adds no questionable assumptions of its own to the premisses we are inferring from.

Besides being reassuring, tautologies offer a convenient way of listing valid inference forms as single-sentence principles. Similarly, logical equivalences can be listed as if-and-only-if sentence forms which are tautologies. Conversely, "if" and "fif" forms can be tested for tautology, and thus for fitness as principles for inference, or for establishment of logical equivalence. (Indeed, it is often of value to test sentences having other main connectives than " ⊃ " or " ≡ " and classify them as tautologies, contradictions, or neither, for other reasons.)

EXERCISES III 4

1. Classify each of the following by truth table, as a tautology, a contradiction, or neither.

   a. $A \supset (\sim A \supset A)$
   *b. $(A \supset \sim A) \supset A$
   c. $(A \supset \sim A) \supset \sim A$
   d. $(A . \sim A) \supset A$
   e. $A . (B \supset B)$
   *f. $(A . B) \supset B$
   g. $A \supset (B \supset A)$
   h. $(A \supset B) \supset B$
   i. $(A \lor B) \supset B$
   j. $B \supset (A \lor B)$
   k. $A \equiv \sim A$
   l. $(A \equiv \sim B) \equiv \sim (A \equiv B)$
   *m. $(A \supset (B \supset C)) \equiv ((A . B) \supset C)$
   n. $(A \lor B) \equiv ((A . \sim B) \lor B)$
   o. $(\sim A \lor (\sim A . B)) . A$

Reference Table of Tautologies

1. $(A.(A \supset B)) \supset B$ Modus Ponens
2. $(\sim B.(A \supset B)) \supset \sim A$ Modus Tollens
3. $((A \supset B).(B \supset C)) \supset (A \supset C)$ Link
4. $((A \supset B).(\sim A \supset B)) \supset B$ Simple Dilemma
5. $((A \vee B).(A \supset C).(B \supset C)) \supset C$ Compound Dilemma
6. $((A \vee B).(A \supset C).(B \supset D)) \supset (C \vee D)$ Complex Dilemma
7. $((A \supset C).(B \supset D).(\sim C \vee \sim D)) \supset (\sim A \vee \sim B)$ Destructive Dilemma
8. $((A \vee B).\sim A) \supset B$, $((A \vee B).\sim B) \supset A$ Elimination
9. $(A.B) \supset A$, $(A.B) \supset B$ Drop
10. $A \supset (A \vee B)$, $B \supset (A \vee B)$ Add
11. $A \supset (B \supset A)$
12. $(A \vee A) \equiv A$, $(A.A) \equiv A$ Redundancy
13. $(A \vee B) \equiv (B \vee A)$, $(A.B) \equiv (B.A)$ Commutativity
14. $(A \supset B) \supset (\sim B \supset \sim A)$ Contraposition
15. $(A.(B \vee C)) \equiv ((A.B) \vee (A.C))$,   Distributivity
    $(A \vee (B.C)) \equiv ((A \vee B).(A \vee C))$
16. $(A \supset B) \equiv (\sim A \vee B)$ Material If
17. $(A \equiv B) \equiv ((A \supset B).(B \supset A))$ Eqi
18. $(A \equiv B) \equiv ((A \supset B).(\sim A \supset \sim B))$
19. $(A \equiv B) \equiv ((A.B) \vee (\sim A.\sim B))$ Eqo
20. $(A \equiv B) \equiv (\sim A \equiv \sim B)$
21. $\sim \sim A \equiv A$ Double Negation
22. $\sim (A \vee B) \equiv (\sim A.\sim B)$ Nor
23. $\sim (A.B) \equiv (\sim A \vee \sim B)$ Nand

(22, 23) De Morgan's Laws

24. $\sim(A \supset B) \equiv (A.\sim B)$ Nif
25. $\sim(A \equiv B) \equiv (\sim A \equiv B)$
26. $\sim(A \equiv B) \equiv ((A.\sim B) \vee (B.\sim A))$
27. $(A.(B \vee A)) \equiv A, \quad (A \vee (B.A)) \equiv A$ Dominance
28. $(A.(B \vee \sim A)) \equiv (A.B), \quad (A \vee (B.\sim A)) \equiv (A \vee B)$ Absorption
29. $(A \supset \sim A) \supset \sim A$
30. $(\sim A \supset A) \supset A$
31. $(A \supset (B \supset C)) \equiv (B \supset (A \supset C))$ Commutation
32. $((A.B) \supset C) \supset (A \supset (B \supset C))$ Exportation
                                                Portation
33. $(A \supset (B \supset C)) \supset ((A.B) \supset C)$ Importation
34. $(A \supset B) \supset ((C.A) \supset B)$
35. $(A \supset B) \supset (A \supset (B \vee C))$
36. $(A \supset B) \supset ((C.A) \supset (C.B))$ Factor Law
37. $(A \supset B) \supset ((C \vee A) \supset (C \vee B))$ Sum Law
38. $(A \supset (B \supset C)) \supset ((A \supset B) \supset (A \supset C))$ Self-Distribution (of $\supset$)
39. $((A \supset B) \supset A) \supset A$ Peirce's Law
40. $((A \supset B).(A \supset C)) \equiv (A \supset (B.C))$ Composition
41. $((A \supset C).(B \supset C)) \equiv ((A \vee B) \supset C)$
42. $((A \supset B) \vee (A \supset C)) \equiv (A \supset (B \vee C))$
43. $((A \supset C) \vee (B \supset C)) \equiv ((A.B) \supset C)$
44. $(A \supset B) \vee (B \supset A)$
45. $(A \vee (B \supset C)) \equiv ((A \vee B) \supset (A \vee C))$
46. $(A \equiv B) \equiv (B \equiv A)$
47. $(A \equiv B) \equiv (\sim A \equiv \sim B)$
48. $\sim(A \equiv B) \equiv (\sim A \equiv B)$
49. $(A \equiv (A.B)) \equiv (A \supset B)$

Optional Further Reading

Other Connectives.

As we noted in the previous section, connectives greatly enhance articulateness. They permit the formulation of alternatives, joint conditions, exceptions, etc. A natural question is: How greatly can articulateness be increased in this way? Is there a limit to the number of connectives we can add? We have already had occasion to observe two phenomena that suggest a limit. On the one hand, many different-sounding English connectives prove to be equivalent (truth-functionally) to others ("but" = "and"; "unless" = "or", etc.). On the other hand, genuinely different truth functions prove so closely related that one may be paraphrased by combining others. (E.g., according to truth tables, exclusive-or ($\not\equiv$) is just the negation of if-and-only-if ($\equiv$).) Indeed, if we limit our attention to binary connectives (that link pairs of sentences), and recall that the meaning of each connective is fixed by its characteristic column of four values, we see there can only be a small, finite number of them. Four choices from two values yield just 2^4 (= 16) possible columns. This is larger than the number of connectives we have considered, but some of the columns yield nothing new, or nothing useful. For example, consider defining connectives for the following unused truth-functions.

	(1st member)	(2nd member)	(tautology)	(contradiction)
A B	A ⊖ B	A ⊖ B	A Ⓣ B	A Ⓕ B
T T	T	T	T	F
F T	F	T	T	F
T F	T	F	T	F
F F	F	F	T	F

III 67
Other Connectives

On the other hand, some genuinely distinct columns such as that for A ⊂ B (A if B) are often avoided by simply symbolizing A if B in reverse, i.e., B ⊃ A.

Rather than speculate further, we can easily survey all sixteen binary truth functions by displaying the usual truth combinations for A, B and listing all possible characteristic columns. Useless ones like those above mentioned can be weeded out. Already familiar ones (for "v", " ⊃ ", etc.) can be tagged. Remaining ones can then be examined. For ease of adding comments, the display of combinations, characteristics columns, etc., are upended:

III 68
Other Connectives

All 16 Possible Binary Truth Functions

| F T F T A | Possible | Kind of |
F F T T B	Readings	Compound
T T T T A Ⓣ B		
F T T T A v B	A or B (or both)	Inclusive Disjunction
T F T T A ⊃ B	If A then B A only if B	Material Implication
F F T T A ⊕→ B	Even if A, B	
T T F T A ⊂ B	A if B	Converse Implication
F T F T A ⊖ B	A (even if B)	
T F F T A ≡ B	A if and only if B	Material Equivalence
F F F T A.B	A and B	Conjunction
T T T F A∣B	A bars B	Exclusion
F T T F A ≢ B	A or B (but not both)	Exclusive Disjunction
T F T F A ⊕ B	Not A (even though B)	
F F T F A ⊄ B	Not A but B	
T T F F A ⊕ B	Even though A, not B	
F T F F A ⫫ B	A without B	
T F F F A↓B	Neither A nor B	Joint Negation
F F F F A Ⓕ B		

Other Connectives

It will be noted that several of the sixteen possible compounds have no commonly accepted names. They are little treated in symbolic logic. Symbols shown for them are, in fact, coined. Still, some seem to correspond to English readings. For example, "We shall swim <u>even if</u> it rains" seems to correspond to S ⊕ R, which is tantamount to asserting the first member.

Before discussing others, it will be instructive to rearrange the foregoing display by putting the lower half, "folded back on itself", in comparison with the upper half.

```
T T T T              F F F F
F T T T    A v B     T F F F     ~(A v B), A↓B   (Peirce Arrow)
T F T T    A ⊃ B     F T F F     ~(A ⊃ B), A.~B, A ⊅ B
F F T T              T T F F
T T F T              F F T F
F T F T              T F T F
T F F T    A ≡ B     F T T F     ~(A ≡ B), A ≢ B
F F F T    A.B       T T T F     ~(A.B), A|B     (Sheffer Stroke)
```

Those on the right are simply the negations of those on the left. The sign for neither-nor, ↓ (coined by Charles Peirce (pronounced purse)) may be regarded as a slashed "or" (v). The sign for but-not (⊅) (coined by Alonzo Church) is a slashed implication sign. The sign for exclusive-or (≢) (also Church's) is a slashed equivalence. The sign of exclusion, |, or not-both (coined by Henry Sheffer) might be regarded as a slashed (and obliterated) dot of conjunction.

It is odd that Sheffer's stroke has no commonly accepted English rendering. Peirce's arrow corresponds to the ancient contraction: N(ot)either-n(ot)or, which jibes well with the tautological equivalence:

~(A v B) ≡ (~A.~B).

For Sheffer's stroke, which is based on the related tautology:

~(A.B) ≡ (~A v ~B),

Other Connectives

one might expect some such contraction as Noth-nand from N(otb)oth-n(ot)-and.

But the evolution of the language has not provided it.

(Computer designers, however, have not hesitated to repair this natural lack, and do, in fact, speak of "nand-gates" - switches which allow output just in case <u>not both</u> inputs are "on".)

The fact that some connectives are just the negations of others, shows that they bring no additional articulateness to language, except as affording <u>abbreviations</u> for what <u>could</u> be said, more lengthily without them. They could, in fact, be thought of as <u>defined</u> as abbreviations. E.g., A↓B could be thought of as defined as meaning the same as $\sim(A \vee B)$. Other possible definitions might be

    A v B   defined as $\sim(\sim A . \sim B)$

    A.B   defined as $\sim(\sim A \vee \sim B)$.

Other definitions made possible by tautological equivalences could be:

    A ⊃ B   defined as $\sim A \vee B$

    A ≡ B   defined as   (A ⊃ B).(B ⊃ A).

It is quickly evident that all sixteen of the binary truth functions are definable from just ($\sim$, v), or just ($\sim$, .). Also possible is ($\sim$, ⊃), since one could define

    A v B as $\sim A \supset B$.

The possibility of "making do" with just two binary connectives was a somewhat surprising and impressive result of the early development of modern logic. It came as a special surprise, therefore, when Henry Sheffer pointed out (in 1913) that even two was more than necessary. His stroke (A|B) function sufficed.

Other Connectives

With its characteristic table,

A B	A∤B
T T	F
F T	T
T F	T
F F	T

and its rule summarizable as

<u>False just in case both are true</u>,

the stroke yielded a definition of "∼":

∼A   as   A∤A

in accordance with the truth table evaluation:

A	A∤A	∼A
T	F	F
F	T	T

⌞ same ⌝

A.B was then definable as ∼(A∤B). The basic set (∼, .) being attained, the rest was straightforward. ↓ proves similarly adequate.

Familiarity with the various interdefinabilities is often clarifying. Suppose, for example, that one wondered whether the following pair were logically equivalent:

$\quad$ A ⊃ (B ⊃ C) $\qquad\qquad$ B ⊃ (A ⊃ C)

Recalling that If A then B could be taken to mean Not A or B, one could express both in terms just of "∼" and "v":

$\quad$ ∼A v (∼B v C) $\qquad\qquad$ ∼B v (∼A v C).

Since disjunction is associative, this may be written:

$\quad$ ∼A v ∼B v C $\qquad\qquad$ ∼B v ∼A v C.

Their equivalence is then obvious from the commutativity of disjunction.

Or consider the pair:

$\quad$ (A.B) ⊃ C $\qquad\qquad$ A ⊃ (B ⊃ C)

Other Connectives

Replacing A.B by its "defining" expression in $(\sim, v)$ we have $\sim(\sim A \vee \sim B) \supset C$. Using the not-or definition of "$\supset$" we have: $\sim\sim(\sim A \vee \sim B) \vee C$ or $\sim A \vee \sim B \vee C$ which is the same as what we get by applying the same definition of the form on the right twice.

Optional Exercise III5

1. Using the definitional equivalences, reexpress each of the following just in terms of $\sim$, ., v.

   a. $A \equiv B$

   b. $A \not\equiv B$

   c. $A \supset (B \supset A)$

   d. $(A \supset B) \supset A$

2. Reexpress each form shown, using successively only the connectives indicated:

   1. $(A . \sim B) \supset C$ a. $(\sim, ., v)$,   b. $(\sim, v)$,   c. $(\sim, .)$.
   2. $(A . B) \vee C$ a. $(\sim, \supset)$
   3. $A \equiv (B \supset C)$ a. $(\sim, ., v)$,
   4. $(A \equiv B) \supset C$ a. $(\sim, ., v)$,

3. Peirce's neither-nor arrow can also serve to define all other connectives. Using it, define $\sim$, v, $\supset$.

4. Express $A \vee \sim A$ using nothing but Sheffer's stroke.

Other Connectives

A next question to arise might well concern the possible need for ternary connectives, or quaternary, or higher. A striking result is quickly obtainable by reconsidering the truth tables. The rows representing the various truth value combinations can be reconstrued as representing conjunctions of the basic components or their negation. For example, one row of truth possibilities for A, B, C, D, such as FTTF could equally well be represented by the conjunction $\sim$A.B.C.$\sim$D. which would be true just in the FTTF case for A, B, C, D. Now suppose Φ(ABCD) represented some quaternary truth function which had the value true just for three cases $\bar{A}BC\bar{D}$, $A\bar{B}C\bar{D}$, and $\bar{A}\bar{B}\bar{C}D$ (here, for brevity, conjunction is represented just by juxtaposition, and negation by overstroke). Φ(ABCD) would be true, then, just in case at least one of those were true. I.e., it would be logically equivalent to

$\bar{A}BC\bar{D}$ v $A\bar{B}C\bar{D}$ v $\bar{A}\bar{B}\bar{C}D$.

In other words, it would be equivalent to an expression in $\sim$, ., and v. Since any n-ary truth function will similarly be equivalent to the disjunction of the conjunctions corresponding to its T cases, it is clear that no n-ary truth function requires (for its expression) anything beyond $\sim$, ., and v. Indeed, a single binary connective, | , or ↓, will suffice, in view of what we have said about them.

The general result is commonly expressed by saying that such selections of connectives as ($\sim$, v), ($\sim$, .), ($\sim$, ⊃), (|), (↓), are <u>truth-functionally complete</u>. Such a set as ($\sim$, ≡) on the other hand would not be complete in this way. (A moment's thought will show why.)

Despite the fact that connectives beyond the binaries are in principle dispensable, one can find some reasons to admit the desirability of some

III 74
Other Connectives

connectives beyond the binary. Some ternary functions can only awkwardly be expressed in unary and binary connectives. Take one of the simplest examples. If we wished to extend exclusive-or to three components by symbolizing it as A ⟂ (B ⟂ C), we might suppose that we had said that one and only one of the three was the case (in contrast to A v B v C which would say that <u>at least one</u> of the three was the case). However, if we examine the truth table, we find that we have not succeeded:

A B C	B ⟂ C	A ⟂ (B ⟂ C)		
T T T	F	T	T T T	A B C
F T T	F	F		
T F T	T	F		
F F T	T	T	F F T	$\bar{A}\,\bar{B}\,C$
T T F	T	F		
F T F	T	T	F T F	$\bar{A}\,B\,\bar{C}$
T F F	F	T	T F F	$A\,\bar{B}\,\bar{C}$
F F F	F	F		

The first case (where all three are true) is admitted! In order to rule it out, we would have to say:

(A ⟂ (B ⟂ C)) . ~(A.B.C).

This oddity of binary exclusive-or may be one of the reasons it is not treated as more basic than the inclusive-or (which is easily extendible to any number: A v B v C v D ...). In practice, one usually (informally) says something like: "Exactly one of the following three situations hold".

Another sort of expression which is often used (especially by such people as logicians, mathematicians, and computer designers) is any of the following, all meant as mutually equivalent:

A if B, otherwise C (strong if)

A if and only if B, otherwise C

If B then A, otherwise C (strong if)

A or C, depending on B

Other Connectives

It may be symbolized as $(A \equiv B).(\sim B \equiv C)$

Using the method of truth tables to represent it just in terms of "not", "and", and "or". We find:

A B C	$(A \equiv B)$	$(\sim B \equiv C)$	$(A \equiv B).(\sim B \equiv C)$	
T T T	T	F	F	
F T T	F	F	F	
T F T	F	T	F	
F F T	T	T	T	} True cases { $\bar{A}\ \bar{B}\ C$
T T F	T	T	T	$A\ B\ \bar{C}$
F T F	F	T	F	
T F F	F	F	F	
F F F	T	F	F	

The function could therefore be equivalently expressed as $(\sim A. \sim B.C) \vee (A.B.\sim C)$. The English expression remains briefer than any purely binary representation, in that each component is mentioned only once. In effect, the English represents a ternary connective.

IV

USING THE LOGIC OF CONNECTIVES

To get the most out of logical symbolism one must be able to relate its simplicities to the complexities of English. This chapter begins with some pointers on English in relation to logic. Then it gives a few applications and shortcuts.

1. <u>Connectives in English Usage</u>.

In order to relate our connective symbols more closely to English usage, it will be worthwhile both to recall some facts about English grammar and also to foreshadow some of the symbolisms we shall be using in later chapters. (This section may be skimmed by readers who feel clear on connectives already.)

We have symbolized the negation of a sentence A simply as $\sim$A which we read as not-A. But of course the English negation of "Detroit is a seaport" is "Detroit is not a seaport", and not "Not Detroit is a seaport". To be sure, the order would be acceptable if $\sim$D were read "It is not the case that D" (and we shall often so read it). But we intend "$\sim$" just to perform the logical task of inverting truth values. That task is indicated in many ways in English. Often these ways indicate not only simple negation but also feelings, attitudes, or expectations. E.g., "Detroit is absolutely not a seaport", "Detroit a seaport? Nonsense!", "Detroit fails to qualify as a seaport", "It is an error to suppose Detroit a seaport". But logic is concerned only with the impersonal matters of truth, validity, etc.

IV 77
Connectives in English

Similarly, the logical task of conjunction is indicated in a variety of ways. The following examples involve applications of predicates to names of cities. To symbolize them we will let small letters stand for cities and use capitals for predicates.

New York: n,   Detroit: d,   Charleston: c.

S: a seaport,   F: a financial center.

And we will ignore the copula "is", the manner in which negation is expressed, and any accompanying "overtones". Thus, $\sim$nS will stand for New York is not a seaport.

(1) "New York is a seaport, <u>while</u> Detroit is not"   nS.$\sim$dS

(2) "Detroit is not a seaport, <u>but</u> New York is" $\sim$dS.nS

(3) "Charleston is a seaport <u>just as</u> New York is"   cS.nS

(4) "New York is a seaport <u>as well as</u> a financial center"   nS.nF

(5) "Charleston is a seaport <u>though</u> not a financial center"   cS.$\sim$cF

The number of other ways of expressing conjunction is, of course, enormous: "nevertheless", "in addition", "also", "however", period-punctuation between sentences, etc.

It will be noticed that in each symbolization above there are two name occurrences and two predicate occurrences. But in the English, avoidance of repetition allows (1), (2), (3) to use a single predicate occurrence (seaport). On the other hand, (4) and (5) each make do with a single name occurrence (with two predicate occurrences). The effect is a bit like "factoring" in algebra. Just as we can factor out the 3 in $3x^2 + 3y^2$ to obtain $3(x^2 + y^2)$, in English we commonly "factor out" a name or a predicate:

Connectives in English

Vincent and Paul are artists.   (Predicate factored out.)
    Vincent is an artist and Paul is an artist.
Allen is a writer and director.   (Name factored out.)
    Allen is a writer and Allen is a director.

Generally accepted logical symbolism does not allow such factoring, for the sake of explicitness, and of simplicity in logic's "grammar". We will follow this practice. There is nothing illogical in factoring, of course, and some special purpose systems have in fact incorporated it. (Factoring provides a pitfall for some students. First they properly symbolize "Vincent and Paul are artists" as V.P., but later try to read V ⊃ K as "Vincent implies..." or to read ∼ P as "not Paul". Always bear in mind that the capital letters (<u>in the logic of connectives</u>) stand for <u>sentences</u> — not for names alone, nor for predicates alone. It may help to read "V ⊃ K" not as "If V then K" but as "If V is so, then K is so". (One would less easily read "If Vincent is so, then...".)

Beside the fact that conjunction is often conveyed by other means than "and", the word "and", itself, is often used to mean something more, or other, than plain conjunction!

The "and" in "Jeff entered and took off his tie" seems like plain conjunction, until we recall that plain conjunction is commutative (A.B is logically equivalent with B.A). If we change the order and consider: "Jeff took off his tie and entered", this describes a different sequence of events. "And" here means something like "and then" or "and subsequently".

Other meanings of "and" can lead to an expression that appears like factoring but is not. Although "John and Donna are bridge players" results by factoring from "John is a bridge player and Donna is a bridge player", the same can not be supposed for "John and Donna are a team". "John is a team and Donna is a team" is hardly what was meant. "And" here forms a name-phrase for a <u>collective</u>: John-and-Donna. Similarly, in "2 and 2 are 4", "and" forms a numerical phrase for a number: 2 <u>plus</u> 2. In "Philadelphia is between New York and Washington" "and" is a grammatical accompaniment of "between". In "John and Donna are two mature personalities" and in "John and Donna are married", "and" is used in still other ways which we will have occasion to examine later on.

We have already used "unless" as synonymous with "or". The dictionary correctly gives "if not" for "unless". But truth tables reveal "if not" also to be simply "or"! Consider "Unless Jane hurries, we'll be late". Change this to "If not Jane hurries, we'll be late", i.e., "If Jane does not hurry, we'll be late". Symbolizing, with H for Jane hurries and L for We'll be late, and following the dictionary's "if not", we see the following:

$$
\begin{array}{ccc}
\text{unless} & & \text{or} \\
\underline{H\ L} & \underline{\sim H \supset L} & \underline{H \vee L} \\
T\ T & F\ \ T\ T & T \\
F\ T & T\ \ T\ T & T \\
T\ F & F\ \ T\ F & T \\
F\ F & T\ \ F\ F & F \\
& \underbrace{\quad\quad\quad\quad\quad}_{\text{same}} &
\end{array}
$$

Just as "or" is ambiguous in English, so is "unless". The exclusive "unless" which is intended in "You will get a bad credit rating unless you pay" would be symbolized as B ≢ P, i.e., just as exclusive-or.

In the above example of "strong unless" we put the "unless" <u>between</u> the components. Would similar placement upset "weak unless"? Consider

IV 80
Connectives in English

"We'll be late unless Jane hurries". The dictionary would make this "We'll be late, if Jane does not hurry". Or: L if not H. So far, we have used "if" only to mark the antecedent. Actually it always does. That is, "L, if not H" is simply a reversed form of "If not H, then L". We could, however, read "A if B" in terms of a distinct truth-function whose truth rules make it a "backward implication". I.e., "A if B" would be false just in the FT case, so that if we represent "A, if B" by $A \subset B$ we would have:

A B	$A \subset B$	$B \supset A$
T T	T	T
F T	F	F
T F	T	T
F F	T	T

↳ same ↵

Then "A unless B" (as "A if not B") would be:

A B	$A \subset \sim B$	$A \vee B$
T T	T F	T
F T	T F	T
T F	T T	T
F F	F T	F

↳ same ↵

We have already remarked in Chapter III on the many uses of "if", and on the fact that whatever use of "if" is intended in asserting If A then B, A's being true with B false makes that if-sentence false. (This prompted defining the truth-functional, "material if" ($\supset$) so as to be true in all cases other than the TF case.) A moment ago we spoke of a "backward (material) implication", "$\subset$". $A \subset B$ would be read A if B, and would be false just in the FT case. "Strong if" ($\equiv$) was read explicitly as "if and only if". This phrase can be seen to arise, in English, from an odd "double factoring":

  A if and only if B   A if (B)   and   (A) only if B
  $A \equiv B$ $(A \subset B)$. $(A \supset B)$

IV 81
Connectives in English

In the above, $A \supset B$ has been given the reading: A <u>only if</u> B. To see the naturalness of this reading consider the following pairs:

    If the triangle is equilateral then it is isoceles. $(E \supset I)$
    The triangle is equilateral only if it is isoceles. $(E \supset I)$

    If Prinz is the killer than his blood type matches
    that on the dagger handle. $(K \supset M)$
    Prinz is the killer only if his blood type matches
    that on the dagger handle. $(K \supset M)$

"Only if", in fact, marks the <u>consequent</u> in the same way that "if" marks the <u>antecedent</u>. Thus, sentences equivalent to the above paired sentences would be:

    Only if the triangle is isoceles is it equilateral. $(E \supset I (\text{or } I \subset E))$.

    Only if Prinz's blood type matches that on the
    dagger handle is he the killer. $(K \supset M (\text{or } M \subset K))$.

With these readings in mind, the relationship can be verified as follows:

		if	only if	
A B	A ≡ B	$(A \subset B)$	.	$(A \supset B)$
T T	T	T	T	T
F T	F	F	F	T
T F	F	T	F	F
F F	T	T	T	T

            ⌒— same —⌒

Since "$\subset$" is seldom used, the Eqi equivalence is more common. "If" is by no means the only English rendition of implications or conditionals.

Consider the following locutions:

In case of rain we will meet at Jack's.
(If it rains then we will meet at Jack's.)

Being equilateral is a sufficient condition for that triangle to be isoceles.
Being isoceles is a necessary condition for that triangle to be equilateral.
(If that triangle is equilateral then it is isoceles.)

Jones' dismissal would mean a strike.
(If Jones is dismissed, there will be a strike.)

Connectives in English

In representing compound sentences in symbols we have avoided ambiguity by indicating grouping by parentheses. English has no one method.

One way, as we saw earlier, is to match each connective with a grouper word - "both" with "and", "either" with "or", etc. Then (A.B) v C can be distinguished from A.(B v C) by properly inserting the groupers, thus:

(A.B) v C   Either both A and B or C.
(A.(B v C)   Both A and either B or C.

Of course, this is more than necessary. The following would suffice:
Either A and B or C.
A and either B or C.

An alternative way is to insert an extra phrase when a larger break is intended:

(A.B) v C   A and B, or _else_ C
A.(B v C)   A, and _furthermore_ B or C.

Often factoring indicates the grouping:

(A.B) v C   Art and Bill are going or Carl is.
A.(B v C)   Art is going and Bill or Carl is.

"If", in "If A,B", is, so to speak, a grouper without a connective. "Then" alone means only "subsequently". This causes no problem for the grouping A ⊃ (B ⊃ C) (If A, then if B then C), but for the grouping (A ⊃ B) ⊃ C, it leads to an unacceptable pile-up: _If if_ A then B, then C. Such pile-ups are avoided in various ways. One such way is to employ "only if" (a connective without a grouper) to obtain If A only if B, then C.

Connectives in English

Another way is to shift from a <u>sentence</u> like "Jones is dismissed" to a verbal-noun <u>phrase</u> like "Jones' dismissal" and use a verb like "means" or "implies". Thus, the following pile-up is avoided:

If if Jones is dismissed then there is a strike, then the Chairman had better overrule Personnel.

The more graceful formulation would be:

If Jones' dismissal means a strike then the Chairman had better overrule Personnel.

The above remarks suggest a few of the possibilities to be considered when applying symbols in the analysis of reasoning expressed in normal English. Others will become apparent as we proceed.

Exercises IV 1

1. The following English sentences are to be put into symbols, using the appropriate connective symbols and parenthesis grouping. Use the various clues offered by English phrasing, as described. The sentences involve only four basic components, symbolized by A, B, C, and D, as follows: A: Arch goes; B: Bea goes; C: Claude goes; D: Della goes. Ignore tense differences. E.g., "A" will serve to symbolize "Arch will go", "Arch is going" etc.

   *a. Arch will go, but Bea won't.

   b. Bea won't go unless Della does.

   c. Claude will go only if Della does.

   d. Bea will go if Claude fails to.

   *e. Della will go provided Arch does.

   f. Claude or Della will go, but not both.

   g. Della will not go. Nevertheless, Bea will go in case Arch does.

   h. Arch's going means Bea will go too.

   i. If Arch's going means Bea's, then Claude will refrain from going.

   j. For Claude to go it is necessary that Bea not go.

   k. Arch will go unless either Claude or Bea does not.

   l. Only if Claude goes will Bea and Della both go.

   *m. Della will not be going, while Claude and Bea will unless Arch does not go either.

   n. Arch will go, and moreover so will Bea, if Claude does.

   o. In the event that either Claude or Arch does not go, Della won't go and Bea won't either.

Exercises IV 1

2. The expression of inferences in English seldom follows the neat P/C pattern. In English, the conclusion may come

      first: C because P,
      last: P; therefore C,
or middle: since P_2, C because P_2.

And there are many rhetorical trimmings that are logically superfluous. The fact that inferences are often made during the course of conversation also effects their expression.

The objective of this exercise is to try and spot the elementary inference form (e.g., MP, MT, etc.) in each of the following. (In a few of the examples the reasoning may be of no form so far encountered, or it may be invalid. Such cases should be so labeled.) Examples that are to be understood as involving two speakers indicate the speakers as "A:", "B:". It may help to symbolize the inferences, using component letters of your choice.

*a. A: If it rains today, the party's off.
    B: Well, it's off, because it's raining now.

*b. A: The case is a sinus infection or malaria.
    B: Malaria is unthinkable, so it has to be a sinus infection.

*c. Jean will miss the countryside. She's going to New York or to Chicago. If it's New York, she'll miss it; and the same thing if she goes to Chicago.

*d. A: If there is an earthquake tomorrow, Jeff won't go to school.
    B: He won't go, then, because there *will* be an earthquake tomorrow.

*e. A: If Green's broker gave good advice, he'd be rich himself.
    B: But Green's broker *is* rich; therefore he gives good advice.

*f. No blip showed. Therefore there were no kappa tachyons present, because if kappa tachyons were present, a blip would show.

*g. It was agreed that if a ship was not sighted tomorrow, we'd take the longboat. But if the typhoon hits tomorrow, we'll see no ship. That would mean that if the typhoon hits tomorrow, we take the longboat!

*h. Beamis has to be in the woods or dead. He escaped over the wall or by swimming. If he went over the wall, he's still in the woods. If he swam, he died in the ebbtide. Obvious.

*i. You owe me a bottle of sack because you said "If Fitzhugh bowls out Cowles, I'll buy you a bottle of sack", and he did.

Exercises IV 1

*j. Rač would not leave his wife in Apheim if he were planning to defect. He sent her to Vienna. Obviously, he plans to defect.

*k. A: If there is a life hereafter, then Myra is happy.
    B: You apparently agree, then, that there is no life hereafter, since you _know_ Myra could not be happy.

*l. If interest rates drop, the market will rise.
    If the energy pinch continues, the market will not rise.
    Therefore it will not be the case that the interest rate drops and the energy pinch continues.

2. Partial Evaluation, Laws, and Contracts

In Chapter III we gave some attention to evaluating compounds for given truth-values for the components. But there are also times when the same evaluating technique is useful when we know the truth-value of only some of the components, especially if it happens that it lies within one's own power to make one or more of the components "come true" (- or false as the case may be.)

In everyday life, we seldom encounter compounds of much complexity. Consequently, we apply the rules subconsicously from our naturally acquired understanding of "and", "or", etc. However, almost everyone who has ever signed a lease, filled out an income tax form, or taken out insurance, has been baffled by involved clauses of some such form as the following (in which the capital letters serve as dummies for various acts, conditions, etc.):

> The tenant may not Q under either condition C or condition D unless E, in which case Q is permitted if and only if W is not the case.

Suppose W and D happen to be the case while E is not, and the tenant wonders whether he can Q without violating that clause. He can decide by symbolizing and partially evaluating the compound on the assumption that Q is permitted (symbolized Q). Symbolizing might proceed in the following steps:

"Not Q under condition (C or D)" becomes "(C v D) $\supset$ ~ Q."

Adding "unless E", he gets "((C v D) $\supset$ ~Q) v E".

The "which case" is E, of course. Therefore he repeats E in a conjunction:-

(((C v D) $\supset$ ~ Q) v E).(In case E then Q $\equiv$ ~W)   or, completely in symbols:

(((C v D) $\supset$ ~ Q) v E).(E $\supset$ (Q $\equiv$ ~ W)).

2. Contracts

Evaluating now for W,D,Q true and E false, we have:

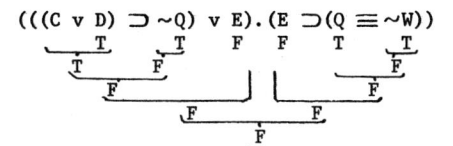

$$(((C \vee D) \supset \sim Q) \vee E) \cdot (E \supset (Q \equiv \sim W))$$

$$\begin{array}{cccccc} T & T & F & F & T & T \\ T & F & & & & F \\ F & & & & F & \\ & F & & F & & \\ & & F & & & \end{array}$$

Thus, Q would violate the clause under the given circumstances. Notice that lack of knowledge of C was unimportant since 'C v D' was already made true by the truth of D. Similarly, the falsity of E sufficed to show the truth of the second member of the conjunction, so that further evaluating steps there were in fact unnecessary.

Other circumstances can be similarly investigated. For example, the tenant may find that with W and D true, Q would still violate the clause even if the exonerating condition E is in effect.

Exercises IV 2

In the following contract-clause problems, the reader should assume that:

(1) the contract-holder prefers not to violate the clause, i.e., he prefers that it be true, if possible;

(2) the contract-holder has some influence on the truth or falsity of the indicated component sentences, but not a reliably decisive influence, so that if there are several ways of making the whole clause true, he might pursue all such ways, rather than rely on any one;

(3) any component whose truth value will not effect the outcome should be ignored (trying to influence a sentence's truth-value ordinarily takes time, energy, or money);

(4) many contract clauses are basically of an if-then form with the antecedent describing some event which the contract maker wishes to avoid, or the consequent describing some sort of punishment or compensation in case it happens. Making the clause true by falsifying the antecedent is naturally, a perfectly acceptable way of making the whole clause true.

*1. A clause in a builder's contract reads:

"If waste asbestos must be buried and the plant operation is not above level B then the contractor must make alteration C within three months unless the overall cost has been less than D dollars and the railroad trunk has been extended to the plant."

Which we may symbolize:

$(A . \sim B) \supset (C \lor (D . E))$

Events have made B and D both false. Indicate what the builder's policy should be toward A, C, and E by placing a check-mark in the appropriate box:

	A	C	E
The builder should try to make true			
The builder should try to make false			
The builder should ignore			

2. A certain lease has a clause of the form:

   (A v (C.~B)) ⊃ ((D.E) v (G.~H))

   Circumstances have made B false and C, D, and H true. I.e., the following values are fixed: $\frac{B\ C\ D\ H}{F\ T\ T\ T}$

   Indicate the policy the tenant should follow in order not to violate the clause (i.e., to keep it true).

	A	E	G
Tenant should try to make true			
Tenant should try to make false			
Tenant should ignore			

3. A contract clause has the form:

   "If A, while B is not done or C is in effect, then E, if D, unless G" which is symbolizable:

   (A.(~B v C)) ⊃ (D ⊃ (E v G))

   Indicate the policy of the contract-holder for B, D, and E in each of the following cases of A, C, G:

   *a. $\frac{A\ C\ G}{T\ T\ F}$ b. $\frac{A\ C\ G}{T\ F\ F}$ c. $\frac{A\ C\ G}{T\ F\ T}$ d. $\frac{A\ C\ G}{F\ T\ T}$

4. For a contract clause of the form A v ~B will be permitted if and only if C.~D, i.e., (A v ~B) ≡ (C.~D), indicate the policy of the contract holder for B and D for the following cases of A and C:

   a. $\frac{A\ C}{T\ T}$ b. $\frac{A\ C}{F\ F}$

As the reader may have already suspected, the foregoing problems have been kept artificially simple. For example, the answer forms given are suitable only for considering a single condition-letter at a time. But often one will need to choose a combination of conditions. Thus, to make $A \equiv B$ true one would have to make A and B jointly both true or both false.

In the general case, to survey all combinations systematically one may have to consider not single-condition tables but combined conditions corresponding to entire rows in the truth table of a contract clause. Furthermore, labeling rows as to truth and falsity of the clauses will often need to be supplemented by considerations of difficulty or cost to the contract holder, and also of probability e.g. of certain emergency conditions. Though more is thus needed, the reader can perhaps see the value of truth-value analysis logic provides.

3. The Loophole Method

3. <u>Testing Validity by the Loophole Method</u>.

The evaluation of compounds affords a remarkably quick method of testing the validity of inferences in the logic of connectives when it happens that either (1) the conclusion can be false in only one way (i.e., it is false for only one combination of truth values), or (2) some premiss(es) can be true in only one way (i.e., true for only one combination of truth values).

For example, the following inference with its eight components would be tedious for the truth table method. But it satisfies the conditions mentioned.

```
1    A v B v C
2    (D v B) ⊃ E
3    A ⊃ ~G
4    C ⊃ (H ≡ J)
5    ~J
     ─────────────
     (~E ⊃ ~G) v ~H
```

The conclusion can be false in only one way. It is a disjunction, so both members would have to be false. Since the first member is an if-sentence, it can be false only if its antecedent, ~E, is true and its consequent, ~G, is false. I.e., the conclusion would be false only for the values

$$\frac{E\ G\ H}{F\ T\ T}.$$

3. The Loophole Method

Recall the earlier remark that a valid inference is one which has no loopholes, (i.e., a possible case where all premisses are true but the conclusion is false). The FTT combination for E, G, H would be a <u>possible</u> loophole. If any assignment of truth values to the other letters (the "atoms" involved) made <u>all</u> premisses <u>true</u>, the overall assignment would be a <u>real</u> loophole, and the inference would be invalid.

The fifth premiss, $\sim J$, can be true only if J is false. But then with H true and J false, the fourth premiss, $C \supset (H \stackrel{T}{\equiv} \stackrel{F}{J})$ can be true only if C is false. If the third premiss, $A \supset \sim G$, is to be true, A must be false, since G is true in the possible loophole. But now with both A and C false, B must be true if the first premiss $A^F \vee B \vee C^F$ is to be true. But B's truth makes the antecedent, $\stackrel{T}{D} \vee \stackrel{T}{B}$, of the second premiss true. But E is false in the possible loophole. So $(\stackrel{T}{D} \vee B)^T \supset E^F$ is false. I.e., we have been led, step by step, from the only possible loophole assignment to E, G, and H to the inescapable falsity of at least one of the premisses. So the inference had no real loopholes at all, and hence is valid!

Our trail can be recorded by listing first the assignment constituting the possible loophole and then the assignments needed for the truth of other premisses until we find one than cannot be made true:

Possible loophole	Pr. 5	Pr. 4	Pr. 3	Pr. 1	Pr. 2		
$\frac{E\ G\ H}{F\ T\ T}$	$\frac{J}{F}$	$\frac{C}{F}$	$\frac{A}{F}$	$\frac{B}{T}$	Forced to be false!		Inference VALID!

In practice, the check is carried out by just marking small Ts and Fs over the critical parts, so that the whole procedure requires few markings and takes little time.

Though especially rapid for the conditions mentioned it can be applied in other cases as well. A general summary of the method follows.

THE LOOPHOLE METHOD (SUMMARY)

A loophole in an inference is an assignment of truth values to the letters which makes the conclusion false and all premisses true.

An inference without loopholes is valid.

The validity of an inference can be tested by examining its possible loopholes (where by "possible loophole" will be meant an assignment of truth values to the letters appearing in the conclusion which makes the conclusion false).

To test for validity:

1. Enumerate all possible loopholes and test them in order as follows:

2. Wherever a conclusion letter appears in the premisses, mark its truth value according to the possible loophole being tested.

3. Seek to assign values to the other letters so as to make each premiss true.

4. If you succeed for any possible loophole, you have found a real loophole and the inference is invalid. (No further possible loopholes need be examined.)

5. If a possible loophole can not be turned into a real one by any assignment to the remaining letters, take up the next possible loophole.

6. If no possible loophole can be turned into a real one, the inference is valid.

The work involved in step 5 can be kept to a minimum by letting the values of the remaining letters be determined as narrowly as possible, sequentially, by examing the premisses in the most strategic order. (Since <u>all</u> premisses must be true for a real loophole, the order in which they are examined is a matter of choice.) Delay examining premisses which can be made true by several different assignments to the remaining variables. Usually some premisses can be found which will determine a unique value for one or more of its remaining letters, if it is to be true. That assignment when carried over to the other premisses will often fix further assignments in another premiss, and so on. If we encounter a premiss which is already made false by previous assignments (each having been forced by the truth requirement of some premiss under the assumption of the possible loophole), then we can see that no assignment for that possible loophole will make all premisses true. (If at any point no premiss fixes a unique assignment to any remaining letter, we must consider the possible assignments separately; but strategic sequencing will at least keep this to a minimum.)

Exercises IV 3

Test the following inferences by the loophole method.

1. (A.B) v (C.D)
    ―――――――――――
    B v C

*2. (B ⊃ A) ⊃ (C v B)
     ―――――――――――――――――
     ~A ⊃ B

3. (B ⊃ A) ⊃ (C.B)
    ―――――――――――――
    ~A ⊃ B

*4. (A v B) ⊃ (A.B)
     A.B
     ―――――――――――――
     A v B

5. (~A ⊃ ~B) v C
    C v ~B
    ―――――――――――
    C v (D ⊃ A)

6. A v B v C
    A ⊃ ~B
    C ⊃ W
    A ⊃ G
    ―――――――
    G v W

The reader may be interested to check the validity of basic stepwise rules by the loophole method and compare its ease with the truth table method of Chapter III. E.g., the simple, compound, and complex dilemmas.

4. Simplification

In using the logic of connectives, occasions arise when it is possible to simplify a given compound (i.e., find a simpler one which is logically equivalent to it). Simplification is desirable not only on general grounds, but it can also have important economic and engineering value. The elaborate switching circuits in computers and telephone systems, for example, are commonly based on elements which combine signals by "and-gates" "or-gates", inverters (nots, switching on to off, or positive to negative). And the complex compound describing a circuit is realized in hardware. Every connective is matched by a device. It costs money and takes space. Simplification can be crucial.

Simplifications may be obvious, as for $\sim\sim A$, $A \vee A$, or $A.A$. Or less obvious, as for $A \equiv (\sim A.B)$, which has the simpler equivalent $\sim A. \sim B$.

Simplification uses logical equivalences. Some equivalences provide direct simplification, as above. Others are preparatory - putting a compound in a form in which directly simplifying equivalences can apply.

The commutativity and associativity of both 'ands' and 'ors', together with their mutual distributivity, makes sentences using them especially easy to arrange. A common preparatory strategy, therefore, is to eliminate all other connectives (except nots) in favor of their "definitional" equivalents. For example, since a material-if can be replaced by a "not-or" formulation,

(1) $(A.(\sim B \vee C)) \supset (B.\sim C)$ becomes

(2) $\sim(A.(\sim B \vee C)) \vee (B.\sim C)$ by Mif.

4. Simplification

Since freedom of rearrangement is hindered by any negation signs outside of parentheses, another preparatory procedure, mentioned earlier, is to <u>internalize negations</u> - by using the de Morgan "Nor" and "Nand" equivalences. For example, if we apply Nand to the first member of the disjunction in (2), $\sim(A.(\sim B \vee C))$, we get: $\sim A \vee \sim(\sim B \vee C)$. Applying Nor to the inner clause, $\sim(\sim B \vee C)$, we get: $\sim \sim B.\sim C$. Cancelling the double negation gives $B.\sim C$.

Example (1) has now been changed to:

(3) $(\sim A \vee (B.\sim C)) \vee (B.\sim C)$, which associativity lets us write:

(4) $\sim A \vee ((B.\sim C) \vee (B.\sim C))$

Now, the simplifying redundancy equivalence gives the obvious, simpler equivalent: $\sim A \vee (B.\sim C)$.

Before proceeding, the reader may wish to refresh his grasp of the process of internalizing negation on the following forms:

(a) $\sim(A \vee \sim B)$ (b) $\sim(\sim(C.D))$ (c) $\sim(A.(B.C))$ (d) $\sim(A.(B \vee C))$

(e) $\sim(\sim A \vee (A.B))$ (f) $\sim(\sim A. \sim(B.C).(\sim A \vee \sim B))$

When negations are internalized (and so appear only before letters), it is often convenient to change the representation of negation from $\sim A$ to $\bar{A}$, and to represent conjunction simply by juxtaposition. With these conventions, the result of the proceeding practice example (a) would be $\bar{A}B$.

Turning now to directly simplifying steps, a common one is afforded by noting and evaluating any tautologies or contradictions that turn up, and taking account of the effects on the compounds in which they appear. E.g.,

4. Simplification

(5) $((A.B) \lor C \lor \sim(A.B)).(D \lor B)$ may (by commutativity and associativity) be written as

(6) $(((A.B) \lor \sim(A.B)) \lor C).(D \lor B)$. The obvious tautology of form $A \lor \sim A$ here may be evaluated as T, so the example becomes

(7) $(T \lor C).(D \lor B)$. Now, treating T as a tautological sentence, note the effects of a tautology in a disjunction and in a conjunction:

$$\frac{T \lor G}{\begin{array}{ccc}T & T & T \\ T & T & F\end{array}} \Longleftrightarrow \frac{T}{\begin{array}{c}T \\ T\end{array}} \qquad \frac{T.G}{\begin{array}{c}TTT \\ TFF\end{array}} \Longleftrightarrow \frac{G}{\begin{array}{c}T \\ F\end{array}}$$

The effect of the tautology in (7), therefore, is to turn the first disjunction into a tautology, which then disappears in the resulting conjunction:

(8) $T.(D \lor B)$ (9) $D \lor B$

A tautology or contradiction may be less obvious. For example, in the internalizing example (e) above, the result of internalizing would be $A(\overline{A} \lor B)$, or $A.(\sim A \lor B)$. Distribution (of conjunct A through the disjunction) gives $(A.\sim A) \lor (A.B)$. Evaluation of the contradiction $A.\sim A$ yields $F \lor (A.B)$. Corresponding to our previous observations on the effect of a tautology in a compound, we note:

$$\frac{F \lor K}{\begin{array}{ccc}F & T & T \\ F & F & F\end{array}} \Longleftrightarrow \frac{K}{\begin{array}{c}T \\ F\end{array}} \qquad \frac{F.K}{\begin{array}{c}FFT \\ FFF\end{array}} \Longleftrightarrow \frac{F}{\begin{array}{c}F \\ F\end{array}}$$

In illustrating the effects of tautologies and contradictions we have been treating T and F as <u>sentences</u> having the <u>values</u> T and F. This is a convenient device, and we will continue to use it. It can be justified technically in various ways. In some treatments, T and F are incorporated as special sentences within the system. In others, they are stand-ins for some convenient tautology and contradiction. They may be regarded as informal practical aids to evaluation, or in other more interesting ways. We need

4. Simplification

not decide, at this point. Their use is clear. To permit ordinary symbolizing of specific sentences by T and F, we will use 𝕋 and 𝔽 for our special Truth and Falsehood, when necessary to avoid ambiguity. Otherwise, plain T and F will serve.

The above equivalences may also be used to introduce a T or an F <u>into</u> a sentence. Oddly, the final result may yet be a simplification. Consider the following transformations:

(A.∼B) v ∼B becomes, on inserting a tautology, T, (A.∼B) v (T.∼B) which gives (A v T).∼B by factoring out ∼B. Since A v T is equivalent to T, we have T.∼B which finally simplifies to ∼B alone!

Actually, such a ploy will not be needed if we remember two simplifying rules. (The above transformations constitute a proof of one instance of one of them. All of them can be proved by truth-table, of course.) The following two rules simply summarize them all. I will call them the two <u>3-2 rules</u>. They simplify compounds of a special sort (which are in internalized and-or form). I will call them the 3-2 compounds. Examples are A.(B v A), A v (B.A), B v (B.∼A), ∼A.(∼B v A), ...

They satisfy the following conditions:

(1) Each has <u>three</u> occurrences of marks, but only <u>two</u> letters, one of which occurs twice.

(2) Each contains <u>both</u> "." and "v".

(3) In each, the recurring letter (with or without negation) is a member of the main connective of the compound.

(The reason for conditions (2) and (3) is that compounds which satisfy (1) but not one of the others is that they can be simplified by already given rules:
Those which violate (2), e.g., A v B v A, A v B v ∼A, A.B.A, A.B.∼A, ... are simplified by redundancy, or contained-tautology or contradiction.
Those which violate (3), e.g., A v (B.B), (A.∼A) v B, B.(A v ∼A). are similarly simplified.)

4. Simplification

The 3-2 compounds fall into two classes:

I. The "same-sign" class: Those in which the two occurrences of the recurring letter have the same sign, e.g., $(A.\sim B) \vee A$, $(\sim B \vee A).\sim B$

II. The "different-sign" class: Those in which the two occurrences of the recurring letter have <u>different</u> signs, e.g., $(\sim A.B) \vee A$, $(\sim B \vee \sim A).A$, etc.

Rule 1: A same-sign compound simplifies to the recurring letter with its "same" sign standing alone. E.g., $(\sim A \vee \sim B).\sim A$ simplifies to $\sim A$. $(B.A) \vee A$ simplifies to A.

Rule 2: A different-sign 3-2 compound is simplified by dropping the <u>inner</u> occurrence of the recurring letter. E.g., $\sim A.(\sim B \vee A)$ simplifies to $\sim A.\sim B$ (dropping A). $B \vee (\sim B.A)$ simplifies to $B \vee A$ (dropping $\sim B$).

The first rule is sometimes called the rule of <u>dominance</u>; the second, the rule of <u>absorption</u>.

Both rules have been stated just with reference to <u>letters</u>, for sake of simplicity. But the letters may be thought of as standing for sentences of any complexity. So the rules may effect a simplification before other preparatory strategies are carried out. For example, $\sim C \vee ((A \supset \sim B).C)$ may be simplified to $\sim C \vee (A \supset \sim B)$ by the different-sign (absorption) rule. Similarly, $(A.B.C.D) \vee (A.C)$ may be simplified by seeing that the first conjunction can be arranged, by commutativity, to $A.C.B.D$ and applying the same-sign (dominance) rule to $(AC.BD) \vee AC$, thus simplifying to $A.C$.

Summary of Simplification Procedures

Preparatory

- Eliminate $\supset$, $\equiv$, etc. in favor of $\sim$, $.$, v.
- Internalize negations.
- Rearrange (distribute, factor, reorder) for steps below.

Simplifying

- Drop redundancies. Cancel double negations.
- Locate and evaluate clauses containing tautologies and contradictions.
- Apply 3-2 rules.

Two last suggestions before exercises in simplification:

(1) The definitional equivalences most convenient for simplification are:

$(A \supset B) \Longleftrightarrow \bar{A} \vee B$ $\qquad$ $A \equiv B \Longleftrightarrow AB \vee \bar{A}\bar{B}$

$\sim(A \supset B) \Longleftrightarrow A\bar{B}$ $\qquad$ $\sim(A \equiv B) \Longleftrightarrow A\bar{B} \vee \bar{A}B$

$\qquad\qquad\qquad\qquad\qquad$ $A \not\equiv B \Longleftrightarrow A\bar{B} \vee \bar{A}B$

(2) Distribution of many-membered conjunctions over many-membered disjunctions or vice-versa, can be done in a style similar to algebraic multiplication, as in the following examples:

<u>Algebraic multiplication</u> of $(a + b + c) \times (p + q)$

$$\begin{array}{l} a + b + c \\ \underline{p + q} \\ pa + pb + pc + qa + qb + qc \end{array}$$

<u>Logical distribution</u> of $(A \vee B \vee C).(P \vee Q)$

$$\begin{array}{l} A \vee B \vee C \\ \underline{P \vee Q} \\ PA \vee PB \vee PC \vee QA \vee QB \vee QC \end{array}$$

<u>Logical distribution</u> of $(A.B.C) \vee (P.Q)$

$$\begin{array}{l} A.B.C \\ \underline{P.Q} \\ (P \vee A).(P \vee B).(P \vee C).(Q \vee A).(Q \vee B).(A \vee C) \end{array}$$

Exercises IV 4

* Simplify:

1. $A.(\sim B \vee A)$
2. $(A.B) \vee (A.\sim B)$
3. $A.(C \vee \sim A)$
4. $(L.M) \vee (M.\sim L)$
5. $(A \vee B) \vee (\sim C \vee B)$
6. $(H \vee J \vee \sim H).K$
7. $(A.B).(A \vee (A.B))$
8. $((A \supset B) \vee A).B.C$
9. $(A.B) \equiv (A.\sim A)$
10. $A \equiv (A.B)$
11. $(A \supset B).(A \vee B)$
12. $\sim(A \supset B) \vee (B.\sim B.C.A)$
13. $(A.(\sim B \vee C)) \vee (C.A) \vee (A.\sim B)$
14. $(A \supset B) \supset (((C.(\sim A \supset B)) \vee ((B.(\sim B \supset A)))$

Distribute:

15. $A.(B \vee \sim C)$
16. $A \vee (\sim B.C)$

Cross-Distribute:

17. $(A.B) \vee (C.\sim D)$
18. $(\sim E \vee G).(H \vee E)$

V
A DEDUCTIVE SYSTEM FOR CONNECTIVE LOGIC

1. Deductive Systems

In this chapter we return to round out the stepwise approach we began in Chapter II. The stepwise method is far older (aside from niceties of record keeping and symbols) than the methods of Chapters III and IV, based on meanings. It was already considerably systematized by the ancient Greeks. And it is more natural; working with truth tables has no close correspondence with natural thought processes. Reasoning tends to be stepwise. To be sure, meanings were always basic. But meanings long tended to be dealt with in terms of the external patterns they gave rise to - elimination, dilemma, absurdity, and the like - rather than in their own terms.

Both methods continue to be developed, and interact. The older method, conentrating on forms of sentences and patterns of deduction, has come to be called deductive, proof-theoretic, or syntactical, while the more basic, but more recently systematized method based on meanings is called the model-theoretic, or semantical method.

There can be many equally good deductive systems, specified by various sets of rules. But they must all pass the test of yielding the same inferences, as certified by meaning relationships. Up to now, we have used "$\Rightarrow$" to stand for logical implication in an informal, general sense. Now we may introduce, in a preliminary way, symbols corresponding to the two different approaches. "$\models$" will stand for the more basic, semantical relation of logical implication in virtue of meaning, while "$\vdash$" will stand for the syntactical relation determined by a specific set of rules. Since many systems are possible, they need to be tagged according to the system used. For example, if we call the system developed in this chapter for connective logic S, then "P $\vdash_S$ C" would mean "C is <u>derivable in system S from</u> premisses P". Needless to say, it is desirable that P $\vdash_S$ C if an only if P $\vDash_T$ C (where "$\vDash_T$" means logically implies in virtue of connective truth-functional meanings). The present system has more than enough rules to ensure this, a matter which will be discussed further on. The present system provides more rules than are strictly necessary in order to keep down the number of steps needed in a deduction without sacrificing their obvious validity.

2. <u>Rules of This System</u>.

In Chapter II, we took note of four basic kinds of rules that could be used to justify a line of a deduction:

1. A line can be justified simply as a premiss (citation: P), or supposition (citation: S) without reference to previous lines.

2. A line can be justified as obtained by a particular form of (one-way) logical <u>implication</u> (e.g., MP) from preceding, cited lines.

3. A line can be justified by replacing all, or any sentential part, of a single preceding line by a sentence which is logically <u>equivalent</u> to the replaced sentence or sub-sentence, according to a cited form of logical equivalence (e.g., double negation) and citing the previous line. (Note that the sort of rule mentioned in 2, does <u>not</u> apply to <u>parts</u> of lines.)

4. A line can be justified by either of the two premiss-discharging rules, Qualification (SQ), and Absurdity (SA), in the manner described

in Chapter II. (Note: A deduction from given premisses is not correct unless all suppositions have been discharged at, or before, the concluding line.)

With this framework in mind, we may fill out the system simply by giving lists of the implication and equivalence forms we will use. Many are already familiar; some are not. Discussions and illustrations of the new forms will follow the listings. In examining the listings bear in mind that the capital letters representing sentences may represent compound sentences of any complexity.

IMPLICATION RULES (⊢)

(i,j, ... are used as dummies for line numbers. Premiss numbers are omitted.)

Modus Ponens

i A ⊃ B
j A
k B   i,j MP

Modus Tollens

i A ⊃ B
j ~ B
k ~ A   i,j MT

Link

i A ⊃ B
j B ⊃ C
k A ⊃ C   i,j Link

Simple Dilemma

i A ⊃ B
j ~A ⊃ B
k B   i,j Dsimp

Compound Dilemma

i A v B
j A ⊃ C
k B ⊃ C
l C   i,j,k Dcomp

Complex Dilemma

i A v B
j A ⊃ C
k B ⊃ D
l C v D   i,j,k Dplex

Elimination   e.g.

i (Any disjunction)   i A v B v C v D
j (Negation of a member)   j ~ C
k (The disjunction without   k A v B v D   i,j Elim
     the negated member)

Add (a disjunct)   e.g.

i A   i A
j (any disjunction   j B v A   i Add
     of which A is a
     member)

Drop (a conjunct)   e.g.

i (Any conjunction)   i A.B.C.D
j (Any member)   j B   i Drop

Join   e.g.

i A   i A
j B   j B
k C   k B.A.   i,j Join
.
.
m (conjunction of preceding
     lines in any order

Ejoin

i A ⊃ B
j B ⊃ A
k A ≡ B   i,j Eqi

Edrop

i A ≡ B
j A ⊃ B   i Edrop

Edrop

i A ≡ B
j B ⊃ A   i Edrop

EQUIVALENCE RULES (⊣⊢)

(Related equivalences are often given a name in common.)

Names		Abbreviations
Redundancy	A.A ⊣⊢ A A v A ⊣⊢ A	Red
Commutativity	A.B ⊣⊢ B.A A v B ⊣⊢ B v A	Com
Contraposition	A ⊃ B ⊣⊢ ~B ⊃ ~A	Con
Associativity	A.(B.C) ⊣⊢ (A.B).C A v (B v C) ⊣⊢ (A v B) v C	As
Distributivity	A.(B v C) ⊣⊢ (A.B) v (A.C) A v (B.C) ⊣⊢ (A v B).(A v C)	Dis
Material if	A ⊃ B ⊣⊢ ~A v B	Mif
Equivalence (.)	A ≡ B ⊣⊢ (B ⊃ A).(A ⊃ B)	Eqi
Equivalence (v)	A ≡ B ⊣⊢ (A.B) v (~A.~B)	Eqo
Double Negation (Not Not)	~~A ⊣⊢ A	N
Not either	~(A v B) ⊣⊢ ~A.~B ⎫ (De Morgan's	Nor
Not both	~(A.B) ⊣⊢ ~A v ~B ⎭ Laws)	Nand
Not if	~(A ⊃ B) ⊣⊢ A.~B	Nif
Not fif	~(A ≡ B) ⊣⊢ ~A ≡ B	Nof
Portation	A ⊃ (B ⊃ C) ⊣⊢ (A.B) ⊃ C	Port

3. Discussion of the Rules

It will be noticed that implication rules have only been moderately increased over Chapter II, while equivalence rules have grown from only double negation to a large number, based on the tautologies established in Chapter III.

The added implication rules are simply Link, which was earlier obtained by using supposition in Chapter II, and validated in III, and three rules for "≡" which often prove convenient

The added equivalence rules will be mostly familiar from corresponding tautologies found in Chapter III.

Another obvious but useful equivalence is Redundancy (Red) A v A ⊣⊢ A (and the similar rule for "."). Its deductive uses go beyond simplification. Consider the inference:

A ⊃ B,   B ⊃ ~A   / ~A

```
1 |1   A ⊃ B            P
2 |2   B ⊃ ~A           P          /~A
1,2|3  A ⊃ ~A           1,2 Link
1,2|4  ~A v ~A          3 Mif (Material if)
1,2|5  ~A               4 Redundancy
```

Note, also, the use of Mif in line 4, above. Our use of it in the preceding chapter was principally as a step in the "definitional" elimination of "⊃". But it is useful in either direction (hence to go from a not-or back to an if). For example, consider the following inference:

Ames or Burns took the blueprints.
If Ames took them, he did not check in at his hotel last night.
<u>If Burns took them, his Delta Maid will have weighed anchor.</u>
If Burns checked in, the Delta Maid has gone.

3. Discussion of Rules

Symbolizing (and allowing for normal English paraphrasings):

A: Ames took the blueprints
B: Burns took the blueprints
C: Ames checked in at his hotel last night
D: The Delta Maid has gone

```
   1|1  A v B          P
   2|2  A ⊃ ~C         P
   3|3  B ⊃ D          P    /C ⊃ D
1,2,3|4  ~C v D        1,2,3 (Complex) Dilemma
1,2,3|5  C ⊃ D         4 Mif
```

An elaboration of the foregoing inference exhibits the rules in cooperation:

```
     1|1   A v B              P
     2|2   (G v A) ⊃ ~C       P
     3|3   B ⊃ (H.D)          P
     4|4   (C ⊃ D) ⊃ E        P    /E
     5|5   A                  S (suppose)
     5|6   G v A              5 Add
   2,5|7   ~C                 2,6 MP
     2|8   A ⊃ ~C             5,7 SQ
     9|9   B                  S
   3,9|10  H.D                3,9 MP
   3,9|11  D                  10 Drop
     3|12  B ⊃ D              9,11 S
 1,2,3|13  ~C v D             1,8,12 Dplex
 1,2,3|14  C ⊃ D              13 Mif
1,2,3,4|15 E                  4,14 MP
```

Lest the inference appear too contrived, it might be imagined to symbolize the following argument:

> Ames or Burns took the print.
> If Gerda is in town or Ames took the print, he did not check in at his hotel (in either case).
> If Burns took it, then Helga will have gone underground and the Delta Maid is gone.
> If Burns' checking in means the Delta Maid is gone, then Eakins, the desk clerk, can tip us on the Delta Maid without knowing he is doing so.
> Eakins can tip us off on the Delta Maid without knowing it.

Exercises V 1

A. The following exercises consist of valid inferences for which deductions are to be constructed, using the rules of the system of this chapter. Since the reader has now some practice in penetrating to the logical forms underlying natural language, they are given without symbolic paraphrase. But occasional hints are given, and letter symbols for component sentences are suggested, with letters underlined in the English to suggest which component sentences they stand for, when not obvious. A good policy is to write out exactly the sentence each letter is to stand for. But bear in mind that shifts in tense and mood may be ignored. (Logical symbolism is capable of representing time relationships, but need not do so unless inference(s) depend on them.)

1. The proposal that the meeting be held at either Athens or Cairo was turned down
The proposal that the meeting be held at either Athens or Belgrade was accepted
The meeting will be held at Belgrade   (A,B,C)
   (Hint: The premisses boil down to:
   The meeting will not be held either at Athens or Cairo
   The meeting will be held either at Athens or Belgrade)

2. If Altair and Betelgeuse are not both visible, the calibration of the rocket's S-system will be made after launch
Betelgeuse is not visible
Calibration will be made after launch   (A,B,C)

*3. If population grows indefinitely, essential resources will be exhausted
If essential resources are exhausted, population will not grow indefinitely
Population will not grow indefinitely   (G,E)

*4. Archer gets the loan or else Bates, Ltd. is bankrupt and Carla stays home
Archer gets the loan or Carla stays home   (A,B,C)

*5. Either Ahmed's victory means Bultz gets the next match or the championship is vacated
It was not the case that the championship was vacated unless Bultz got the next match
Ahmed was not victorious   (A,B,C)

6. If it was arson then, if Binns' policy applies, his loss is covered
If it was arson, then Binns' policy applies
If it was arson, then Binns' loss is covered   (A,B,C)

Exercises V 1

7. If Alexander were alive, he'd use nuclear weapons (He'd stop at nothing!)
   If Alexander were alive, he'd not use nuclear weapons (His tactics never involved them!)
   Alexander is not alive   (A,N)
   (Hint: The remarks in parenthesis may be omitted.)

*8. If Akins takes archaeology he will have to master Benton's text and dig civilization
   If Akins masters Benton's text, he won't dig civilization
   Akins will not take archaeology   (A,B,C)

9. It is not so that if Alan is a musician, then Fido is a virtuoso!
   Alan is a musician   (M,V)

10. It can't be that the suspect is both the arsonist and the burglar
    The suspect is the arsonist (according to latest evidence)
    The suspect is not the burglar   (A,B)

11. If Tamiland does not yield on the air access issue, then the African resolution does not pass unless a compromise with Tamiland's neighbor is worked out
    Tamiland will not yield, and a compromise will not be worked out
    The African resolution does not pass   (T,A,C)

12. The act is passed or else if the bank fails to grant the loan, the company must close
    If the bank grants the loan, the act will be passed
    If there is a delay, the act will not be passed
    If there is a delay, the company must close   (A,B,C,**D**)

13. The proposed tariff will not both control domestic prices and please our allies
    Either the proposed tariff controls domestic prices or it will further inflation
    If the proposed tariff pleases our allies, it will further inflation   (C,A,I)

14. Either Barovia is too ill-equipped or else such a confiscation means war
    But Barovia can't both have received an American loan and be too ill-equipped
    If she has received an American loan, then, if there is to be no war, there must be no such confiscation   (B,C,W,L)

*15. Prof. McFiend has taken over the rocket controls, but if he does
     not notice Alan's absence, we will be able to shut off the
     power before we reach position C
     Prof. McFiend can't both have taken over the controls and also
        notice Alan's absence
     We will fail to make Mars only if we are not able to shut off
        the power before we reach position C
     We will make Mars   (P,N,S,M)

16. Agents are in Ankara, Belgrade, or Cairo
    If they are in Ankara, then either Davros has not been contacted
       or they are in Belgrade too
    Either Davros has been contacted or if agents are not in Belgrade
       then they are not in Ankara either
    If agents are not in Belgrade, they are in Cairo   (A,B,C,D)

17. If the Venus module fails to arrive, then loss of position Q or Z
       means disaster unless Ulg keeps his word
    Ulg will keep his word only if either position Z is not lost or
       the Venus module arrives
    Position Q is lost
    The Venus module does not arrive
    We face disaster if Ulg fails to keep his word
       (Hint: Use the following letters with the readings shown:
       V: The Venus Module arrives
       Q: Position Q is lost
       Z: Position Z is lost
       D: Disaster occurs
       U: Ulg keeps his word)

18. Bond is in Singapore or Laos or in Goldfinger's clutches
    Tai Fu is on her beat
    Bond has not been in touch with Wang nor has HQ been alerted
    If Bond is in Singapore, he is either making love or is in touch
       with Wang
    If he were in Singapore and making love, Tai Fu would not be
       on her beat
    If he were in Laos, he would not be in touch with Wang, but
       HQ would be alerted
    If he is in Goldfinger's clutches, he is not making love
    Bond is in Goldfinger's clutches
       (Hint: Symbols with readings:
       S: Bond is in Singapore
       L: Bond is in Laos
       G: Bond is in Goldfinger's clutches
       B: Tai Fu is on her beat
       W: Bond is in touch with Wang
       H: HQ is alerted
       M: Bond is making love
       D: Bond is in Djakarta

Exercises V 1

B. To stress the fact that the letters used in representing the basic rules may be taken to stand for compounds of any complexity, some of the following problems require far shorter deductions than would first appear. A simple form may apply, though the compounds have many components.

*1. (A v B) ⊃ (C ⊃ D)
     ~(A v B) ⊃ (C ⊃ D)
     ─────────────────
     C ⊃ D

*2. (A ⊃ B) v C v (D.E)
     ~(D.E)
     ~C
     ─────────────────
     A ⊃ B

*3. (A v B) ⊃ (C ≡ D)
     D ⊃ (A v B)
     ─────────────────
     D ⊃ (C ≡ D)

4.   A v (B.~C) v D
     ~D
     ─────────────────
     ~A ⊃ (B.~C)

5.   A v (B ⊃ C)
     A ⊃ (B ⊃ D)
     (B ⊃ C) ⊃ (B ⊃ D)
     ─────────────────
     B ⊃ D

6.   A v B v C
     ~B
     A ⊃ D
     ─────────────────
     (C ⊃ D) ⊃ D

7.   ~A ⊃ B
     (D v E) ⊃ C
     (D v E) v ~A
     ─────────────────
     B v C

3. Discussion of Rules

After constructing deductions for valid inferences, the reader may feel the need of practice in spotting invalid ones. Systematic methods, such as finding loopholes, exist. But skill in quickly _spotting_ bad moves will improve by becoming closely familiar with correct patterns. Perhaps the most common actual mistakes (in connective logic inference) are those that stem from (a) treating if like strong-if ($\equiv$), in particular, the "fallacy of simple conversion": $A \supset B \ / B \supset A$, the "fallacy of affirming the consequent": $A \supset B, B \ / A$, and the "fallacy of denying the antecedent": $A \supset B, \sim A \ / \sim B$, and (b) treating or (v) like "strong" or ($\not\equiv$), e.g., $A \vee B, A \ / \sim B$,

    (A: Either Addison or Bronf have been taking graft.

    B: Addison was just caught at it.

    A: Well that lets Bronf off the hook.).

V 115
Derived Rules

Optional Further Reading

Derived Rules of Inference

It was remarked at the beginning of this chapter that many alternative deductive systems are possible which yield the same, semantically valid inferences. If one system yields a certain pattern, such as compound dilemma, by listing it among its basic rules, then another system which did not list it as basic would have to be able to reproduce it by steps. For example, a system B like the one in this chapter, S, but omitting compound dilemma, could reproduce it by steps from the complex dilemma, e.g.:

```
    1|1   A v B
    2|2   A ⊃ C
    3|3   B ⊃ C       /C
1,2,3|4   C v C       1,2,3 Dplex
1,2,3|5   C           4 Red
```

Once having shown how to reproduce it in the original system B, one could adopt the compound dilemma as a <u>derived rule</u> of B. That is, one could assign the rule a name (such as Dcomp) and record the stepwise method above in a file marked Dcomp. Then a deduction with a step justified by "Dcomp" could be regarded not only as a deduction of system S, but also as a deduction of <u>B - as extended by the rule on file</u>.

A given deduction-system may, in fact, be successively extended by adopting further derived rules, christening them with appropriate tags, and recording the stepwise way of reproducing them, in a file. Such recorded deductions can utilize earlier derived rules, for sake of brevity, provided that the records are kept in strict order, each utilizing only derived rules whose records precede it in the file. Thus, a deductive system B which starts with a given supply of rules can extend itself by converting any of its deductions into derived rules, thus providing a shortcut for future deductions. Of course, any such abbreviated deduction will not be of the bare, original system B, but of a kind of grown "dialect" of B, namely, of the extension of B-relative-to-Rule-File-R. (As extensions of various sorts are spoken of, this sort may be distinguished as a (<u>deductive</u>) <u>rule extension</u>. (Adding a rule that a system B could <u>not</u> reproduce is also said to be a (rule) extension; but it would be called, technically, a <u>nonconservative extension</u>, i.e., an innovative one.))

Our adoption of the shortcut of writing (N) after various rules to indicate an omitted N step was, in effect, an informal adoption of a number of derived rules, MT(N), Elim(N), etc.

Axiomatics

At the beginning of this chapter, the deductive method was sharply contrasted with the truth-table method of Chapters III and IV. The first was said to be syntactic, concerned with patterns of symbols, and the second was said to be semantic, concerned with what the symbols stood for.

The importance of the contrast has become evident only gradually in the development of logic. The seeds for the realization were planted by Euclid's systematization of geometry. Reasoning about geometry (at first involving much drawing of diagrams and intuitive grasp of relationships) early acquired a body of rules. Some rules followed from others. Euclid set out to systematize them into a deductive system. A small set of rules, found to be very basic, were selected as <u>axioms</u>, and the others were arranged as <u>theorems</u>, with explicit deductions, or proofs. Concepts, similarly, were given explicit definitions, leading back to a set of explicitly recognized basic concepts. The intent was to make every rule or concept explicit - so explicit, in fact, that diagrams, and appeals to natural understanding, never <u>had</u> to be depended on in any proof. This had the effect that deductions could be carried out by citing linguistically specified rules, manipulating symbols, without really understanding what they stood for. Making a deduction could be regarded as a game, a kind of more elaborate solitaire. This possibility was not the intention, to be sure, but rather an effect of making everything explicit. The possibility began to be exploited, however, (after many centuries) by geometers studying the deductive effects of altering Euclid's parallel postulate.

Even then, it was not thought of as a serious divorce from meaning. But when the advent of relativity showed that some of the altered geometries

Axiomatics

could be used in theories of the physical world, and furthermore that some of the theories seemed to defy natural understanding, the possible utility of purely syntactical deductive systems, to bridge gaps where human insight seemed to fail, was driven home. At the same time, axiomatic systems which were developed for one branch of mathematics, were increasingly found to be applicable to many, and soon were developed on their own, independently of any one interpretation (abstract algebra).

Because of the influence of these developments in geometry and algebra, modern logic, also, was first developed as a deductive development of a set of axioms. (For connective logic, the axioms consisted of a certain selection of what are now recognized as tautologies by the semantics of truth tables. With these, only MP and a rule of substitution were used as rules.)

At first, the axiomatic systems of logic could only be justified as "standing to (natural) reason". But with the development of a systematic semantics (of truth-functional meanings, in the case of connective logic), one could ask such things as whether a given deductive system for connective logic could justify all, and only, inferences justified by truth-table, or whether the sentences deducible from the axioms alone consisted of all tautologies, and of no non-tautologies.

For the logic of connectives, the results were satisfying, but unexciting: A number of deductive systems were indeed proved to be sound, in the sense that _only_ truth-functionally valid inferences could be made by a deduction of the system, i.e., for the system in question:

If $P \vdash C$ then $P \models C$ **Soundness**.

And they were proved __complete__ in the sense that __all__ truth-functionally valid inferences were attainable by a deduction of the system, i.e.:

If $P \models_T C$ then $P \vdash C$ **Completeness**.

(Optional) Exercises V 2

1. It was shown above how Dcomp could be obtained as a derived rule from Dplex. Show how Dsimp can be similarly obtained. (Hint: Neither Dcomp nor Dplex are needed. Use Absurdity.)

2. Our deductive system s contains more rules than necessary, as remarked. A less generous one would consist just of the two suppositional methods, no equivalence rules, and only the following implication rules:

   Ncanc(ellation)

   $$\frac{\sim\sim A}{A}$$

   Join

   $$\frac{A, B}{A \cdot B}$$

   Add

   $$\frac{A}{A \vee B} \quad \frac{A}{B \vee A}$$

   MP

   $$\frac{A, A \supset B}{B}$$

   Drop

   $$\frac{A \cdot B}{A} \quad \frac{A \cdot B}{B}$$

   Elim

   $$\frac{\sim A, A \vee B}{B} \quad \frac{\sim A, B \vee A}{B}$$

   The reader may wish, at his leisure, to obtain others as derived rules (treating equivalences as pairs of implication rules - going both directions). As it helps to use earlier derived rules to get later ones, we may, as a starter, group some of them in three classes I, II, and III. Those in class I can be obtained directly. Those in class II are more conveniently gotten with the help of one or more of class I. Class III uses one or more of class II.

   I. $A / \sim \sim A$ (Nad), Com (for .), MT, Nor, Red (both . and v), Assoc (.)

   II. Contra, Dilemmas, MT, Mif, Com (v)

   III. Nand, Nif, Assoc (v), Distributivities.

Results for more powerful branches of logic, however, proved more surprising. Certain powerful logics were not only proved incomplete, but, in a sense, incompletable. Even a somewhat weaker logic (the one we shall be studying) was found wanting in certain sense: Although it was proved sound and complete, it was found insufficiently strong to prove all the consequences which a set of axioms of number theory had (in the semantical sense). It was results of this sort that led to the sharpened distinction between syntactic deducibility, $\vdash$ (studied in proof theory) and semantic having-as-consequence, $\vDash$ (studied in model theory).

Model Theory Concepts for Connective Logic

Out of the development of a systematic semantics for logic, and the study of its relations to (the syntax of) deduction, there has grown a discipline of great profundity and complexity known as model theory. We can get a first glimpse of it in connection with connective logic, though that glimpse will seem hardly exciting.

To begin with, let us imagine all sentence letters in alphabetical order, and imagine each to be assigned a T or an F. Such a assignment could be regarded as one row in a large truth-table display of possible truth-value combinations (2^{26} rows!). Now even if we make the list infinitely long (by adding numerical subscripts to the letters: $A, B, \ldots A_1, B_1 \ldots A_2, B_2, \ldots$), we can still speak of assignments, in general, though unable to list them all. Then the following definitions can be made, in accord with earlier discussions:

Tautology

A sentence s is a tautology fif it is (evaluates to) true

under every assignment.

V 121
Model Theory

Truth-Functional Validity

An inference, P/C, is truth-functionally valid (P $\models_T$ C) fif

C is true every assignment which makes every sentence

in P true.

Note that under this definition, P may contain infinitely many sentences. The display rows we wrote in Chapter III for a particular inference can be regarded simply as part of overall assignments, which display the values assigned to the letters in the given inference.

And, not as yet defined:

Model

A <u>model</u> of a set of sentences, P, is an **assignment** under which

every sentence of P is true.

The assignments can be regarded as representing any of the following:

(a) possible matters of fact, cases, or "outcomes", the sentence letters being regarded as having fixed meanings;

(b) other "possible worlds", in which the sentences with the same meanings have other truth-values;

(c) the truth-values which the letters might have under other possible interpretations of the letters.

Because of these variations in viewing "assignment", we often hear of the following (operationally equivalent) formulations:

A tautology is $\begin{cases} \text{true independently of facts} \\ \text{true in all possible worlds} \\ \text{true under all interpretations} \end{cases}$

A valid inference, P/C, is one such that in

$\Bigg[$ Every eventuality in which the premisses are true, the conclusion is true;

Every possible world in which the premisses are true, the conclusion is true;

Every interpretation under which the premisses are true, the conclusion is true.

VI
PREDICATION AND QUANTIFICATION

1. <u>Predication</u>

We will now step beyond the logic of connectives to the logic of quantifiers. The logic of quantifiers, is based on the notions of <u>all</u> and <u>some</u>. It incorporates the logic of connectives and adds only a few notions, and basic rules. But adding them turns out to be a giant step, both in the power of inference attained and in the intricacy of analysis made possible.

To begin with, it requires that we look more deeply into the structure of sentences. Simple capital letters in compounds will not do.

A basic essential of any language is the ability to say something about individual things. For this we need <u>names</u> and <u>predicates</u>. Names are symbolized as small letters, a, b, c, ... and predicates by capitals, A, B, C, ... (The use of capitals for <u>sentences</u>, as in preceding chapters, is different, of course. Some writers distinguish the two uses by different kinds of symbols, e.g., Greek letters for predicates. But we will allow ourselves the familiarity of the ordinary capitals, relying usually upon context to make clear which use is intended.)

In logic, the predicate is written first, and the name of what it applies to is written second. Thus "John walks" is symbolized as Wj. This order has no essential logical justification. It has only a small systematic advantage, which will become clear presently. Historically, it was prompted by analogy to the mathematical practice of writing a function symbol followed by an "argument" symbol, e.g., "cosine $(\frac{\pi}{2})$". In fact, the name following the

1. Predication

predicate is often spoken of as designating the <u>argument</u> of the predicate; and the predicate itself is often spoken of as designating a <u>function</u>. As in mathematics, the argument symbol is commonly set off by parentheses: Walks(john). This proves useful later on, but for the time being, we will do without such parentheses.

The English "parts of speech", verbs, adjectives, and nouns do not correspond to any clearcut logical distinctions. All predications are symbolized simply by predicate letters, whether verb, adjective, or noun. For example, the following predications vary only slightly in meaning. The different parts of speech simply call for different grammatical treatment:

Part of Speech	English Affirmative	English Negative
Verb	John walks	John does not walk
Adjective	John is ambulant	John is not ambulant
Noun	John is a pedestrian	John is not a pedestrian

In logic, the symbolizations of the above are the same in form (though different predicate letters are used, to reflect the slight differences in meaning):

$$Wj \qquad \sim Wj$$
$$Aj \qquad \sim Aj$$
$$Pj \qquad \sim Pj$$

Differences in tense are ignored (for the present). All symbolizations refer to "tenseless" or non-committal "present", or to a time left tacit.

Differences in person are inappropriate to logic, since a sentence using "I", "we", "you" would not be the sort of context-independent sentence having a fixed truth value, which logic requires. In practice, we may reason with such sentences, with the tacit understanding that "I" and "you" are

1. Predication

<u>understood</u> in a given context as referring to definite persons whose proper names could be supplied.

Plurals serve various uses in English. But logic is able to express each such use without recourse to special "plural" symbols.

In short, logic requires only a third-person, singular, no-tense predication.

Certain other grammatical distinctions, however, are given very explicit treatment. Logic goes beyond traditional grammar, in fact, in other directions. Traditional grammar distinguishes between "transitive" and "intransitive verbs". From the standpoint of logic, the difference is that intransitive verbs, like "breathe", or "sleep" apply only to a single "subject", while transitive verbs, like "hit", "love", etc., involve a second, "object" individual. Logic calls predicates which apply to one individual <u>one-place</u> (<u>monadic</u>, or <u>singulary</u>). Predicates which apply to two individuals are called <u>two-place</u> (<u>dyadic</u>, or <u>binary</u>). Thus, intransitive verbs are one-place predicates, while transitive verbs are two-place. But there are also two-place nouns: Don is a friend of Bob, symbolized as Fdb (or F(d,b)). And many "prepositions" are, in effect, two-place adjectives: Jackson is near Lansing (Njl).

Logic goes beyond natural grammar in permitting systematic treatment of predicates of any finite number of places. (The number of places which a given predicate has (i.e., the number of individuals it applies to) is called the <u>degree</u> of that predicate). Thus, if we symbolize a verb which takes an "indirect object", in a pattern such as "a gives b to c" by Gabc, G is said to be a predicate of degree three. Similarly, "between" is three-place, triadic, or of degree three. "Philadelphia is between New York and Washington" may accordingly be symbolized: Bpnw. For "between", some writers prefer

1. Predication

to incorporate the spatial analogy into the order of names and write Bnpw. In either case, the significance of the order one chooses must be carefully specified - usually be providing a "reading" for the symbol. Under the first reading, Bnpw would be false; under the second (e.g., "New York has Philadelphia between it and Washington") true.

A four-place predicate would be called for to symbolize "New York is farther from Detroit than Chicago is from Lansing", e.g., as $F(n,d,c,l)$, or, more shortly, as Fndcl. Predicates of degree higher than four are less common.

To keep the "grammar" of the symbolism simple, we continue to treat the connectives "externally". That is, connectives are not to connect names, or to connect predicates. When they appear to do so in English, the meaning must be paraphrased. We have already noted English "factoring out", and will easily make the following symbolizations:

    John and Don are newsmen   Nj.Nd

    Don is a newsman and a linguist   Nd.Ld

But things are not always as simple. For example, in the following symbolization,

    John and Don are neighbors $\neq$ Nj.Nd

The compound Nj.Nd would translate back into English as "John is a neighbor and Don is a neighbor". I.e., each is a neighbor of someone, but not necessarily of each other. What is wanted is a two-place predicate for the relation of being a <u>neighbor of</u>. Treating N as such a predicate, it suffices to symbolize as follows:

    John and Don are neighbors   Njd (John is a neighbor of Don)

The "and" does not appear. We need not express it by making it Njd.Ndj because of the meaning of "neighbor". On the other hand, the meanings of other relation words are not as obliging. Consider the following:

Don and Pat are brothers   Bdp (Don is a brother of Pat)

The meaning of "brother of" does not automatically make Pat a brother of Don. Pat might be Don's sister. The English rules that out. The proper symbolization of the English, then, is Bdp.Bpd. The question of when to rely on meanings in symbolizing will become clearer as we proceed. A safe working rule is not to depend on them. Thus, even the neighbor example would most straightforwardly be Njd.Ndj.

Exercises VI 1

1. Symbolize. Use the predicate and name symbols indicated. The degree of the predicate needed is for you to decide.

   *a. Alex and Bea are juniors.   (a,b,J)

   *b. Alex and Bea are cousins.   (a,b,C)

   *c. Alex likes Bette or Della.   (a,b,d,L)

   *d. Alex gave Rover, but not Spot, to Bea.   (a,r,s,b,G)

    e. Alex or Craig gave Rover or Spot to Bea or Della.   (a,c,r,s,b,d,G)

2. Quantification

Many familiar sentences make no reference to specific individuals. Examples are: "Nothing lasts", "Some officials are helpful", "Not all critics are informed". Furthermore, we often wish to reason hypothetically about an unknown x (and perhaps y and z...). For these purposes, logic adds to its symbols a class of signs called <u>variables</u>. We shall be concerned, at first, with variables of one kind, called <u>individual</u> variables. For these, we will use small letters from the end of the alphabet: x, y, z, w, ..., (with numerical subscripts, if necessary).

Individual variables act like names. Predicates are applied to them. For example, if "Hj" is read "John is hungry", then "Hx" would be read "x is hungry". Or if "∼G(3,8)" is read "3 is not greater than 8", then "∼G(x,y)" would be read "x is not greater than y". In fact, variables are commonly used with predicate letters in order to provide them with a precise reading (meaning) in a given problem. For example, in a problem involving "G" in the above sense, a reading would be provided by writing G(x,y): x is greater than y. Thereby, corresponding readings are provided for G(8,3), G(3,8), G(y,5), G(y,x) as 8 is greater than 3, 3 is greater than 8 (false, of course), y is greater than 5, and y is greater than x. This device is especially useful when a predicate letter is being used to convey a complex idea having no simple English correlate. (Predicate letters, like letters in connective logic, may be used to pack in information whose analysis is not relevant to a particular inference.) For example, the reading of Px might be: x gets pugnacious everytime someone mentions poetic license to x, when x is not sober. Or the reading of Ixy might be: x ignores y in favor of anyone who flatters x and belittles y.

2. Quantification

Of course, Hx and Gxy by themselves are not sentences, capable of having a truth value independent of context. We shall call them <u>open clauses</u>. But compounds can be formed of open clauses, just as well as from sentences. And connective logic can be applied to them in the following sense. Suppose we extend our conception of inference to include hypothetical inferences about unspecified individuals, and in an inference, P/C, permit both C and members of P to be open clauses. Then the principle, P ⊃ C, of the inference is also an open clause. If its form is tautological, it will be logically true whatever its individual variables are taken to stand for. (Variables in an open clause act like names in the sense that if a variable, x, is taken to stand for a thing, every occurrence of x stands for the same thing.) Therefore, if we reason correctly by connective logic from Ax to Bx, the inference is valid in the sense that whatever x may be taken to be, if "Ax" is true of it, then "Bx" must, logically, be true of the same thing.

Besides being able to reason hypothetically with open clauses, we can form complete sentences (<u>closed</u> clauses) from them by adding ways to symbolize the ideas of "all" and "some", as follows. We add two new symbols, the <u>universal quantifier symbol</u> "∀" and the <u>existential quantifier symbol</u> "∃". The significance of these two quantifier symbols can be most quickly suggested by presenting each in its typical context and providing the whole with an "official reading". For the sake of illustration, "Hx" will be taken to mean <u>x is happy</u>.

2. Quantification

The Universal Sentence:	∀xHx	Readings
For every (individual) x, x is happy.		Official
For all x, x is happy.		Alternative
Everyone is happy; Everybody is happy; All are happy; ...		Informal
The Existential Sentence:	∃xHx	Readings
There exists at least one (individual), x, such that x is happy.		Official
For some x, x is happy.		Alternative
Someone (at least) is happy; Some are happy; There are happy individuals; ...		Informal

An occurrence of "∀" followed by some variable, u, is called an occurrence of a <u>universal quantifier on u</u>. E.g., in "Ha v ∀xHx", "∀x" is a universal quantifier on x. Similarly, ∃u is an <u>existential quantifier on u</u>.

In both quantifiers, the following variable, at a given occurrence, may also be called the <u>variable of quantification</u> at that occurrence.

To make the meaning of a quantified sentence more exact, one must specify the <u>universe of discourse</u>. If a person says "Everyone is happy", it is unlikely that he means to include everyone in the world. More probably, he means to refer to a quite limited universe of discourse. It may be composed, for example, just of people attending a party he is giving and just at the time he utters the sentence. In informal communication, the universe of discourse is left as tacitly understood.

For purposes of becoming familiar with the logic of quantifiers, let us consider a UD (Universe of Discourse) consisting of certain persons: a, b, c, . . ., and note certain analogies with the logic of connectives.

2. Quantification

A universal sentence, such as ∀xHx is like a long conjunction: Ha.Hb.Hc... . Informally, the sentence "Everyone is happy" is like saying "Alex is happy and Brenda is happy and Clare is happy and ...".

This similarity suggests one of the central implicational rules of the logic of quantifiers. The Drop Rule of the logic of connectives permits the obviously valid step from a conjunction to any of its members. Similarly, a universal sentence, viewed as a long conjunction, permits the inference to any member of that conjunction:

∀xHx   (like)   Ha.Hb.Hc....
Hb   Hb   Drop

The universal quantifier cannot be actually <u>defined</u> by ".". Different definitions would be required for different finite universes of discourse. And infinite UDs would call for infinitely long conjunctions! Consequently, the universal quantifier symbol is taken as an added basic sign of logic. And its rule which is "similar" to the Drop Rule is given its own name: <u>Universal Instantiation</u>. In a stepwise inference, such a step will be justified by the abbreviation <u>UI</u>. And Hb in the example below will be said to be an <u>instance</u> of Hx (which ∀x entitles us to infer by UI):

```
  ..  ..   ..
2,3  7   ∀xHx
2,3  8   Hb        7 UI
  ..  ..   ..
```

In contrast to a universal sentence, an existential sentence, such as ∃xHx, is like a long <u>dis</u>junction: Ha v Hb v Hc ... . Informally, to say "Someone is happy" is like saying "Alex is happy or Brenda is happy or Clare is happy or ...". I.e., at least one of the individuals in the universe of discourse is happy.

2. Quantification

Just as the Universal Instantiation rule corresponded to the Drop Rule for conjunctions, so a basic rule for <u>existential</u> sentences is suggested by the Add Rule for disjunctions: <u>Existential Generalization</u> (EG).

$$\frac{Hb}{\exists x Hx} \text{ EG} \quad \text{(like)} \quad \frac{Hb}{Ha \lor Hb \lor Hc \ldots} \quad \text{Add}$$

Two further rules are suggested by analogies with rules for the <u>negations</u> of conjunctions and disjunctions, namely the de Morgan Nand and Nor equivalences.

The Nand rule says the negation of a <u>con</u>junction is a <u>dis</u>junction of the negations of the components of the conjunction. Since universal and existential sentences resemble conjunctions and disjunctions, respectively, one anticipates that the negation of a universal sentence (long conjunction) should be equivalent to an existential sentence (long disjunction) which corresponds to having each member of the disjunction negated. The relationship may be portrayed informally as follows:

$$\sim \forall x Hx \quad \text{(like)} \quad \sim(Ha.Hb.Hc\ldots) \iff \sim Ha \lor \sim Hb \lor \sim Hc \quad \text{(like)} \quad \exists x \sim Hx$$

In accordance with the analogy, we shall take the logical equivalence as a basic equivalence rule of the logic of quantifiers: <u>(Universal) Quantifier Negation (QN)</u>

$$\sim \forall x Hx \iff \exists x \sim Hx$$

Informally: "Not everyone is happy" $\iff$ "Someone is not happy". (Or, in our "official" reading: It is not the case that for every x, x is happy $\iff$ There exists at least one x such that x is not happy.)

VI 132
3. Quantifying Compounds

In a parallel way, the Nor equivalence suggests a companion equivalence for negated existential sentences:

$\sim \exists x Hx$ (like) $\sim(Ha \lor Hb \lor Hc...) \Longleftrightarrow \sim Ha.\sim Hb.\sim Hc...$ (like) $\forall x \sim Hx$

The equivalence, stated in its own right, is:

$\sim \exists x Hx \Longleftrightarrow \forall x \sim Hx$ (Existential) Quantifier Negation (QN)

Informally: It is not so that at least one person is happy $\Longleftrightarrow$ No one is happy.

(It will have been noticed that we have reverted to the informal $\Longleftrightarrow$. Although, we have been speaking of meanings, we have used analogies, and have not provided full semantical truth rules for the quantifiers. We are, in fact, proceeding in the spirit of Chapter II. That is, while appealing to an intuitive validity in terms of meanings, we will focus first on useful rules (e.g., of deduction). Then we will draw these together into a particular deductive system. The justifying basis in semantics will become progressively clearer.)

3. <u>Quantifying Compounds</u>.

Such sentences as "Everybody is happy", valuable in speaking of very limited universes of discourse, must be qualified for larger UDs. Such a qualified universal sentence might be "Everybody at Jeff's 1978 New Year's party is happy". To symbolize this, we may introduce another predicate letter P, with Px meaning that x is at the party in question. We wish to say that every x at that party is happy. Since every such x is at the party <u>and</u> happy, a common first attempt at symbolization is: $\forall x(Px.Hx)$. But the official reading for this is "For every x; x is at the party and (the same) x is happy", where x now covers the very large UD of all persons. As a long conjunction, it means "A.A.Albert is at the party and is happy and Paul

3. Quantifying Compounds

Bernays is at the party and is happy and ...". By Universal Instantiation, this implies of each person, e.g., the U.S. Ambassador to Portugal, that he is at the party and is happy. Clearly, the symbolization asserts too much. All that is wanted is to say of every person that he is happy <u>if</u> he is at the party (in the weak sense of "if", of course). Accordingly, the appropriate symbolization is: $\forall x(Px \supset Hx)$. The reading is: "For every x, <u>if</u> x is at the party then x is happy". The corresponding "long conjunction" would be $(Pa \supset Ha).(Pb \supset Hb).(Pc \supset Hc)$ ...etc. Universal Instantiation for the Ambassador (whom we will symbolize as "a") yields $Pa \supset Ha$. I.e., if a is at the party, he is happy. By Mif, this claims no more than that either a is not at the party or is happy (or both). We see, then, that all simple universal sentences which say something about all of a specified class of things can be symbolized as saying something about everything <u>if</u> it fulfills the qualifications of belonging to the specified class:

Every lion is carnivorous $\forall x(Lx \supset Cx)$

All athletes exercise $\forall x(Ax \supset Ex)$

Each quasar broadcasts $\forall x(Qx \supset Bx)$

In the preceding discussion, we have been applying quantifiers to open clauses. As earlier indicated, all occurrences of a given variable in an open clause (with no other quantifiers) are taken to have the same reference. For example, in the clause foll ing the quantifier in the sentence about lions, the two occurrences of "x" refer to the <u>same</u> individual, (whatever individual it happens to be). E.g., the sentence implies, among other things, that if a certain dog named Toby is a lion, then <u>Toby</u> is carnivorous!

3. Quantifying Compounds

The same variable can occur in separately quantified clauses, however, without making common reference. For example, we can symbolize "Dogs bark but wolves howl" as $\forall x(Dx \supset Bx).\forall x(Wx \supset Hx)$. The reading for the symbolism is: "For every x, if x is a dog then x barks, and furthermore, for every x, if x is a wolf then x howls". We shall say that the two occurrences of "$\forall x$" have distinct scopes. The scope of a quantifier occurrence is the clause that immediately follows it.

We turn now to existential sentences. Suppose we wish to make the transition from a limited UD assertion such as "Some are overloud" to the more explicit "Some who are at the party are overloud". The change is achieved by existentially quantifying a compound of the clauses Px and Ox. Here, however, it is not an if-compound that is called for but a simple conjunction. The symbolization is: $\exists x(Px.Ox)$. The official reading is "There exists at least one x such that x is at the party and x is overloud". The corresponding "long disjunction" is $(Pa.Oa) \lor (Pb.Ob) \lor (\ldots$. Given any instance of someone who is both at the party and overloud, "Some at the party are overloud" follows by Existential Generalization.

A momentary temptation may have been felt to symbolize the existential sentence with an if, in superficial analogy with the universal symbolization. But $\exists x(Px \supset Ox)$ reads "There exists at least one x (in the UD of persons) such that if x is at the party, then x is overloud". But that does not actually imply that anyone at the party is overloud. And the English sentence clearly does imply it. All the symbolization says is (by Mif) that there is some person, somewhere, who is either not at the party or else is overloud, i.e., $\exists x(\sim Px \lor Ox)$. But this feeble statement is true merely if there is anyone

3. Quantifying Compounds

not at the party, loud or not. (These two mistranslations (i.e., using a conjunction in universals and an implication in existentials, as the main connective) have been treated at this length of forestall frequent initial misconceptions).

Words like "every", "some", "any", etc., are called <u>determiners</u> by some modern linguists. Another determiner is "no", as in "No guest at the party is bored". To symbolize sentences using "no" we do not need a new quantifier. A sentence of the above form has in fact long been referred to as a <u>universal negative</u>. It calls for a universal quantifier and a negation. But the desired effect depends on correct placement of the negation sign. Putting the negation in front, e.g., $\sim \forall x(Px \supset Bx)$, merely denies that <u>everyone</u> at the party is bored. The correct symbolization, therefore, is $\forall x(Px \supset \sim Bx)$. One may feel that it is just as well symbolized as the negation of an existential sentence, i.e., $\sim \exists x(Px.Bx)$. The feeling is right. The two symbolizations are equivalent. Consider the following equivalence transformations:

$\sim \exists x(Px.Bx)$
$\forall x \sim (Px.Bx)$ QN (Quantifier Negation)
$\forall x(\sim Px \; v \sim Bx)$ Nand
$\forall x(Px \supset \sim Bx)$ Mif

While each symbolization has advantages in given situations, tradition favors the universal symbolization of the "universal negative", other things being equal.

Traditional logic gave special prominence to four types of simple quantified sentences. Their forms were <u>All As are Bs</u>, <u>Some As are Bs</u>, <u>No As are Bs</u>, and <u>Some As are not Bs</u>. We have already covered the first three, called, respectively the <u>universal affirmative</u>, the <u>particular affirmative</u>, and the <u>universal negative</u>. To round out the account of the

3. Quantifying Compounds

four types, it will suffice to remark that the fourth type, the <u>particular negative</u>, Some As are not Bs, is symbolized as an existentially quantified conjunction with negated second component. E.g., "Some guests at the party are not sober" is $\exists x(Px \cdot \sim Sx)$. I.e., "There exists at least one x who is a guest at the party such that x is not sober".

The four types of sentences were arranged in a pattern called <u>The Square of Opposition</u>. Each type is exemplified below using the predicate letters, G,H interpreted in terms of "guest", and "happy".

A (from <u>A</u>ffirmo)   E (from N<u>E</u>go)

<u>Universal Affirmative</u>   <u>Universal Negative</u>

$\forall x(Gx \supset Hx)$ $\forall x(Gx \supset \sim Hx)$

All guests are happy ←——— contrary ———→ No guests are happy

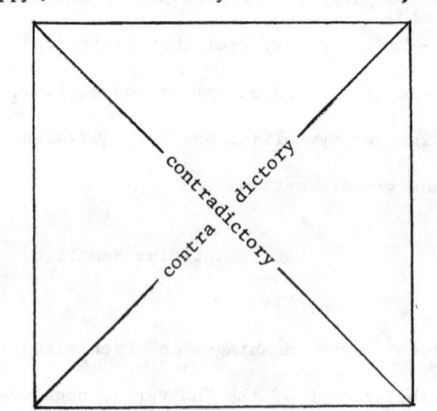

contradictory
contradictory

Some guests are happy   Some guests are not happy

$\exists x(Gx \cdot Hx)$ $\exists x(Gx \cdot \sim Hx)$

<u>Particular Affirmative</u>   <u>Particular Negative</u>

I (from Aff<u>I</u>rmo)   O (from Neg<u>O</u>)

3. Quantifying Compounds

The Square of Opposition played an important role in traditional logic. Other relations beside those of being contrary and contradictory were indicated between other pairs. But the development of modern logic required modifications which need not concern us for the present.

Beside historical interest, however, the Square makes graphic the important distinction between stating a contrary to a sentence, and stating its simple negation (contradictory). Both are "opposites", but in different senses. The contraries on the Square are opposite in the sense that if one is true the other cannot be. But both may be false. They are all-or-none extremes with a range of intermediate possibilities. The contradictories on the Square are also contraries in the sense of each excluding the other. But at least one of two contradictories must be true, in the light of what was said in Chapter I about truth and negation.

Confusion between the two relationships, sometimes deliberate, is frequent in quarrels. E.g.,

A: All politicians are crooked.
B: That's not so!
A: Oh, so you think no politician is crooked! I suppose you think they are all saints!

A here unjustifiably takes B's negation as the extreme contrary. A's second sentence, which jumps from crook to saint, unjustifiably introduces another contrary (not in the sense of the Square, but in the sense of excluding crook by an extreme opposite, not simple contradiction).

3. Quantifying Compounds

The two quantifiers of logic serve to symbolize many different ways of speaking in English. Sentences using the determiners "all", "some", "no", etc. are only a few of them. To use logic effectively, one must become increasingly familiar with them. The following remarks may serve as a starter.

∃xLx (with reading: There is an x such that x lives) can symbolize not only "Something lives", "Something is living", but also "There are things which live", "There are living things", and, in an "abstract mode", "There is life in the universe (of discourse)", "Life exists."

∀x(Lx ⊃ Cx) (with reading: For every x, if x is a lion then x is carnivorous) can not only symbolize "Every lion is carnivorous", "All lions are carnivorous", but also "Lions are carnivorous", "The lion is carnivorous", "A lion is carnivorous", and colloquially, e.g., by a zookeeper, "Your lion is carnivorous".

Notice that universality must be inferred from context and meaning, since similar grammatical forms can at times call for an existential quantifier, as in "Lions are loose", "The lion is loose", "A lion is loose", "Your lion is loose".

The word "only" is often used for universality. It is attached to the predicate that appears in the consequent in the usual symbolization, just as "only if" does in symbolizations using " ⊃ ". Thus ∀x(Sx ⊃ Px) (reading: For every x, if x is a successful person then x is persistent) can symbolize not only "Every successful person is persistent", but also "Only the persistent are successful", or "The successful are only the persistent", or "A person is successful only if he is persistent".

3. Quantifying Compounds

Other ways of expressing universality use

a. "one" or "you", as in "If one travels, one matures", or "If you travel, you mature";

b. "whatever", "whoever", "whenever", etc., as in "Whatever goes up comes down";

c. "he who", as in "He who hesitates is lost";

d. a shifted determiner, as in "Politicians are all showmen";

e. a temporal determiner, possibly shifted, as in "Mammals are always warm blooded."

Summary of Quantifier Rules So Far

In this summary, Cu will stand for any clause containing one or more occurrences of some variable u which are not within the scope of a quantifier on u, and Cb will stand for the same clause with some name b substituted for each such occurrence of u.

Universal Instantiation (UI)　　Existential Generalization (EG)
to name instances　　　　　　　　from name instances

$\forall u Cu$　　　　　　　　　　　　Cb
Cb　　UI　　　　　　　　　　　　$\exists u Cu$　　EG

Quantifier Negation Equivalences (QN)

$\sim \forall u Cu \iff \exists u \sim Cu$

$\sim \exists u Cu \iff \forall u \sim Cu$

Exercises VI 2

1. Symbolize each of the following sentences. Use only the indicated predicate letters. A word like "thing" ordinarily does not require a predicate symbol. Such words are usually "universe of discourse words", indicating (and applying trivially to everything in) the universe of discourse, or they are simply to provide nouns, to fulfill the demands of English grammar.

*a. Everything falls. (F)
 b. Nothing lasts. (L)
 c. Something thinks. (T)
 d. Some things are not flawless. (F)
*e. There are no ogres. (O)
 f. Every giraffe is herbivorous. (G,H)
*g. Not all animals are herbivorous. (A,H)
*h. No lions are herbivorous. (L,H)
 i. Some animals hibernate. (A,H)
 j. Some animals do not migrate. (A,M)
*k. Nothing that is not sealed will be mailed. (S,M)
 l. Some things that are not flawless are nevertheless valuable. (F,V)
 m. Any student can read. (S,R)
 n. No businessman does not gamble. (B,G)
 o. Not every businessman gambles. (B,G)

Exercises VI 2

2. Provide the following valid inferences with stepwise deductions. Bear in mind that connective logic is a part of the logic of quantifiers. UI, EG and QN are simply added steps.

*a. All lions are carnivorous
    Rex is a lion
    Rex is carnivorous   (L,C,r)

*b. Rex is a lion
    Rex does not howl
    Some lions do not howl   (r,L,H)

c. All lions roar
   Fido does not roar
   Fido is not a lion   (L,R,f)

*d. All wolves howl
    Fido howls
    Fido is not a wolf
    Not everything that howls
       is a wolf   (W,H,f)
    (Hint: Use Absurdity)

*e. Every applicant who speaks
       Spanish will be considered
    Jane speaks Spanish
    If Jane applies, she will
       be considered   (A,S,C,j)

f. All actors are temperamental
   Todd is an actor, but not
      fickle
   Not everyone who is
      temperamental is fickle (A,T,t,F)
   (Hint: Use Absurdity)

g. Every creature in the cage is a bird of prey or an aquatic scavenger
   Queenie, in the cage there, is aquatic but not a scavenger
   Some birds of prey are not scavengers

   (Symbolized:) $\forall x(Cx \supset (Bx \lor (Ax \cdot Sx)))$
                  $Cq \cdot Aq \cdot {\sim}Sq$
                  $\exists x(Bx \cdot {\sim} Sx)$

3. Symbolize each of the following so that the first symbol is a negation sign. Then internalize the negation by first using one of the QN laws and then using familiar steps of connective logic (e.g., Nif, Nor, Mif, etc.) Translate the resulting symbolization back into normal English.

   *a. Not all germs are harmful. (G,H)

   *b. It is not so that some members are not honest. (M,H)

   c. It is not so that some members are lazy. (M,L)

   d. It is not so that no student is ambitious. (S,A)

Exercises VI 2

    e. It is not so that no one who is not a genius can write. (G,W)

4. Symbolize, using the predicate letters indicated:

    *a. Politicians will always compromise. (P,C)

    *b. Wolves do not bark. (W,B)

    *c. There are lazy people who are nevertheless intelligent. (L,I)

    *d. Poverty doesn't always mean laziness. (P,L)

    *e. Every voter is a Republican or a Democrat. (V,R,D)

    *f. Horses and cows are mammals. (H,C,M)

    *g. He who plans, survives. (P,S)

    *h. Only Ph.D.s or teachers will be considered. (P,T,C)

    *i. Whoever graduates will be jobless unless he hustles. (G,J,H)

    *j. A scout is outside. (S,O)

    *k. A scout is reverent. (S,R)

    *l. The governor is an elected official. (G,E,O)

    *m. A governor is a successful politician. (G,S,P)

    *n. A governor is speaking and is on television. (G,S,T)

    *o. Any promoter who is clever or at least glib will succeed, if he is not overconsiderate. (P,C,G,S,O)

4. Diagrams

4. Diagrams and Classes

Some aspects of quantificational logic can be made vivid by diagrams. Imagine that we symbolize a clause, containing one free variable, as Ax. The clause may be true of all the individuals x in the universe of discourse, or true of some, or of none. Those of which it is true may be regarded as forming a <u>class</u> — the class of those of which A is true, or the class of As, for short. The class may be represented by a circle in a square, the square representing the universe of discourse (UD): Quantified statements about A may then be represented as shown below:

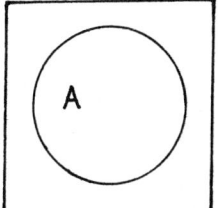

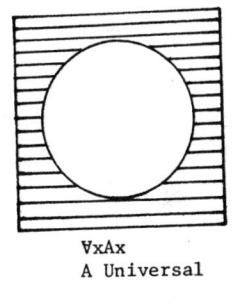

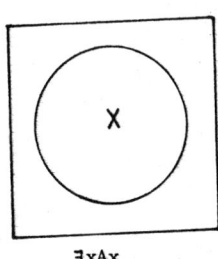

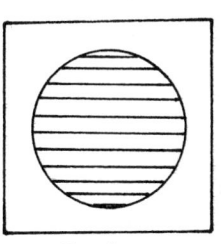

∀xAx
A Universal

∀x ~Ax
A Empty

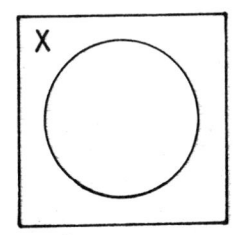

∃xAx
A non-empty

∃x ~Ax
A non-universal

4. Diagrams

The four diagrams above are arranged to show contraries and contradictories, as in the Square of Opposition mentioned in the preceding section. Note the following conventions.

<u>Everything is A</u> is shown by blacking out the region outside the circle to show that there is nothing in it. The UD is confined to class A, which is therefore said to be <u>universal</u>.

<u>Nothing is A</u> blacks out the inside of the circle. Class A is then said to be <u>empty</u>.

<u>Something is A</u> is shown by placing a cross in the circle. Class A is said to be <u>non-empty</u>. (A region with neither cross nor black-out is simply left uncommitted.)

<u>Something is not A</u> places a cross outside the circle. Class A is then said to be <u>non-universal</u>.

The method is extended to sentences involving two predicates, A and B, by drawing overlapping circles for A and B, omitting the UD frame when not needed, and blacking out as before to show emptiness and placing a cross to show existence:

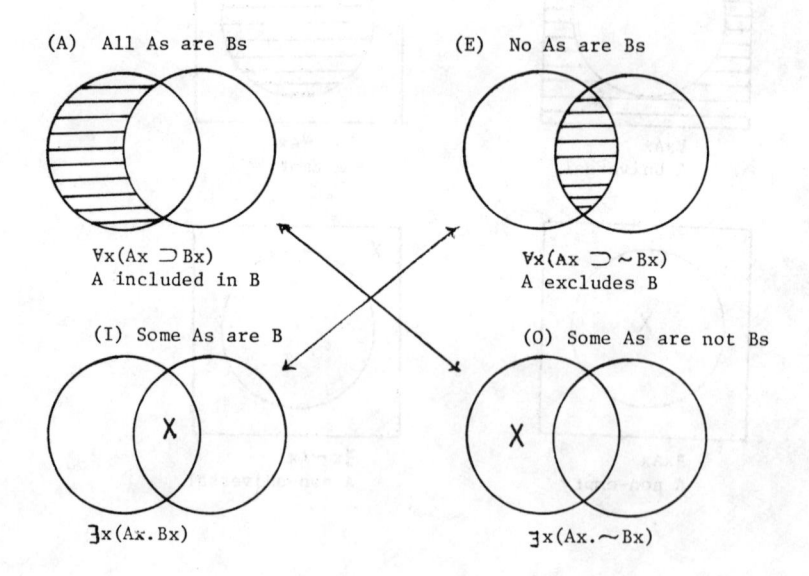

(A) All As are Bs

$\forall x(Ax \supset Bx)$
A included in B

(E) No As are Bs

$\forall x(Ax \supset \sim Bx)$
A excludes B

(I) Some As are B

$\exists x(Ax \cdot Bx)$

(O) Some As are not Bs

$\exists x(Ax \cdot \sim Bx)$

4. Diagrams

These are the four traditional <u>categorical</u> forms, A, E, I, O, earlier mentioned.

(A) <u>All As are Bs</u>. A's, if any, are confined to the B-region by blacking out the region which might show the existence of As which are not Bs. Class A is said to be <u>included</u> in class B.

(E) <u>No As are Bs</u>. The overlapping region is blacked out. This rules out things which are both A and B. (The symmetry of the diagram shows it could equally well represent <u>No Bs are As</u>. In other words, simple conversion of the universal negative is no fallacy, as it would be for the universal affirmative (A). Instead, it yields a logical equivalent.) Class A is said to <u>exclude</u> class B.

(I) <u>Some As are Bs</u>. The existence cross is placed in the overlapping region (the same region blacked out by I's contradictory, E). Here again, symmetry indicates the logical equivalence of <u>Some Bs are As</u> -- a simple conversion rule for I sentences.

(O) <u>Some As are not Bs</u>. The existence cross is placed in the A-but-not-B region (which was blacked out by the A sentence, the contradictory of O).

Diagrams provide an easy test for inferences with two premises and a conclusion each of one of the four categorical forms A, E, I, and O. Such inferences have long been famous as <u>categorical syllogisms</u>. A theory of categorical syllogisms was the first part of logic to be formulated (by Aristotle, circa 350 B.C.), preceding systematizations of connective logic (by the Stoics, circa 250 B.C.). Aristotle's rules did not refer to quantifiers or connectives. Indeed, the rules for quantifiers given so far are not quite adequate to the deductions. The needed strengthening is given shortly, but the method of diagrams is so quick and instructive, that it is worth learning by itself. Systems of diagrams using neither Aristotle's rules nor those of quantificational logic developed only in recent centuries, culminating in the system here described (developed by John Venn near the end of the nineteenth century).

4. Diagrams

Syllogisms involve three predicates (traditionally called terms). The two that appear in the conclusion were called the <u>subject</u> and the <u>predicate</u>, though in our present terminology both were predicates. The one called the <u>subject</u> was the one that appeared first. For example, "poet" is the subject term of each of the following, "All poets are sensitive", "Some poets are famous", "No poets are financiers". The premisses of a categorical syllogism each involve the third predicate, called the <u>middle term</u>. In keeping with tradition, we will often use S, P, and M for predicate letters in describing the form of syllogisms, and in labelling the corresponding diagrams, — now three in number.

As a first example, consider:

(A) All upwardly <u>m</u>obile persons are poseurs $\quad \forall x(Mx \supset Px)$
(A) All <u>s</u>nobs are upwardly mobile $\quad \forall x(Sx \supset Mx)$
(A) All snobs are poseurs $\quad \forall x(Sx \supset Px)$

The first premiss, of form A, blacks out all "mobiles" which are not poseurs: The second premiss, also of form A, blacks out snobs that are not upwardly mobile: Together, the two premisses have blacked out all snobs but those in the poseur region. That is, the premisses have confined the "subject" region to the "predicate" region. The conclusion is forced to be true, if both premisses are true. The validity of this inference,

4. Diagrams

which takes at least six lines by deduction (as will be seen in the next chapter), is seen directly from the diagram.

Example 2:

(A)	All poseurs are Machiavellian	$\forall x(Px \supset Mx)$
(A)	All Machiavellian people are snobs	$\forall x(Mx \supset Sx)$
(A)	All snobs are poseurs	$\forall x(Sx \supset Px)$

Crossing out areas in accord with the premisses, we have: but here the snob region has not been confined to the poseur region. Both premisses could be true and the conclusion false. The invalidity may perhaps be more readily seen by comparing it to the following inference, which has the same form:

(A)	All pigs are mammals	$\forall x(Px \supset Mx)$
(A)	All mammals have spines	$\forall x(Mx \supset Sx)$
(A)	All things with spines are pigs	$\forall x(Sx \supset Px)$

The diagram method supplies a test for syllogisms, in fact, revealing both validity and invalidity.

Example 3:

(I)	Some students are militants	$\exists x(Sx.Mx)$
(A)	All militants are potential neurotics	$\forall x(Mx \supset Px)$
(O)	Some students are not potential neurotics	$\exists x(Sx.\sim Px)$

It is best to black out as much as possible first, so that places for existence crosses are narrowed down. Blacking out the M-but-not-P region in accord with the universal (second) premiss, and placing the existence cross in the only S-and-M region left gives   No x is provided in the student (S) region which is not in the potential neurotic (P) region as asserted by the conclusion, so the inference is invalid.

4. Diagrams

Example 4:

Some <u>s</u>tudents <u>m</u>editate (transcendentally) $\exists x(Sx.Mx)$
No one who me<u>d</u>itates is <u>p</u>rim $\forall x(Mx \supset \sim Px)$
Some students are not prim $\exists x(Sx.\sim Px)$

    Blacking out the M-and-P region in accord with the universal premiss, and placing the cross in the only S-and-M area left: puts the cross, simultaneously, in the S-and-not-P region. The inference is therefore obviously <u>valid</u>.

    Sometimes the premisses will leave more than one region available for placing an existence cross. In that case, put a cross in both places and connect them by a line. This is to show that existence in either region, alone or together, is consistent with the premisses. For the inference to be valid, the conclusion must not be false in <u>any</u> of these allowed circumstances. (A valid conclusion is not merely one which is consistent with the premisses; it is one whose truth is necessitated by the truth of the premisses.)

Exercises VI 3

Decide the validity of the following inferences by Venn diagram. Letters suggested for labelling circles are shown underlined in the English inferences.

*1. Every scholar likes footnotes (S,F,U)
    Some scholars are untidy
    ─────────────────────────────
    Some who are untidy like footnotes

*2. Every robin lays blue eggs (R,B,G)
    Some birds in my garden lay blue eggs
    ─────────────────────────────────────
    Some birds in my garden are robins

*3. No spy seeks publicity (S,P,A)
    All actors seek publicity
    ─────────────────────────
    No actors are spies

*4. No spy seeks publicity (S,P,T)
    No timid person seeks publicity
    ───────────────────────────────
    No spy is timid

*5. All cats are mammals (C,M,L)
    Only mammals produce live young
    ───────────────────────────────
    All cats produce live young

6. All murderers are psychopaths (M,P,S)
   Some spies are murderers
   ────────────────────────
   Some spies are psychopaths

7. All scientists are rationalists (S,R,E)
   No existentialist is a rationalist
   ──────────────────────────────────
   No scientist is an existentialist

8. No positivists are metaphysicians (P,M,S)
   Some scholars are not metaphysicians
   ────────────────────────────────────
   Some scholars are positivists

9. Some millionaires are not polite (M,P,S)
   All millionaires are socialites
   ───────────────────────────────
   Some socialites are not polite

10. All market analysts are practical (M,P,S)
    No scholars are market analysts
    ───────────────────────────────
    No scholars are practical

11. Some males are not playboys (M,P,S)
    All males are sex-conscious
    ───────────────────────────
    Some sex-conscious people are not playboys

12. Some poets are moody (P,M,S)
    All moody people are shunned
    ────────────────────────────
    Some shunned people are poets

OPTIONAL FURTHER READING
Quantifiers and Inductive Inference.

The "laws of nature" which scientists seek are universal sentences. Typically, they assert some property of Q (possibly involving quantitative relationships) of everything which as a property P. The typical form, then, is simply $\forall x(Px \supset Qx)$. Viewed as a "long conjunction", it is like $(Pa \supset Qa).(Pb \supset Qb).(...$ Equivalently, it is like $(\sim Pa \vee Qa).(\sim Pb \vee Qb).(...$ Each member of the conjunction can be regarded as an *instance* of the property of either not being P or being Q. Although the universal sentence implies each instance, by Universal Instantiation, no finite number of instances suffices to "prove" the law. Scientists may pile up instances, and grow increasingly confident that the universal sentence is true, but the inference from the instances to the universal will always be inductive. It will yield a certain measure of probability of confirmation, but the truth of the universal is never guaranteed by the truth of the instances (the evidence sentences). The very next observation may yield a negative instance - something that has property P but does not have property Q. Suppose the next observed object is d, and $Pd. \sim Qa$. This is equivalent to $\sim(\sim Pd \vee Qd)$, by Nor. Thus, it is the negation of one of the members of the "long conjunction". A conjunction, however long, is false if even one of its components is. Similarly, a single negative instance suffices to falsify the universal.

In practice, if a single observation appears to contradict a highly confirmed law, it is common to suspect an error in the observation, - in the instruments used, in the observer, etc., and to demand further observations. But the logic of the matter is clear. If the single instance *was* negative, the universal is false. The falsified universal would not necessarily simply be discarded. It might be "demoted" to a still very valuable statement of high statistical frequency, or it might be slightly revised. But unaltered, it would be false.

An existential sentence, by contrast, can be verified by one instance. An existential sentence such as "Some porpoises can speak high-school-level English", symbolized as $\exists x(Px.Ex)$ is like a long disjunction which ascribes the property of being an English-speaking porpoise to one or another individual in the universe. A single instance of that property, i.e., a single English-speaking porpoise, suffices to verify the existential sentence, just as a single true component of a disjunction makes the entire disjunction true. On the other hand, no amount of negative instances can disprove it. The negation of the existential $\exists x(Px.Ex)$ is the universal $\forall x(Px \supset \sim Ex)$, and a universal is not fully provable from instances, as we have seen. A frequently heard pronouncement is "You can't prove a negative". Stated in this way, such a pronouncement is no truth of logic. But if applied to existentials, it has the justification indicated above. On the other hand, the negation of an existential sentential sentence can, at least, become highly confirmed, just as a universal can.

VII

MORE COMPLEX QUANTIFICATION

The basic elements of quantificational symbolism were introduced in the preceding chapter. But attention was focused mainly on one-place predicates, and on single quantifications and their negations. Indeed, traditional logic, from Aristotle into the nineteenth century, went no further, in any systematic way. But just as compounds can be built up by compounding compounds, so quantificational clauses can be quantified again, or compounded in turn.

In this chapter, we will first survey some of the possibilities informally, and then study a systematic grammar for the symbolism.

1. Relational Quantifications

Consider the two-place predicate "loves". With two names it forms a complete sentence: "Greg loves Clare", symbolized Lgc. To symbolize "Greg loves someone" (for a universe of discourse of people) the second name is replaced by a variable and the result prefixed with an existential quantifier on that variable: $\exists x Lgx$. To symbolize "Someone loves Clare" would be $\exists x Lxc$.

To symbolize "Everyone loves someone", an additional quantifier is needed. Also a new variable is needed, to prevent confusion. The symbolization would be $\forall x \exists y Lxy$. The reading is given simply by a repeated application of the readings for single quantifications: For every x there is a y such that x loves y. The scope of the universal quantifier is the immediately following clause. This might suggest the symbolism $\forall x(\exists y Lxy)$, just as $\sim(\sim A)$ might seem

1. Relational Quantifications

suggested for double negation. But the parentheses are unnecessary in both cases, because the extent of the immediately following clause is always unambiguous.

It is important to notice that the order of the quantifiers is important to the meaning of this double quantification. That is, $\forall x \exists y Lxy$ and $\exists y \forall x Lxy$ are not equivalent. The first symbolized sentence says that every x in the universe of discourse loves someone; but that does not logically imply that there is some y in the universe of discourse whom everyone loves, which is a correct reading for the second. (Another correct reading for the second, in which Lxy is thought of, in passive voice, as "y is loved by x", would be "Someone is loved by everyone".)

Other quantificational patterns yield other meanings, of course. The reader may wish to study the following, for comparison. For each, the reader should recall the full official reading and relate it to the shorter, informal English reading given.

$\forall x \exists y Lxy$
Everyone loves someone

$\exists x \forall y Lxy$
Someone loves everyone

$\exists y \forall x Lxy$
Someone is loved by everyone

$\forall y \exists x Lxy$
Everyone is loved by someone

$\forall x \forall y Lxy$
Everyone loves everyone

$\exists x \exists y Lxy$
Someone loves someone

$\forall x Lxx$
Everyone loves himself

$\exists x Lxx$
Someone loves himself

2. Combining Quantifiers and Connectives

The QN rules for the negation of quantifiers, applied to single quantifications in the preceding chapter, can be applied to multiple quantifications by recalling that in showing $\sim \forall u C$ as logically equivalent to $\exists u \sim C$, and $\sim \exists u C$ as logically equivalent to $\forall u \sim C$, C was intended to stand for <u>any</u> clause, possibly an already quantified clause. Thus, if C is taken to be the already quantified clause $\exists y L x y$, the rule for $\sim \forall x C$ applies to $\sim \forall x \exists y L x y$, and yields $\exists x \sim \exists y L x y$. In other words, denying that everyone loves someone is equivalent to asserting that there is someone, x, such that it is not so that x loves someone. The inner clause can be transformed, in turn, to $\forall y \sim L x y$ by another application of QN, taking C to be Lxy in $\sim \exists y C \Leftrightarrow \forall y \sim C$. The result is $\exists x \forall y \sim L x y$, which can be read informally as "Someone loves no one". The method can easily be seen to extend to a negation standing before any string of quantifiers (which stand before a single clause.) Such a negation can thus be <u>internalized</u> "wholesale" simply by changing each quantifier to its opposite and moving the negation sign inward past all the quantifiers. Quantifications can also appear as members of compounds, for example "Either Greg is daydreaming or he loves someone", symbolizable as $Dg \lor \exists x L g x$. And quantifiers may have more complex scopes. Before taking up the systematic grammar of notation, the following examples can be studied on the basis of what has been already said.

Everyone Grant hires, he bullies.
    $\forall x (Hgx \supset Bgx)$ (Reading: "For every x, if Grant hires x then Grant bullies x.")

Exercises VII 1

Not everyone you love will love you.
  ∼∀x∀y(Lxy ⊃ Lyx) (Reading: "It is not the case that for every x, for every y if x loves y then y loves x." Note that the "you" in this example is not "second person" but is a familiar way of expressing universality. Similarly, the "will" is acting not as a future tense but also as a universality indicator.)

One's younger brothers always pester one.
  ∀x∀y((Yxy.Bxy) ⊃ Pxy) (Reading: "For every x for every y, <u>if</u> x is younger than y and x is a brother of y, then x pesters y.")

If every supporter of Drake votes for him, he will win.
  ∀x(Sxd ⊃ Vxd) ⊃ Wd (Reading: "If for every x, if x is a supporter of Drake then x votes for Drake, then Drake wins." Note that the scope of the quantifier, the immediately following clause, does not include the consequent.)

No tourist comes to Nerja unless someone advertises it.
  ∀x(Tx ⊃ ∼Cxn) v ∃xAxn (Informally: "Either every x who is a tourist refrains from coming to Nerja or else some x advertises Nerja.")

Some celebrities are admired by every faddist.
  ∃x(Cx.∀y(Fy ⊃ Ayx))

Every crackpot is admired by someone gullible.
  ∀x(Cx ⊃ ∃y(Gy.Ayx))

Exercises VII 1

1. Internalize negations for each of the following.

  *a. ∼∀x∃y∀zRxyz   *d. ∼∀x∃y(Hxy ⊃ Rzb)

  *b. ∼(Pb ⊃ ∀xHbx)   *e. ∼∀x(Px ⊃ ∃ySyx)

  *c. ∼(∀x∃yRxy ⊃ Hzb)   *f. ∼∀x(∃ySyx ⊃ Px)

Exercises VII 1

*2. Symbolize the following. Use the symbols indicated. Universe of discourse may be taken to be people where convenient.

   a. Bruce smiles at someone. (b,S)

   b. Everyone smiles at Bruce. (b,S)

   c. Bruce envies no one. (b,E)

   d. If Bruce is glum, he smiles at no one. (b,G,S)

   e. If no one smiles at Bruce, he is glum. (b,S,G)

   f. Bruce is anxious unless someone smiles at him. (b,A,S)

   g. Not everyone envies someone. (E)

   h. Every celebrity is envied by someone. (E, in same sense as above)

   i. Everyone Bruce smiles at likes him. (b,S,L)

   j. Bruce smiles at every girl who is pretty. (b,S,G,P)

   k. Whoever smiles at everyone is not liked by some. (S,L (for likes))

   l. Mary has a lamb. (Choose your own symbols.)

   m. Mary has an uncle. (Choose your own symbols.)

   n. Everyone who has a pool has friends. (Choose your own symbols.)

*3. Write deductions for the following valid inferences.

   a. Schulz has no in at City Hall $\qquad$ $\sim Is$
      Meara employs only people with an in at $\qquad$ $\forall x(Emx \supset Ix)$
      $\underline{\text{City Hall}}$ $\qquad$ $\sim Ems$
      Schulz is not one of Meara's employees

   b. If King contributed, so did everyone $\qquad$ $Ck \supset \forall xCx$
      $\underline{\text{Benson and Jones did not both contribute}}$ $\qquad$ $\sim(Cb \cdot Cj)$
      King did not contribute $\qquad$ $\sim Ck$

   c. Jane is sober, if anyone is
      $\underline{\text{Bill is sober}}$
      Jane is sober $\qquad$ (j,S,b)

   d. Every new boy on the block teases Debbie
      If someone teases Debbie, Debbie cries
      $\underline{\text{Benny is a new boy on the block}}$
      Debbie will cry $\qquad$ (B,T,d,C,b)

3. Syntax for Quantificational Symbolism

Despite the many combinations of connectives and quantifiers that can occur in a symbolized sentence (and there is no upper limit unless a limit is set to sentence length), quantificational syntax can be given as a fairly brief sequence of definitions. The definitions culminate in a definition of "sentence", given any particular selection of names and predicates of various degrees. The definitions are important, not only for characterizing exactly what are, and are not, sentences, but also for the exact statement of rules of deduction. The definitions formulated are precise enough for a computer to check symbol strings for sentencehood.

Because a particular selection of names and predicates of various degrees must be specified to make the definitions complete, places where they would appear in the definitions are left open, to be filled in. A particular selection of names and predicates may be viewed as the basic, or non-logical, vocabulary of a mini-language, which we will call a Q-language. Thus, definitions below (with such a vocabulary filled in), can be thought of as giving the syntax of a single Q-language (i.e., specifying exactly what a sentence of that language may consist of). The terms being defined are underlined. Some of the definitions are given simply by lists of what the defined term is to apply to.

(Vocabulary of Q-Language)

1. a. Names: (E.g., a, b, c, ...)
   b. 1-place predicates: (E.g., P, Q,...)
   c. 2-place predicates: (E.g., R, S,...)
   d. 3-place predicates: (E.g., H, K,...)
      (etc., as needed)

3. Syntax

2. **Variables**: $x, y, z, \ldots x_1, y_1, z_1, \ldots$
3. **Binary Connectives**: $.\,, \vee, \supset, \equiv$
4. **Connectives**: $\sim$, binary connectives
5. **Quantifier symbols**: $A, \exists$
6. **Auxiliary Symbols**: comma, parentheses

(Formational Syntax of Q-language)

7. A <u>term</u> is a name or a variable
8. An <u>n-place argument</u> consists of n terms (separated by commas, if more than one)
9. A <u>predication</u> is an n-place predicate followed by a parenthesis-enclosed n-place argument.
10. A <u>clause</u> is one of the following:
    a. a predication
    b. "$\sim$" followed by a clause
    c. parentheses enclosing a string consisting of a clause followed by a binary connective followed by a clause
    d. a quantifier symbol followed by a variable followed by a clause
11. Qu is a <u>quantifier on</u> (a variable) u, and (a clause) C is the <u>scope of</u> Qu, in any occurrence of QuC.
12. An occurrence of a variable u within an occurrence of QuC is <u>bound</u> in QuC.
13. An occurrence in C of a variable which is not bound in C is <u>free</u> in C.
14. A clause is <u>open</u> if some occurrence of a variable in it is free, otherwise <u>closed</u>.
15. A <u>sentence</u> is a closed clause.

3. Syntax

Examples and Discussions of the Definitions

Definition 8 (<u>n-place argument</u>). Examples: "x" and "a" are 1-place arguments; "z,z,b" and "y,b,y" are 3-place arguments.

Definition 9 (<u>Predication</u>). Examples: "P(b)" and "R(g,x,y)" are predications. Although we have written simply "Pb" and "Rgxy", and will continue to do so informally, parentheses and commas are important for clarity at all times. For example, "83 is greater than 9" is clearly symbolized by "G(83,9)" but not by "G839".

Definition 10 (<u>Clause</u>) is what is called a recursive definition. It uses not only previously defined terms, but also the word being defined! But it avoids circularity by allowing only a finite number of repeated applications (recursions). Like all recursive definitions, not all of its parts contain the defined term: Part a. speaks only of predication. To have an example, let us consider a Q-language, $Q^†$, whose names are c,g; whose predicates are L,K, (1-place), and M (2-place). Part a. suffices to establish, e.g., L(x), K(g), and M(x,c) as clauses without recursion. Parts b,c and d then serve to establish as clauses, e.g., ∼L(x), (L(x) v M(x,c)), ∀yK(y), and by further applications, also (∼L(x) v ∀yK(y)), etc. The definition thus provides both a starting point and ways to build up sentences of any length and complexity. Indeed, all the clauses of $Q^†$ can be generated. Definition 10 may be viewed not only as a method of generating clauses, but also as a test which a string of symbols must pass to be a $Q^†$ clause, i.e., a so-called recognition procedure. Thus, a symbol string may be examined (by human or computer) to see if the first symbol is (a) a predicate listed as belonging to $Q^†$, (b) a negation sign, (c) a left

3. Syntax

parenthesis, or (d) a quantifier symbol. In case (a), one goes on to check whether parentheses enclose an argument of the number of places specified in the $Q^\dagger$ list. In each of the other cases one is led to recursions to check whether some smaller string(s) is a clause. Since each recursion examines shorter strings, recursion must ultimately terminate by leading to predications or rejection of the string as a non-clause.

It should be noticed that 10c requires that parentheses enclose every pair of clauses joined by a connective. This is convenient for the statement of rules. But informally, we will continue to omit outermost parentheses and those that separate members of a disjunction, or members of a conjunction, in accord with the rules given in Chapter II, p. 35. To follow rules presupposing them, of course, we must imagine all parentheses in place. (Various sets of rules for omitting parentheses are in use, often allowing more extensive omission than ours.)

> It may be of interest to note that two parentheses and a connective are not strictly needed to prevent ambiguity. With a connective, either the first or the last parenthesis can be systematically omitted without ambiguity. Moreover, both parentheses can be omitted if a binary grouper word is used instead of a connective. Thus A v (B.C), (A v B).C, A ⊃ ~(B ⊃ C) could be rendered, respectively, either A both BC, both either ABC, If A not if BC. This possibility was first observed by the Polish logician J. Lukiasiewicz, who based a famous logical notation on it, called Polish notation. Instead of a leading, "grouper" symbol, a trailing symbol would do as well, and is used, in fact, by computer engineers who call the resulting notation "Reverse Polish".

<u>Definition 11</u> (<u>Scope</u> (of a quantifier)). The scope of a given occurrence of a quantifier is only the immediately following clause. For example, in ∀x(∃yRyx ⊃ (Hyx.∃xQx)) ⊃ Lx the scope of ∀x is not "(∃yRyx" which

is not a clause; nor is it any shorter expression than $(\exists y Ryx \supset (Hyx. \exists x Qx))$. On the other hand, the scope cannot be the longer expression $(\exists y Ryx \supset (Hyx. \exists x Qx)) \supset Hx$ for although this looks like a clause with its outermost parentheses omitted, such omission would be impossible following $\forall x$, since only the outermost parentheses of the entire sentences may be omitted. By a similar argument, the scope of $\exists y$ is only the clause Ryx.

Definition 12 (occurrences bound in (an occurrence of) a clause). Notice that the wording makes a variable occurrence immediately after a quantifier symbol is bound in the whole quantified clause.

Definition 13 (occurrence free in (an occurrence of) a clause). Example: In $\forall y(Rxy \supset \exists x Px)$, the first occurrence of x is free, but the second two are not. However, the last occurrence of x is free in the subclause Px, even though it is not free in $\exists x Px$, or in the larger, containing clauses.

Exercises VII 2

In a certain language, a,b,c, are names, and P,Q are 1-place, R,H 2-place, and G 3-place, predicates. Copy the expressions below and for each, do any of the following which are appropriate.

a. Mark it C if it is a clause (whether open or closed, allowing arguments to lack parentheses and commas, and outermost parentheses to be omitted), otherwise mark X.

b. For each occurrence of a variable in a clause, other than immediately following quantifiers: if free in the clause, mark it f; if bound, draw an arrow to the variable of the quantifier it is bound by (that is, in whose scope it is free.)

c. Underline the scope of each quantifier in a clause (with more inclusive scopes marked below included ones, if necessary.)

d. Mark it O, of open, S (for sentence) if closed.

*1. ∃xRxb

*2. ∀x(Px ⊃ Rgx)

*3. ∀xPx ⊃ Qx

*4. ∀x(Qxb ⊃ Ry)

*5. ∀x(Px ⊃ ∃y(Gayx v Pb))

*6. Rax ⊃ ∃x∀y(Rxy ⊃ ∀xGyzx)

*7. Pa v ∀xQx ⊃ Px

*8. ∀x(Px v (∀xSxx.∃yGxyz))

OPTIONAL FURTHER READING

Finite Expansions

The resemblance of universal and existential quantifications to (long) conjunctions and disjunctions, respectively, has already been used in explaining several points. It is sometimes helpful to keep them short by supposing the universe of discourse to contain just a finite number of named or numbered individuals. Quantifications can then be taken to correspond to definite, finite conjunctions or disjunctions called <u>finite expansions</u>. For example, for a universe consisting of just a and b, a finite expansion can be given not only for ∀xPx and ∃xPx but also for combinations of quantifiers and connectives. The effect may be seen from studying the following list of expansions. The first few are already familiar, but the others may be revealing:

Finite Expansions for {a,b}

1.	∀xPx	Pa.Pb	Everything is P
2.	∃xPx	Pa v Pb	Something is P
3.	~∀xPx	~(Pa.Pb)	Not everything is P
4.	∀x~Px	~Pa.~Pb	Nothing is P
5.	∀xPx.∀xQx	Pa.Pb.Qa.Qb	Everything is P and everything is Q
6.	∀x(Px.Qx)	Pa.Qa.Pb.Qb	Everything is both P and Q
7.	∃xPx.∃xQx	(Pa v Pb).(Qa v Qb)	There are Ps and there are Qs
8.	∃x(Px.Qx)	(Pa.Qa) v (Pb.Qb)	Something is both P and Q
9.	∀xPx ⊃ Qb	(Pa.Pb) ⊃ Qb	If everything P, b is Q
10.	∀x(Px ⊃ Qb)	(Pa ⊃ Qb).(Pb ⊃ Qb)	For everything, if it is P, then b is Q

Finite Expansions

11. $\exists x Px \supset Qb$ $(Pa \lor Pb) \supset Qb$

12. $\exists x(Px \supset Qb)$ $(Pa \supset Qb) \lor (Pb \supset Qb)$

13. $\forall x \forall y Rxy$: $\forall y Ray . \forall y Rby$; $Raa.Rab.Rba.Rbb$

14. $\forall x \exists y Rxy$: $\exists y Ray . \exists y Rby$; $(Raa \lor Rab).(Rba \lor Rbb)$

15. $\exists x \forall y Rxy$: $\forall y Ray \lor \forall y Rby$: $(Raa.Rab) \lor (Rba.Rbb)$

16. $\forall x(\exists y Rxy \supset Qb)$: $(\exists y Ray \supset Qb).(\exists y Rby \supset Qb)$:
    $((Raa \lor Rab) \supset Qb).((Rba \lor Rbb) \supset Qb)$

17. $\forall x \exists y (Rxy \supset Qb)$: $\exists y(Ray \supset Qb).\exists y(Rby \supset Qb)$
                    : $((Raa \supset Qb) \lor (Rab \supset Qb)).((Rba \supset Qb) \lor (Rbb \supset Qb))$

18. $\forall x \forall y (Rxy \supset Qb)$: $\forall y(Ray \supset Qb).\forall y(Rby \supset Qb)$
                       $(Raa \supset Qb).(Rab \supset Qb).(Rba \supset Qb).(Rbb \supset Qb)$

It will be noticed that the scope of the quantifiers plays a vital part in meaning. It causes an important difference, for example, between 9 and 10. By connective logic, one can see that 9 is logically equivalent, not with 10, but with 12. Similarly, 16 is equivalent, not to 17, but to 18. We shall return to such matters in a more general way presently. For the moment, these expansions should suffice, at least, to emphasize the importance of scope (and of parentheses which indicate it).

Ignoring scope leads, for instance, to an error such as the following:

$\forall x(Sx \supset Tx) \supset Lj$

$(Sb \supset Tb) \supset Lj$ UI

The first sentence is not a universal sentence but a compound with a universal premiss: $\forall x\underline{(Sx \supset Tx)} \supset Lj$. Suppose it symbolizes: If every seat is taken, then
                      scope

Jeff leaves. The second sentence is not implied by the premiss; consider

Exercises VII 3

the equivalence transformations:

   $(Sb \supset Tb) \supset Lj$
   $\sim Lj \supset \sim (Sb \supset Tb)$ Contraposition
   $\sim Lj \supset (Sb . \sim Tb)$ Nif

I.e., if Jeff does not leave, then b is a seat which is not taken!

(Optional) Exercises VII 3

1. Give the finite expansions for {a,b} of the following:

   *a. Pb v ∃xQx   *b. ∃x(Pb v Qx)

    c. ∃x(Px v Qx)   d. ∃xPx v ∃xQx

   *e. ∃x∀yRxy v Pb

VIII

FURTHER METHODS

1. New Quantifier Rules: Hypothetical Individuals

The value of hypothetical reasoning was remarked upon in Chapter I, and illustrated by the supposing techniques of Chapter II. Early in Chapter VI we noted the possibility of reasoning with open clauses, whose free variables might be taken as provisional names for unspecified, hypothetical individuals. However, such reasoning was not actually called for in any of the exercises. And the rules UI, EG, and QN were stated using only bound variables and proper names. Such uses are indeed the most common ones, that is, reasoning from a universal to a specific instance, or from a specific instance to an existence statement. However, we do often have occasion to carry on our reasoning as though concerning hypothetical individuals - not "naming names". We are familiar with the process in algebra, where "the unknown" is called x, and reasoned about as if known. Similarly, we are familiar with the mystery fiction detective who says "Suppose we call the murderer Mr. X", and proceeds to jot down facts about Mr. X indicated by the available evidence, and then to draw inferences from them. Everyone makes similar inferences, though without using variables such as "x". Instead, we may reason about "Whoever it was that borrowed my sweater".

Quantificational logic incorporates the strategy of reasoning about hypothetical individuals by permitting inferences with clauses containing free variables as well as with genuine sentences. That is, at a certain line in a stepwise inference we may have symbols for "x shot y" or "x shot Greene" as readily as for "Someone shot Greene" or "Brown shot Greene". Justification

1. New Rules

of such reasoning was touched upon in the previous chapter. If the principle of such an inference is tautological in form, though an open clause, it was said to be logically true <u>whatever the free variables were taken to stand for</u>. (A phrase we shall soon find technically more convenient is "for every (possible) <u>assignment</u> of individuals in the universe of discourse to (all) variables".)

To implement reasoning about hypothetical individuals we will extend our UI, EG, and QN rules to open clauses, and add two new rules: Existential Instantiation (EI) and Universal Generalization (UG). Both of the latter rules also correspond to basic moves in informal reasoning - although they are usually moves of a more sophisticated and deliberate sort, as is all hypothetical reasoning.

<u>Existential Instantiation (EI)</u>

EI is a move from an existential to a hypothetical instance obtained by uniformly substituting a variable (called the variable of instantiation) for the variable of quantification and dropping the quantifier. Informally, its principle might be expressed as "What holds for something, holds for some particular (but unspecified) thing". It is the move taken by a detective who begins speaking of a hypothetical Mr. X when in possession of facts about <u>some</u> criminal - or by a mathematician who knows that some number satisfies a number of conditions and says "Let x_o be such a number". By dissolving the existential quantification, it permits reasoning with single clauses about the hypothetical individual. It is not a logically conclusive step in itself, of course. It would be absurd, for example, for the detective to announce that he had solved the case by identifying the criminal as Mr. X, or for the mathematician to claim a solution to his problem. (It would be even more absurd, of course, to permit EI to yield an instance with a proper name - as if the detective were

1. New Rules

to infer from the fact that someone embezzled from a bank to the conclusion that Wells, the teller, did it.) Instead, EI is a transitional step, taken in the context of a course of reasoning. And it must be hedged about by restrictions to prevent miscontrual of the free-variable-containing clause which it generates. For example, we shall require that each variable introduced by an EI be different from all similarly introduced variables appearing in previous steps. The unreasonableness of existentially instantiating to the same variable twice may be felt by imagining a detective who had christened an unknown embezzler, Mr. X, and then learns that the embezzler had a conspirator and decides to call the conspirator Mr. X also! Thus, although at some point in a course of reasoning it may be possible, as in UI, to make an EI step by simply dropping the quantifier: (i.e., letting the hypothetical individual be named by the same variables used in the quantifier): $\begin{vmatrix} \exists x(Ax.Bx) \\ Ax.Bx \end{vmatrix}$ EI, one cannot then do the same in applying EI to, E.G., $\exists x(Cx.Dx)$. There will be other restrictions too, but we can postpone discussing them for the moment. As an example of the use of EI consider the inference: Every genius has an eccentric patron; Some geniuses are boors / Some boors have patrons. Using Gx for <u>x is a genius</u>, Ex for <u>x is eccentric</u>, Pxy for <u>x is a patron of y</u>, Bx for <u>x is a boor</u>, the inference would proceed as follows:

```
 1│1    ∀x(Gx ⊃ ∃y(Ey.Pyx))         /∃x∃y(Bx.Pyx)
 2│2    ∃x(Gx.Bx)                    2 EI
 2│3    Gx.Bx                        3 Drop
 3│4    Gx                           1 UI (to hypothetical x!)
 1│5    Gx ⊃ ∃y(Ey.Pyx)              4,5 MP
1,2│6   ∃y(Ey.Pyx)                   6 EI (different variable)
1,2│7   Ey.Pyx                       7 Drop
1,2│8   Pyx                          3 Drop
 2│9    Bx                           8,9 Join
1,2│10  Bx.Pyx                       10 EG (from hypothetical y!)
1,2│11  ∃y(Bx.Pyx)                   11 EG (from hypothetical x!)
1,2│12  ∃x∃y(Bx.Pyx)
```

Universal Generalization (UG)

UG is a move from a clause containing a variable, say w, which, according to premisses and prior reasoning, holds no matter what individual w is taken to stand for, to a universal sentence of whose scope the clause was an instance. Informally, the principle underlying UG might be expressed as "What is shown to hold of anything, is thereby shown to hold of everything". In other words, if we show that Fx (where x is <u>any</u> hypothetical individual) follows from certain premisses or suppositions, then we may conclude ∀xFx (or ∀yFy) from the same premisses or suppositions.

A clause about a hypothetical x which has been introduced by EI has not been shown to be true of <u>any</u> x, of course. Therefore, we shall require restrictions which prevent UG from applying to such a clause. Such a restriction would ban the following invalid inference, for example:

1	∃x (x is a number less than twelve)	
2	x is a number less than twelve	1 EI
3	∀x (x is a number less than twelve)	2 UG

We can now begin using UG on the basis of the explanation given and the above restriction (that a UG may not be made by universally quantifying a variable which was introduced by an EI). (A more thorough treatment of restrictions will be forthcoming.)

Example of the use of UG:

All philosophers are quiet and serene; No serene person is worried or tense / No tense person is a philosopher. Using an obvious choice of symbols:

VIII 170
1. New Rules

```
    1 |1    ∀x(Px ⊃ (Qx.Sx))
    2 |2    ∀x(Sx ⊃ ~(Wx v Tx))         /∀x(Tx ⊃ ~Px)
    1 |3    Px ⊃ (Qx.Sx)                1 UI
    4 |4    Px                          4 S (Contraposition foreseen)
  1,4 |5    Qx.Sx                       3,4 MP
  1,4 |6    Sx                          5 Drop
    2 |7    Sx ⊃ ~(Wx v Tx)             2 UI
1,2,4 |8    ~(Wx v Tx)                  6,7 MP
1,2,4 |9    ~Wx.~Tx                     8 Nor
1,2,4 |10   ~Tx                         9 Drop
  1,2 |11   Px ⊃ ~Tx                    4,10 SQ
  1,2 |12   ~~Tx ⊃ ~Px                  11 Contra
  1,2 |13   Tx ⊃ ~Px                    12 N
  1,2 |14   ∀x(Tx ⊃ ~Px)                13 UG
```

We already have some familiarity with UI and EG, but extending them to open clauses calls for some additional remarks:

Universal Instantiation (UI)

Informally, the principle underlying UI may be expressed as "What holds of everything holds of any particular thing". It is reasoning from a universal to an instance. We now add that the particular thing in the instance may be hypothetical, and represented by a variable. In permitting UI to something unspecified we must assume there to be <u>something</u> in the UD. This is important for extended EG, as we shall see.

Existential Generalization (EG)

Informally, the principle underlying EG may be expressed as "What holds of any particular thing holds of something". It is reasoning from particular instance of some condition to the indefinite existence of <u>some</u> instance of that condition. We now add that the particular thing may be hypothetical. To infer existence, e.g., ∃xFx, from a statement about a hypothetical individual, y, e.g., Fy / ∃xFx, may seem odd. But consider the ways in which such a line

1. New Rules

as Fx might appear:

(1) Fx might appear as a supposition. Then it follows *from* that supposition. E.g., suppose a certain x was a fairy; it follows that there would be at least one fairy. If we discharged the supposition by qualification we would only have $Fx \supset \exists xFx$, i.e., if anything is a fairy then there are fairies. True enough.

(2) If Fx were a premiss and not discharged, it would have to be shown true before the conclusion need be accepted. For an open clause, truth is meaningless, unless we either took it as tacitly existential, in which case we might as well write the premiss explicitly as $\exists xFx$, which would logically imply $\exists xFx$, of course, or we took it to be tacitly universal, in which case we might as well write the premiss explicitly as $\forall xFx$. Fx would follow from $\forall xFx$, of course, and existence would follow from that. (As mentioned above, our logic for extended UI requires that there be at least one individual in the universe of discourse.)

(3) Finally, Fx might appear as the result of a previous EI. For example:

```
| 1  ∃x(Fx.Gx)
| 2  Fx.Gx         1 EI
| 3  Fx            2 Drop
```

But then existence is already provided by the original existential sentence.

An important feature of existential generalization (from name or variable) is that different existential generalization steps may be made from the same line. If a clause mentions a certain individual more than once the individual may be regarded as an instance of several conditions. For example, if Bob

VIII 172
1. New Rules

loves himself (in symbols Lbb), we can take him as an instance of the condition of (1) loving oneself, (2) loving Bob, and (3) being loved by Bob. Accordingly, Lbb can serve as the premiss for three correct EG steps:

```
Lbb                  Lbb                  Lbb
∃xLxx    EG          ∃xLxb    EG          ∃xLbx    EG
```

By contrast, UI provides only a single instantiation for a given term from its universal premiss.

Preliminary Safeguards

The net effect of our basic quantificational rules, aside from QN, can be viewed simply as a way of taking off quantifiers and putting them back on again. Representing each by a simple example, the effect is displayed below:

```
Quantifier Off    ∀xFx              ∃xFx
                  Fy       UI       Fy       EI

Quantifier On     Fy                Fy
                  ∀xFx     UG       ∃xFx     EG
```

In other words, reasoning about hypothetical individual permits us to strip off quantifiers, carry out deductions with clauses, open or closed, by the logic of connectives, and then put the desired quantifiers back in the desired places.

The process must be carefully hedged about with restrictions, however, And the restrictions involve record-keeping. After all, complexities are bound to arise when (1) several hypothetical individuals are being reasoned about simultaneously, and when (2) some clauses involving a hypothetical individual must be construed as particular predications about <u>some</u>

VIII 173
1. New Rules

unspecified indiviudal obtained by EI, while others are construed as predications about <u>any</u> individual in the universe of discourse, obtained by UI.

Various systems of restrictions can be used in setting up a deductive system. A deductive system is syntactical. It prescribes ways of manipulating symbols. Any way will do as long as it is sound (that is, the deductions permitted by the system ($P \vdash C$) are only those which are semantically valid ($P \models C$)) and, if possible, complete (that is, if $P \models C$ then $P \vdash C$). The system we shall use (which is provably sound and complete) is based on a method developed by W. V. Quine as a simplification of earlier methods. It will be called the Q-system. Deductions using it will be called Q-deductions, if necessary to distinguish them from those of other systems. (The "Q" may be thought of as standing for Quine or Quantification, or both.)

The basic addition to the record-keeping needed is that at each line obtained directly by EI or by UG one writes, immediately to the right of the citation, the variable in the <u>instance</u> involved (which we may call the <u>instantial variable</u>). For example.

```
1   ∃x(Px.Ryx)              1   Fx ⊃ Sxz
2   Pz.Ryz      1 EIz       2   ∀y(Fy ⊃ Syz)    1 UGx
                 ↑                                    ↑
                 └─── the instantial variable ───────┘
```

The instantial variable is said to be <u>flagged</u> at any step where it is thus recorded. The restrictions, then, are as follows:

VIII 174
1. New Rules

Preliminary Safeguard Rules

For a Q-deduction to be regarded as asserting

$P \vdash_Q C$ (C is Q-deducible from P) the following conditions must be met:

1. No variable can be flagged at more than one line.

2. No variable which is flagged at any line may have a free occurrence
   (a) in the last line, C, or
   (b) in any premiss of C.

3. All suppositions must be discharged by the time C is reached (i.e., the premiss numbers of C must include no line number of a supposition).

These restrictions are efficient. Restriction 1, in not allowing a variable to be flagged more than once, prevents two missteps. It prevents (a) making an EI twice to the same variable; and it prevents (b) universally generalizing from an instance introduced by EI.

```
(a)    1| 1  ∃xFx        P              (b)   1| 1  ∃xFx
       2| 2  ∃x~Fx       P                    1| 2  Fy         1 EIy
       1| 3  Fy          1 EIy                1| 3  ∀xFy       2 UGy
       2| 4  ~Fy         2 EIy
       1,2| 5 Fy.~Fy     3,4 Join
       1,2| 6 ∃x(Fx.~Fx) 5 EG
```

Restriction 2a, in not allowing the last line, C, to contain a free occurrence of a flagged variable, ensures that EI is a transitional step. (EI produces a free but flagged variable.)

Restriction 2b, in not allowing any premiss of C to contain a free occurrence of a flagged variable prevents an inference from Fx to ∀xFx,

```
1| 1  Fx     P
1| 2  ∀xFy   1 UGx
```

(But note that a somewhat surprising <u>transitional</u> UG from a supposition <u>is</u> allowed: 1| 1 Fx   S   But suppositions must be discharged. If
                                                 1| 2 ∀xFy 1 UGx
we discharge Fx by SQ we get the line Fx ⊃ ∀yFy, which appears to assert the falsehood that <u>if any x is F, everything is F</u>, but this contains flagged variable x, and so it can not be the last line, C. Discharging an open clause

1. New Rules

by Absurdity yields the negation of that clause and nothing about the universal. A fuller account of the use and justification of such transitional UGs will be given later on.)

Restriction 3 is already familiar from connective logic.

While some final safeguards will be detailed presently, we can, with the above understandings, summarize our present quantificational rules in a very general symbolism by using:

C for any clause,
r and s for any terms (names or variables),
u and w for any variables, and
C(r/u) for the result of substituting r for every free occurrence of u in C.
With this notation, the format of steps by each of the rules may be given as below:

<u>Universal Instantiation</u>

i $\forall u C$
j $C(r/u)$ i UI

<u>Existential Instantiation</u>

i $\exists u C$
j $C(w/u)$ i EIw

<u>(Universal) Quantifier Negation</u>

i $\sim \forall u C$
j $\exists u \sim C$ i QN

<u>Existential Generalization</u>

i $C(r/u)$
j $\exists u C$ i EG

<u>Universal Generalization</u>

i $C(w/u)$
j $\forall u C$ i UGw

<u>(Existential) Quantifier Negation</u>

i $\sim \exists u C$
j $\forall u \sim C$ i QN

It should be especially noted that the notation <u>rules out</u> making an EI step <u>to</u> a name instance, or making a UG step <u>from</u> a name instance. Both involve variables <u>only</u> (for hypothetical individuals), while UI and EG instances show an r (for name <u>or</u> variable), and flag neither. Also, C(r/u) or C(w/u) call for substitution for every free instance of u. However, in EG, although every instance of u in C must be a place occupied by r in the instance, not every occurrence of r in C need be replaced by a u. (Recall the 'Bobby loves Bobby' example.)

Exercises VIII 1

Provide deductions for the inferences below, if you can. Be careful not to violate safeguard rules. If a deduction seems to call for violating a safeguard, say which it is, and try to show it invalid by any means you can think of, e.g., Venn diagrams.

In deducing with open clauses and the EI and UG rules, suppositional strategy can often be applied by using suppositions about hypothetical individuals (open clauses). For example, to reach a conclusion of the form $\forall x(Fx \supset Gx)$, it may be useful to suppose Fy, infer stepwise to Gy, discharge the supposition to get $Fy \supset Gy$, and then apply UG to get $\forall x(Fx \supset Gx)$. The answer section for the first few asterisked examples will supply examples, if needed.

*1. Every case of pneumonia is a case of bacterial infection
Every case of bacterial infection is curable by antibiotics
Every case of pneumonia is curable by antibiotics   (P,B,C)

*2. Some prisoners are not stupid
Everyone who is not stupid enjoys reading
Some prisoners enjoy reading   (P,S,R)

*3. No private eye is a mystic
All seers are mystics
No seer is a private eye   (P,M,S)

*4. $\forall x(Ax \supset (Bx \cdot Cx))$
$\exists y(Py \cdot Ay)$ /$\exists z(Pz \cdot Cz)$

*5. $\forall x((Cx \lor \sim Gx) \supset Tx)$
$\exists z(Bz \cdot \sim Gz)$ /$\exists x(Tx \cdot Bx)$

*6. $\exists x Ax \supset \forall y(Cy \supset By)$
$\forall x(Gx \supset (Ax \cdot Cx))$ /$\forall x(Gx \supset Bx)$

*7. There are white sea birds
There are eel-eating sea birds
There are white, eel-eating sea birds   (W,E,S)

8. If a new prophet appears, the day of judgment is at hand $\exists x Px \supset D$
   ───
   Choose anyone, if he is a new prophet the day of judgment $\forall x(Px \supset D)$
   is at hand

9. If a witness was lying, some federal judge will reverse $\exists x(Wx.Lx) \supset \exists x(Jx.Rx)$
   the decision before New Year's
   No federal judge reversed the decision before New Year's $\forall x(Jx \supset \sim Rx)$
   ───   ─────────────────────────
   No witness was lying $\forall x(Wx \supset \sim Lx)$

2. <u>Quantifier Shifting</u>.

Quantifiers can often be shifted, yielding a logically equivalent paraphrase. This is useful - in reading symbolized results, and in other ways. In this section we will take note of a number of laws for the shifting of quantifiers. We could, if we chose, incorporate them as (derived) rules in our system of Q-deduction. But for the moment we may consider them informally on their own account, as we did the diagrams of the preceding section.

We are already familiar with one pair of quantifier shift-laws: the QN equivalences. They permit a quantifier to be shifted past a negation sign, in one direction or the other, while simultaneously changing from universal to existential, or vice-versa.

Other laws are available for shifting quantifiers past the other, binary, connectives. In speaking of binary compounds we may speak of a first component and a second. A quantifier on x (or whatever the variable of quantification happens to be) binds all free occurrences of x in its scope; therefore it will be important to distinguish the case where x has a free occurrence in both components from cases where x occurs free just in one of the two components. In the latter case, we will speak informally of the component in which the variable of quantification has no free occurrence as the <u>blind</u> component. For example, the second component is blind in both of the following: (1) $\forall x(Fx \supset Gb)$ and (2) $\forall x(Fx \supset \exists xGx)$. (In the second example, neither of the occurrences of x in the second component are free.) We will let a blind component be represented simply by P in the discussions that follow (bearing in mind that in any particular case P may in fact be a complex quantified clause, possibly with free variables (other than x).)

2. Quantifier Shifting

The case where a quantifier's entire scope is blind to the variable of quantification is possible, of course, according to the syntactical definitions of the preceding chapter. For example, we might symbolize "There exists at least one x such that the world is round" and "For every x, the world is round" as ∃xRw and ∀xRw, respectively. Both say no more or less than Rw. Such cases are called <u>vacuous</u> quantifications. Using P for a blind component, we may write ∀xP ⟺ ∃xP ⟺ P.

Compounds with one blind component are, for the most part, the easiest. For both . and v, both quantifiers can include or exclude the blind component from its scope. For example, to say of every x that P is the case and that x is F is clearly the same as saying that P is the case and for every x, x is F. In symbols: ∀x(P.Fx) ⟺ P.∀xFx. The commutativity of '.' provides similar equivalences for blind P being the second component: ∀xFx.P ⟺ ∀x(Fx.P).
⎿ Scope of ∀x

For disjunction also, if it is true that for some x either x is F or P is the case it is also obviously true that either some x is F or else P is the case, and vice-versa: ∃x(Fx v P) ⟺ ∃xFx v P

The various quantifier shifts can all be carried out by stepwise deductions. For example, for disjunction we could proceed as follows:

```
1|1   ∃x(Fx v P)          /∃xFx v P         1|1   ∃xFx v P           /∃x(Fx v P)
1|2   Fy v P              1 EI y            2|2   ∃xFx               S
3|3   Fy                  S                 2|3   Fy                 2 EI y
3|4   ∃xFx                3 EG              2|4   Fy v P              3 Add
3|5   ∃xFx v P            4 Add             5|5   P                  S
6|6   P                   S                 5|6   Fy v P             5 Add
6|7   ∃xFx v P            6 Add              |7   ∃xFx ⊃ (Fy v P)    2,4 SQ
 |8   Fy ⊃ (∃xFx v P)     3,5 SQ             |8   P ⊃ (Fy v P)       5,6 SQ
 |9   P ⊃ (∃xFx v P)      6,7 SQ            1|9   Fy v P             1,7,8 Dcomp
1|10  ∃xFx v P            2,8,9 Dcomp       1|10  ∃x(Fx v P)         9 EG
```

Moreover, the deductions shown above can be easily transformed into a deduction of the equivalence: (∃xFx v P) ≡ ∃x(Fx v P). Number the two deductions as one long one (first taking care to use a different variable for the EI step at line 3 in the righthand deduction, and in affected lines, to avoid flagging y twice). Discharge the two premises by SQ, getting the additional lines 21 and 22,

2. Quantifier Shifting

and use Ejoin as shown:

```
|21   ∃x(Fx v P) ⊃ (∃xFx v P)      SQ
|22   (∃xFx v P) ⊃ ∃x(Fx v P)      SQ
|23   (∃xFx v P) ≡ ∃x(Fx v P)      i,j E join
```

Premiss numbers are lacking for all three above steps. They were discharged by the two qualifications. This means that they are conclusions that follow from no premisses (or from any premisses - superfluous ones!). To express the fact that a clause C is deduced from no premisses we write ⊢ C. More exactly, since this was carried out in system Q, we write that it is deducible from no premisses in system Q: ⊢$_Q$ C.

A deduction of C from no premisses is said to be a (deductive) <u>proof</u> of C. Provided the system is sound (as this one can be proved to be), the proven sentence will be a logical truth. The logical truths of connective logic are called tautologies, as mentioned in Chapter III. But, as Chapter III also warned, not all logical truths are tautologies. The equivalence above is a logical truth of quantification theory. Like a tautology it is necessarily true (in virtue of the meaning of connectives and quantifiers) — but is true under all circumstances and so is uninformative as to matters of fact.

It is possible to prove an open clause. "Logically <u>true</u>" seems improper to apply to an open clause. Some logicians speak of them as <u>universally valid</u>, or just valid. But "valid" has been traditionally used for inferences as opposed to sentences. For want of a better term, we will continue to use "logically true".

For ⊃ , proofs are easily given for the cases in which the <u>antecedent</u> is the blind component. That is, (P ⊃ ∀xFx) ≡ ∀x(P ⊃ Fx)

$$(P ⊃ ∃xFx) ≡ ∃x(P ⊃ Fx).$$

But implication is not commutative, and when the <u>consequent</u> is blind, the

2. Quantifier Shifting

the results are surprising at first sight.

(1) $\forall x Fx \supset P \iff \exists x(Fx \supset P)$

(2) $\exists x Fx \supset P \iff \forall x(Fx \supset P)$

But using the shift for v, discussed above, together with QN and Mif, yields the following two columns of reversible, equivalence steps, one each for (1) and for (2):

	(1)				(2)	
↑ Mif	$\forall x Fx \supset P$			$\exists x Fx \supset P$		Mif ↑
QN	$\sim \forall x Fx \lor P$	←	Mif →	$\sim \exists x Fx \lor P$		QN
Shift(v)	$\exists x \sim Fx \lor P$	←	QN →	$\forall x \sim Fx \lor P$		Shift(v)
Mif	$\exists x(\sim Fx \lor P)$	←	Shift(v) →	$\forall x(\sim Fx \lor P)$		Mif
	$\exists x(Fx \supset P)$	←	↓ Mif →	$\forall x(Fx \supset P)$		

As remarked at the outset of this section, the equivalences just discussed could be incorporated as derived rules of inference. On the other hand, they could be formulated as logically true material equivalences. Those involving binary compounds with one blind component have often been called, since 1928 (Herbrand), the <u>Rules of Passage</u>. As logically true material equivalences, it might be more appropriate to call them <u>Laws</u> of Passage. They are listed under the latter heading in the summarizing table at the end of next section.

Exercises VIII 2

*1. Write the (deductive) proof of $(\forall xFx.P) \supset \forall x(Fx.P)$.

2. Prove   a. $(\forall xFx \supset P) \equiv \exists x(Fx \supset P)$

   and   b. $(\exists xFx \supset P) \equiv \forall x(Fx \supset P)$

   (by carrying out the plan given informally in the text, by pairs of deductions.)

For each of the English sentences in the problems below, indicate any of the accompanying symbolizations which are acceptable (e.g., by marking "A")(from some suitable UD). All, some, or none may be acceptable. If several symbolizations are acceptable, they should all be logically equivalent with one another. (Ambiguities have been avoided, as much as possible.) If one seems especially appropriate to a given English sentence, mark it with an asterisk.

*3. If anyone enters, Clyde is trapped.

   Ex: x enters;   c: Clyde;   Tx: x is trapped

   a. $\forall xEx \supset Tc$
   b. $\exists xEx \supset Tc$
   c. $\forall x(Ex \supset Tc)$
   d. $\exists x(Ex \supset Tc)$

*4. If anyone enters, he is a suspect.

   a. $\forall xEx \supset Sx$
   b. $\forall x(Ex \supset Sx)$
   c. $\exists xEx \supset Sx$
   d. $\exists x(Ex \supset Sx)$

*5. Everyone is safe unless Clyde has escaped.

   a. $\forall xSx \lor Ec$
   b. $\forall x(Sx \lor Ec)$
   c. $\exists x(Sx \lor Ec)$
   d. $\sim Ec \supset \exists xSx$
   e. $\forall x(\sim Ec \supset Sx)$

*6. If someone enters, Clyde hides.

   a. $\exists x(Ex \supset Hc)$
   b. $\forall x(Ex \supset Hc)$
   c. $\exists xEx \supset Hc$
   d. $\forall xEx \supset Hc$

3. Fission and Fusion of Quantifiers

When neither component of a binary compound is blind, shifting quantifiers typically does not merely move a single quantifier, but distributes it across the connective, i.e., splitting it into two quantifier occurrences (fission), or it "factors out" two occurrences into one (fusion). For example:

$\forall x(Fx.Gx) \Rightarrow \forall xFx.\forall xGx$ fission

$\forall xFx.\forall xGx \Rightarrow \forall x(Fx.Gx)$ fusion

For example (in a limited UD: persons at a particular diplomatic gathering): If <u>everyone</u> [is a French-speaking gourmet] then it follows:

that <u>everyone</u> [speaks French] and <u>everyone</u> [is a gourmet]

(The inference is obviously valid also in the opposite direction.)

Furthermore, the process is less simple in that it does not always proceed in both directions as simply as in the case of conjunction, above. For example, in the pair of sentences below, logical implication holds in only one direction. To test your ability to understand symbolism, and your native logical ability, try to decide the direction ($\Rightarrow$ or $\Leftarrow$) before reading the discussion that follows the pair:

$\forall x(Fx \lor Gx)$ $\forall xFx \lor \forall xGx$

A useful way to read such symbolic sentences is to use the natural language indefinite pronoun "everything", and the device of factoring out. In this way, the sentence on the left could be read: "Everything is F or G. The sentence on the right becomes: Either everything is F or everything is G. If the direction of logical implication is not yet clear, try the following readings. Left: Everything is animate or inanimate. Right: Either everything is animate or everything is inanimate. The left hand sentence is true

3. Fission-Fusion

but it can clearly not imply the false right-hand sentence. On the other hand, if a sentence proclaiming at least one of two sweeping alternatives (as in the right hand form) is true, the more modest assertion on the left is guaranteed. For example, if I have reason to believe that the gumdrops in a bag are either all strawberry or all licorice I can safely infer that each gumdrop is either strawberry or licorice.

Consider deductions in both directions:

```
1|1  ∀xFx v ∀xGx      /∀x(Fx v Gx)          1|1  ∀x(Fx v Gx)      /∀xFx v ∀xGx
2|2  ∀xFx             S                     1|2  Fy v Gy          1 UI
2|3  Fy               2 UI                  3|3  Fy               S
4|4  ∀xGx             S                     3|4  ∀xFx             3 UGy
4|5  Gy               4 UI                  5|5  Gy               S
 |6  ∀xFx ⊃ Fy        2,3 SQ                5|6  ∀xGx             5 UGy
 |7  ∀xGx ⊃ Gy        4,5 SQ                 |7  Fy ⊃ ∀xFx        3,4 SQ
1|8  Fy v Gy          1,6,7 Dplex            |8  Gy ⊃ ∀xGx        5,6 SQ
1|9  ∀x(Fx v Gx)      8 UGy                 1|9  ∀xFx v ∀xGx      2,7,8 Dplex
```

The deduction on the left is trouble-free, but the one on the right, for the invalid direction, flags y twice - at lines 4 and 6. The deduction at the right, then, does not constitute a correct Q-deduction (⊢_Q).

Nevertheless, an equivalence <u>can</u> be proved for a slightly altered pair: ∀xFx v ∀xGx ⟺ ∀x∀y(Fx v Gy).

Instead of proceeding further, connective by connective, to examine the relations of logical implication and logical equivalence between forms obtained by fission or fusion, or other quantifier shifts, the most used ones are displayed in the following table. Material, rather than logical implication and equivalence are used, so that the principles are all expressed as logically true forms.

Logically True Forms

In the forms below, P stands for any clause which contains no free occurrence of the variable of quantification.

If the main connective is "⊃", the converse is not logically true.

I.   Vacuous Quantification $\forall x P \equiv P$ $\exists x P \equiv P$

II.   Quantifier Negation $\sim \forall x Fx \equiv \exists x \sim Fx$ $\sim \exists x Fx \equiv \forall x \sim Fx$

III. Laws of Passage

    1a $(P . \forall x Fx) \equiv \forall x (P . Fx)$ $(P . \exists x Fx) \equiv \exists x (P . Fx)$
      b $(\forall x Fx . P) \equiv \forall x (Fx . P)$ $(\exists x Fx . P) \equiv \exists x (Fx . P)$

    2a $(P \vee \forall x Fx) \equiv \forall x (P \vee Fx)$ $(P \vee \exists x Fx) \equiv \exists x (P \vee Fx)$
      b $(\forall x Fx \vee P) \equiv \forall x (Fx \vee P)$ $(\exists x Fx \vee P) \equiv \exists x (Fx \vee P)$

    3a $(P \supset \forall x Fx) \equiv \forall x (P \supset Fx)$ $(P \supset \exists x Fx) \equiv \exists x (P \supset Fx)$
      b $(\forall x Fx \supset P) \equiv \exists x (Fx \supset P)$ $(\exists x Fx \supset P) \equiv \forall x (Fx \supset P)$

IV. Quantifier Order

    1. $\forall x \forall y Rxy \equiv \forall y \forall x Rxy$ $\exists x \exists y Rxy \equiv \exists y \exists x Rxy$
    2. $\exists x \forall y Rxy \supset \forall y \exists x Rxy$ $\forall x \exists y (Fx . Gy) \equiv \exists y \forall x (Fx . Gy)$

V.   Fission-Fusion Laws

    1. $(\forall x Fx . \forall x Gx) \equiv \forall x (Fx . Gx)$ $\exists x (Fx . Gx) \supset (\exists x Fx . \exists x Gx)$
    2. $(\forall x Fx \vee \forall x Gx) \supset \forall x (Fx \vee Gx)$ $\exists x (Fx \vee Gx) \equiv (\exists x Fx \vee \exists x Gx)$
    3. $\forall x (Fx \supset Gx) \supset (\forall x Fx \supset \forall x Gx)$ $(\exists x Fx \supset \exists x Gx) \supset \exists x (Fx \supset Gx)$

VI. Principles of the Four Quantifier Rules

    UI: $\forall y (\forall x Fx \supset Fy)$ EG: $\forall y (Fy \supset \exists x Fx)$

    EI: $\exists y (\exists x Fx \supset Fy)$ UG: $\exists y (Fy \supset \forall x Fx)$

Exercises VIII 3

1. Prove by deduction each of the quantifier shift laws below in our given deductive system (i.e., without any of the quantifier shifts as steps).

   a. $(\forall xFx . \forall xGx) \supset \forall x(Fx . Gx)$

   *b. $\forall x(Fx . Gx) \supset (\forall xFx . \forall xGx)$

   c. $\forall x(Fx \supset Gx) \supset (\forall xFx \supset \forall xGx)$

   d. $\exists x(Fx \lor Gx) \supset (\exists xFx \lor \exists xGx)$

   *e. $(\exists xFx \lor \exists xGx) \supset \exists x(Fx \lor Gx)$

   *f. $\forall x \forall y(Fx \lor Gy) \supset (\forall xFx \lor \forall xGx)$

*2. Assume our deductive system is expanded to permit equivalence replacement for any of the equivalences listed among our laws of passage on fission-fusion, and write deductions of the expanded system for inferences a and b, using as citations QP (for passage) and QF (for fission-fusion) together with the numbers of the laws from the preceding table.

   a. $\forall x(Fx \supset Gx)$
       $\forall xFx$ /$\forall xGx$

   b. $\exists xFx \lor \exists xGx$
       $\forall x((Fx \lor Gx) \supset Pb)$ /Pb

3. Using equivalence steps as in 2., transform each of the four "principles" listed under VI in the preceding table to clauses having the tautologous form: $A \supset A$.

4. Prenex Form

An interesting property of the quantifier shift equivalences is that they permit one to take any symbolized clause, no matter how complex, and shift quantifiers leftward and increase scopes rightward until a logical equivalent of the original clause is reached in which all quantifiers are gathered in an initial string (with the scope of each extending over everything that follows), so that the string of quantifiers stands before a quantifier-free clause. A clause which thus consists of a string of zero or more quantifiers, followed by a quantifier-free clause is said to be in prenex form. As may be expected, prenex forms have proved of importance for theoretical investigations of logic.

A sentence or clause has more than one prenex equivalent. If desired, a fixed procedure can be used to determine just one of them as a unique, "official" prenex equivalent. But there are sometimes reasons to prefer one of the other prenex equivalents.

Recalling the role of "blind" components in the laws of passage, one can see that it can be important to make, or keep, components blind if possible. For example, although a fusion step easily leads from ∀xFx.∀xGx to the prenex equivalent ∀x(Fx.Gx), one cannot similarly go from ∃xFx.∃xGx to ∃x(Fx.Gx). We can first extend the scope of the first quantifier backward (by the righthand role of III 1 b, p. 185) to ∃x(Fx.∃xGx) since the closed clause ∃xGx is blind to an external quantification. In order to shift the second quantifier forward, we may observe that we can reexpress the second quantification as ∃yGy. Then, since Fx is a blind component for ∃y, it can be shifted forward (by the righthand side of III 1 a), which yields the prenex equivalent: ∃x∃y(Fx.Gy). Reexpressing a quantification with a different variable, as was done in the preceding example, to obtain a blind component is so useful in quantifier shifting that it will be well to state the rule more exactly for reference.

<u>Rule for Relettering Bound Variables (RBV)</u>

In a quantified clause, QuC, u may be replaced throughout QuC by any other variable which has no occurrence already in C. The result is logically equivalent with the original, and may replace it in any context.

The RBV rule will not be proven here, but the reader may wish to prove by deduction that ∀xPx ≡ ∀yPy and ∃xPx ≡ ∃yPy. Also the proviso that the new variable not already occur in C can be appreciated by studying the non-equivalent results of trying to reletter the ∀x quantification with y in the two sentences ∀xRxy and ∀x∃yRxy.

A step by step transformation to prenex form can be roughly described as having some or all of the following stages.

1. Eliminate all occurrences of ≡ by eqo

1a. It is often, but not always, good to eliminate some or all occurrences of ⊃.

2. Internalize negations.

3. Apply fusion equivalences where possible.

4. Reletter bound variables (RBV) so that
   a. No two quantifiers are on the same variable
   b. No quantifier is on a variable which also has a free occurrence.

5. Apply rules of passage, extending scopes, step by step, until prenex form is reached.

A more mechanical method is the following:

Exercises VIII 4

1. Eliminate all occurrences of $\equiv$ and $\supset$;
2. Internalize negations;
3. Reletter as in step 4 above.
4. Prefix all quantifiers in order of occurrences in the clause.

This method, while more mechanical, has the disadvantage that the resulting number of quantifiers may be greater, since all opportunities for fusion have been ignored. Furthermore, various purposes may be better served by other orders of quantifiers than this method gives.

Exercises VIII 4

1. Put the following in prenex form.

   a. $\exists xFx \lor \exists xGx$ f. $\forall xFx \supset \forall xGx$

   b. $\exists xFx . \exists xGx$ *g. $\exists xFx \supset \exists xGx$

   c. $Ax \supset \forall x(Px \supset \exists yRxy)$ *h. $\forall xFx \equiv \forall xGx$

   d. $\exists xFx \supset \forall yRxy$ i. $\exists xFx \equiv \exists xGx$

   e. $\forall x(Fx \supset {\sim}Hx) \supset {\sim}\forall x(Gx \supset Hx)$ j. $\forall xFx \equiv \exists xGx$

Optional Further Reading

Semantics for Q-Languages

Although the meaning of quantifiers has been made reasonably clear by means of analogies with long conjunctions and disjunctions, greater precision is desirable and possible. Although "all" and "some" will be used in giving the rules, just as "and", "or", etc. were used in making clear the truth-functional meanings of connectives, we shall see that just as truth tables cleared away ambiguities in the connectives being used, so an account can be given of the meaning of quantifiers which will provide a more exact basis for quantificational logic. For example, it will permit a definition of a semantical concept of logical implication to be defined, which we have already been symbolizing as $P \vDash C$, (corresponding to our deducibility concept, $P \vdash C$).

It will prove convenient to speak of two sorts of interpretation of a Q-language B which will be called intensional and extensional. An <u>intensional interpretation, i, for language B</u> will be said to be given if:

(1) a class is specified as the universe of discourse of the interpretation, to be represented by iU;

(2) an object in iU is identified as what is named by each name, b, to be denoted by ib (the interpretation of b);

(3) a reading is specified for each predicate, P, to be represented by iP (the interpretation of P).

Let us suppose an object in iU is assigned to each term, variable or name, with the proviso that each name is assigned the thing it names. Such an assignment will be called a <u>term-assignment</u> under the interpretation, and the object assigned to a term, r, will be denoted by ar. Although one can not ordinarily speak of an open clause as true or false, an open clause

Semantics for Q-Languages

.can be given a truth value in a relative sense if one speaks of assignments. That is, it can be said to have a truth value relative to an assignment. With respect to fixed assignment, variables can be treated like names which name the thing assigned to them. Thus, while "Brother(x,y)" has no determinate truth value in an absolute sense, it can be said to be true for an assignment a, if ax(the thing assigned to x) happens to be the brother of ay(the thing assigned to y). With this idea in mind, we can extend it to all clauses (whether compound or quantified) as follows:

1. A clause C (of language B) is <u>true for</u> (an assignment) a under (an interpretation) i under any one of the following circumstances:

   a. C is an n-place predication P $(r_1, r_2,\ldots r_n)$ and iP holds for the individuals assigned by a to each term r, that is, $iP(ar_1, ar_2,\ldots ar_n)$;

   b. C is a negation $\sim$A, and A is not true-for-a-under-i;

   c. C is a conjunction A.B, and A and B are both true-for-a-under i;

   d. C is a disjunction A v B, and A or B, or both, are true-for-a-under-i;

   e. C is an implication A $\supset$ B, and either A is not true-for-a-under-i, or B is true-for-a-under-i;

   f. C is an equivalence A $\equiv$ B, and Both A $\supset$ B and B $\supset$ A are true-for-a-under-i;

   g. C is a universal clause $\forall$uA, and A is true, under i, for every assignment a' which differs from a, at most, in what is assigned to u (in other words, informally, A is true for everything in iU (which may be assigned to u), while all other free variables in A are fixed, i.e., continue to refer to what was assigned to them by a);

   h. C is an existential clause $\exists$uA, and A is true, under i, for at least one assignment a' which differs from a, at most, in what is assigned to u (informally, A is true for something in iU while all other free variables in A are fixed.

Truth of a sentence (under the given interpretation) can now be defined as follows:

2. A sentence (closed clause) is **true** (under interpretation i) fif it is true for every assignment a under interpretation i, and **false** otherwise.

The definition of truth for an assignment under an interpretation, is a recursive definition (like the syntactical definition of clause). The truth of a complex quantified sentence is reduced by stages, through iterated uses of the various cases listed, as they prove applicable to the various subclauses encountered, until the truth of predications are reached. Predications are true (in the words of an apt idiom) fif they tell it like it is. This part of the definition is the essence of what has been called **the correspondence theory of truth**, originally put forward by Aristotle. Since the truth of a predication (even for an assignment) will depend on the way things are, i.e., non-linguistic fact, the recursive character of this definition, unlike that for "clause", does not provide a mechanical way to decide whether the defined phrase applies.

In order to define a semantic concept of logical implication we turn to the other sort of interpretation, the extensional one. The class of objects of which a 1-place predicate is true is said to be the **extension** of the predicate. Two predicates can thus happen to have the same extension even though their meanings, in some sense, are different. A famous example is a predicate given the reading "human", and another given the reading "featherless biped". The extension of a 2-place predicate can be regarded as the class of ordered couples of individuals to which the predicate can be said truly to apply. Similarly, the extension of an n-place predicate would be a class of ordered n-tuples.

Semantics for Q-Languages

Just as tautologies were compounds to which the truth-functional meanings of its connectives assigned the value true for every combination of truth values that can be assigned to the components, so a logical truth of a quantificational sentence can be defined as one which is true for all possible extensions (in every universe of discourse) that can be assigned to its predicates. I.e., no matter what the facts, an extensional interpretation, then, is an assignment of extensions to predicates (in a class acting as universe of discourse).

A more explicit definition is:

An <u>extensional interpretation</u>, i, of a language B consists of:

(1) a class, iU (the universe or domain of the interpretation)

(2) an assignment of an object, ib in U, to each name b, and

(3) an assignment of a class, iP, of n-tuples of members of iU to each n-place predicate P in language B.

Since the concept of term-assignment is unchanged, the definition of <u>truth of a clause for a assignment a under an interpretation i</u> will apply equally well for extensional interpretation if, in the predication clause, a., we understand "$iP(ar_1, ar_2, \ldots ar_n)$" to mean that the n-tuple $\langle ar_1, ar_2, \ldots \rangle$ is in the extension, iP, of P (whether determined by meaning or assigned).

With this broadening, semantical concepts of logic can be defined for a class, P, of (premiss) clauses, and a (conclusion) clause, C, of a Q-language, B. The most basic are as follows.

Semantics for Q-Languages

3. An inference P/C is <u>valid</u> (or P <u>logically implies</u> C (P ⊧ C)) fif for every term-assignment a and interpretation i, if every clause in P is true-for-a-under-i then C is true-for-a-under-i.

4. C is <u>logically true</u> fif for every term-assignment a and interpretation i, C is true-for-a-under-i.

IX
FINAL SAFEGUARDS

1. <u>Variable Capture, Kinds of Instances</u>.

Up to this point, we have managed to steer clear of certain complexities which can arise when clauses involve (1) nested quantifiers (i.e., some quantifiers within the scope of others), (2) predicates of two or more places, and (3) several variables. In such cases the rules so far given do not prevent certain missteps. For example, consider $\forall x \exists y Gyx$. This is of the form $\forall x C$ where C contains the quantifier $\exists y$. According to the rules so far given, we should be able to move by UI to $C(y/x)$ by substituting y for every occurrence of x which is free in C, (i.e., in $\exists y Gyx$). Since the occurrence of x is free here, the result would be $\exists y Gyy$. But this is not a valid step. Read Gyx as <u>y is greater than x</u> (in the UD of numbers). With this interpretation, $\forall x \exists y Gyx$ reads "For every number x there is a y which is greater". The apparent conclusion, $\exists y Gyy$, reads, "Some number is greater than itself!".

The trouble arises in this example because a free occurrence of x (for which we wished to substitute y) is <u>within the scope</u> of the "internal" quantifier, $\exists y$. What we need to do is to prohibit instantiating to a variable that some internal quantifier is on. If we substitute y for the free x in $\exists y Gyx$ we are substituting y at an occurrence of x which is within the scope of a quantifier on y. At that position y becomes bound! Informally, y is said to be <u>captured</u>. To prevent capture, we shall require of the four rules UI, EG, EI, and UG, that the instances involved be clear instances, defining clear as follows:

1. Instances

Clear Instance

An instance of a clause C obtained by substituting a term r for a variable u at every free occurrence of u in C [i.e., C(r/u)] is a <u>clear instance</u> fif no such occurrence of u is within the scope of a quantifier on r in C.

Since a quantifier is never on a name, the wording of the definition makes every name-instance a clear instance. Therefore, it is only reasoning with hypothetical individuals represented by variables that can lead to instances that are not clear.

For EI and UG, even the proviso against capture is not enough. Starting from our earlier premiss that every number had a greater, EI can still lead to the following unwanted inference:

1. ∀x∃yGyx
2. ∃yGyx   1 UI
3. Gxx   2 EI
4. ∃xGxx   3 EG

Here the Gxx of step 3 is a clear instance of Gyx, but ∃yGyx at line 2 came from the universal, and so merely claims that however x is chosen, there is a number greater than x. We should not be able to infer that the number could be x itself. What we want for EI instances is that the variable instantiated <u>to</u> must be distinct from variables already in the scope, C, of the quantifier. One way to insure distinctness is to require that the original clause be recoverable by the reverse substitution.

In our example Gxx is a perfectly good instance of Gyx, putting x for y. But Gyx can not be recovered as an instance of Gxx, since putting y for x gives Gyy. To facilitate formulation of the needed rule, we will define <u>distinct</u> instance:

1. Instances

Distinct Instance

$C(w/u)$ is a <u>distinct</u> instance of C fif

(1) it is a clear instance of C

(2) C is recoverable as a clear instance of $C(w/u)$ by the reverse substitution of u for w.

Put another way:

A is a distinct w-for-u (w/u) instance of B fif

A is a clear (w/u) instance of B and

B is a clear (u/w) instance of A.

    An example of the type of error blocked by requiring that EI instances must be distinct has already been given.

    Imposing the distinctness requirement on UG blocks an inference such as:

```
1   ∀xExx
2     Exx      1 UI
3   ∀yEyx      2 UG
```

Here, the Exx of line 2 is an (x/y) instance of Eyx (the scope of $\forall y$ on line 3). But Eyx is not a (y/x) instance of Exx. Hence line 3 is not from a distinct instance. (Reading Eyx as <u>y equals x</u> has the step from 2 to 3 go from "x equals itself" to "Everything equals x!".)

1. Instances

In studying examples of $C(r/u)$ where C is an actual, symbolized sentence, the sign (r/u), calling for substitution of a term r for variable u, may be written after the symbolized sentence and shown as "equal" to the result of carrying out the substitution. For example, $Px(a/x) = Pa$, $Px(y/x) = Py$, $Px(x/x) = Px$.

<u>Examples of various instances</u>.

$\exists xRxyz(w/y) = \exists xRxwz$ clear and distinct
$\exists xRxyz(y/z) = \exists xRxyy$ clear but not distinct
$\exists xRxyz(x/z) = \exists xRxyx$ not clear
               ↑———— captured
$\forall xRxyz \lor Szb(x/z) = \forall xRxyx \lor Sxb$ not clear

Exercises IX 1

1. Give the y/x instances of:

   *a. (Px.Rxay) v ∃xSxby

   *b. ∃x(Pyx v Rx)

   *c. Pyz

   *d. (∀xRxy v ∀yRxy).∃zRxy

2. Which of the instances indicated below will be distinct instances?

   *a. R(x,y,z)(w/z)   *b. R(x,y,z)(x/z)

   *c. ∃xHxy(x/y)   *d. (∃xKxy ⊃ Szy)(x/y)

3. Which of the following sequences of steps are correct? For those which are not, give the reason.

   *a. 1|1 ∀x∃yGyx
        1|2 ∃yGyx   1 UI
        1|3 Gyx   2 EI
        1|4 ∃xGxx   3 EG

   *b. ∃xRxy
       Rby   EI

   *c. ∀x(Pxy ⊃ Gxzx)
       Pxy ⊃ Gwzw   UI

   *d. ∀x∀y(Rxy ⊃ Rxz)
       ∀y(Ryy ⊃ Ryz)   UI

   *e. Rxyx
       ∀zRzyz   UG

   *f. (∀xPx ⊃ Qx)
       Pa ⊃ Qa   UI

    g. ∀xRxyz
       ∀w∀xRwyz   UG

    h. ∀y∀x(Rxy v Ryx)
       ∀y(Rxy v Ryx)   UI

2. **Quantifier Order and Dependencies Among Hypothetical Individuals**

Suppose we are told (with respect to a certain small universe of discourse) that someone is admired by everyone. It follows that everyone admires someone (if only the universally admired person). On the other hand, if we are told that everyone irritates someone, we could not rightly infer that someone is irritated by everyone. (Each might be irritated only by a neighbor.) Using symbols with the following readings - Axy: x admires y; Ixy: x irritates y - the two inferences are:

$$\text{Valid: } \frac{\exists x \forall y A y x}{\forall y \exists x A y x} \qquad \text{Invalid: } \frac{\forall y \exists x I y x}{\exists x \forall y I y x}$$

The logical difference does not hinge on the predicate readings, of course. What matters is the order of the quantifiers. The premiss of the first inference says that there is some x about whom a <u>universal</u> clause, $\forall y A y x$, is true. The second premiss of the second inference says of every y that an <u>existential</u> clause, $\exists x I y z$, is true of him. The contrasting situations can be represented by <u>arrow diagrams</u>. In such an arrow diagram, individuals are shown as dots (and/or name-letters). If a admires b, for example, it is shown by an arrow from a to b: a⟶b. If they admire each other, the arrow is double-headed: a⟵⟶b. If a admires himself, a "self arrow" points back at a: a↺ . Limiting the UD to four, the universal clause about hypothetical x might have an arrow diagram like this:

(Since <u>everyone</u> admires x, he must admire himself, as shown by the self arrow.) Since an arrow points <u>from</u> <u>every</u> dot, everyone admires someone. The conclusion of the inference is obvious.

2. Quantifier Order

Now the fact that the premiss of the second inference says of every y that y irritates someone means only that in an arrow diagram for I, an arrow must point from every dot. That is true in an arrow diagram like the preceding, to be sure. But it is also true in an arrow diagram like the following:

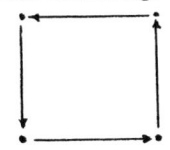

But in this diagram there is no one dot pointed at by every dot.

The premiss of the second inference could be true while the conclusion was false.

Now let us examine the following two deductions:

```
1|1    ∃x∀yAyx                      1|1    ∀y∃xIyx
1|2    ∀yAyx         1 EIx          1|2    ∃xIyx         1 UI
1|3    Ayx           2 UI           1|3    Iyx           2 EIx
1|4    ∃xAyx         3 EG           1|4    ∀yIyx         3 UGy
1|5    ∀y∃xAyx       4 UGy          1|5    ∃x∀yIyx       4 EG
```

The conclusion of the invalid inference is reached by the righthand sequence of steps as correctly as the valid one is on the left, accordingly to the safeguards so far given. A final safeguard to rule it out will be specified shortly. But first it will be worthwhile to examine the righthand sequence of steps more closely. Line one says that for any choice of y there is an x satisfying a certain condition. For different choices of y there may be different choices of x. When we arrive at line 3, Iyx says that a hypothetical y, chosen at random, so to speak, irritates a hypothetical x. But the hypothetical x is not chosen quite at random. He is one of the individuals that _that_ chosen y irritates. Therefore

2. Quantifier Order

the choice of x <u>depends</u> on the choice of y, in a sense. Therefore, it is hardly justified to move to line 4 and infer that everyone irritates that particular x. The appearance of x on line 3 was only in virtue of his being irritated by a hypothetical y chosen at random.

The general point illustrated by the above example is that in stripping off quantifiers we arrive at clauses about hypotheticals some of which depend on others. Various ways are used to keep track of such dependencies. One such way (not the one we will use) is to show that a hypothetical x depends on a hypothetical y by writing y(x). (y is then said to be a Skolem function of x.)

The way we will keep track of dependencies is less obviously appropriate, but it has the merit of simultaneously accomplishing something else, as will be seen presently. The method of our Q-system involves, first, an additional bit of bookkeeping. At every line where a variable is flagged we follow the flagged variable by a list of all other variables which are free in that line. Such variables will be said to be <u>semi-flagged</u> at that line. Examples:

```
∃x(Ryx v VwSwz)
Ryu v VwSuwz         EIuyz
                          ⎱ = semi-flagged
Sxy ⊃ ∃uHxuw              ⎰
∀z(Sxz ⊃ ∃uHxu)      UGyxw
```

For a deduction to be regarded as establishing the relation $P \vdash_Q C$ between its premises and its last line, C, it must also pass a <u>flag test</u> which is applied to the flag lists (flagged followed by semi-flaggeds) as follows:

2. Quantifier Order

Flag Test

a. Cross out all semi-flagged variables that never got flagged.

b. If no flagged variable now stands alone, unaccompanied by any (uncrossed out) semi-flagged variable, the test is failed, otherwise continue.

c. Choose a lone variable and cross it out and cross it out wherever semi-flagged.

d. If all flagged variables have now been crossed out, the test is passed, otherwise return to b.

This sounds complex, but it is easy to apply. To begin with, let us apply this last safeguard to the two sequences of steps we were examining.

```
1|1  ∃xVyAyx      P           1|1  Vy∃xIyx     P
1|2  VyAyx        1 EIx       1|2  ∃xIyx       1 UI
1|3  Ayx          2 UI        1|3  Iyx         2 EIxy
1|4  ∃xAyx        3 EG        1|4  VyIyx       3 UGyx
1|5  VyExAyx      4 UGy       1|5  ∃xVyIyx     4 EG
```

The lefthand deduction passes the flag test because both flagged variables are already "lone". The righthand deduction fails the test because no flagged variable is lone and no crossing out can begin. (The xy following EI at line 3 can be regarded as recording the dependence of x on y, as a (Skolem) function x(y). But the yx after UG at line 4 suggests a different sort of dependence - that the permissibility of UG on y depends on the status of x.)

In the light of the foregoing, one may now appreciate the fact that quantifier order law IV 2 (left) in the table of <u>Logically True Forms</u> in the preceding chapter has only $\supset$ rather than $\equiv$. In other words, the order of quantifiers in a prefix composed purely of universal quantifiers or of existential quantifiers may be changed at will, as indicated in laws IV 1 (left and right). But an existential quantifier may not, in general, exchange positions with a universal quantifier, and have a logically equivalent result. Nevertheless, this warning was qualified by the phrase "in general". The reason for the qualification may be perceived in the following deduction,

2. Quantifier Order

which at first glance seems much like the previous one, going from $\forall y \exists x$ to $\exists x \forall y$, which we just arranged to be blocked:

```
1|1    ∀x∃y(Rxz.Szy)      /∃y∀x(Rxz.Szy)
1|2    ∃y(Rxz.Szy)        1 UI
1|3    Rxz.Szy            2 EI yxz
1|4    Rxz                3 Drop
1|5    Szy                3 Drop
1|6    ∀wRwz              4 UG xz
1|7    Rwz                6 UI
1|8    Rwz.Szy            5,7 Join
1|9    ∀x(Rxz.Szy)        8 UG wzy
1|10   ∃y∀x(Rxz.Szy)      9 EG
```

Does this pass the new flag test? To see the steps taken for the flag test, it is sometimes convenient to assemble the various flaggings separately (instead of crossing variables out directly in the flaggings of the deduction). Accordingly, we may assemble the flaggings at lines 3,6,9 and display the steps of the flag test as follows:

	Step 1	Step 2	Step 3	Step 4
	Crossing out the semi-flagged z which never got flagged	Crossing out x which is now a lone variable	Crossing out lone y	Crossing out lone w
Line 3	y x z̶	y x̶ z̶	y̶ x̶ z̶	y̶ x̶ z̶
Line 6	x z̶	x z̶	x z̶	x̶ z̶
Line 9	w z̶ y	w z̶ y	w z̶ y̶	w̶ z̶ y̶

The flag test is passed!

What made it possible to dodge the crossed flaggings which blocked the previous deduction was the fact that the two quantified variables, x and y, could be separated <u>in different predications on separate lines</u> (4 and 5). This made it possible to change variables from x to w, by moving from Rxz at 4 to ∀xRwz at 6 (by UG xz), and getting Rwz at 7 by UI. Rwz was then joined to Szy so that the UG at 9 flagged w instead of x (as in the previous, blocked example).

2. Quantifier Order

The moral of all of this is that a move from $\forall x \exists y$ to $\exists y \forall x$ is blocked only when the two variables appear in some one predication. That is, the hypothetical individuals involved must be explicitly <u>related</u>. With this in mind, we may note that in dealing with sentences containing only one-place predicates, <u>all</u> permutations of quantifiers in a prefix of quantifiers yield logical equivalents.

We end this section by carrying out the foregoing inference by informal use of the rules of passage.

1 $\forall x \exists y (Rxz.Szy)$

2 $\forall x (Rxz.\exists y Szy)$ $\exists y$ shifted back, across blind Rxz

3 $\forall x Rxz.\exists y Szy$ Scope of $\forall x$ shortened forward, across blind $\exists y Szy$

4 $\exists y (\forall x Rxz.Szy)$ $\exists y$ shifted forward, across blind $\forall x Rxz$

5 $\exists y \forall x (Rxz.Szy)$ Scope of $\forall x$ extended backward, across blind Szy

The same result is obtained in five lines, instead of ten! As earlier remarked, we could, if we chose, incorporate the various quantifier shift moves as derivative rules in our Q-system. In any case, they are obviously useful.

Summary of Safeguards for Q-Deductions

Clear and distinct instances: An <u>instance</u> of a clause C obtained by
    substituting a term r for a variable u at every free occurrence
    of u is a <u>clear</u> instance fif no such occurrence is within the
    scope of a quantifier on r (where r would be <u>captured</u>). A clear
    "r for u" instance, C', of C is a <u>distinct</u> instance fif C is
    recoverable as a clear "u for r" instance of C'.

Restrictions on Instances:
    All instances must be clear.
    Instances for EI and UG must be distinct (use variables only, no names).

Flagging: In EI and UG the instantial variable must be "<u>flagged</u>" by
    writing it immediately to the right of the citation, e.g.,
    ∃xFx   Fz
    Fy   EIy   ∀xFx   UGz
    and all other variables with free occurrence in the clauses
    involved must be <u>semiflagged</u> by listing them to the right of
    the flagged variable, e.g.,
    ∃xRzxw   Rwzy
    Rzyw   EI yzw   ∀xRwxy   UG zwy

Restrictions on Flagging: P ⊦_Q C only if
    1. No flagged variable is free in the last line, or in any of its
        premisses.
    2. No variable is flagged twice.
    3. The flag test is passed. The test is applied as follows:
        a. Cross out all semiflagged variables that never got flagged.
        b. If no flagged variable now stands alone, unaccompanied
           by any (uncrossed out) semiflagged variables, the test
           is failed, otherwise
        c. Choose a lone variable and cross it out and cross it out
           wherever semi-flagged.
        d. If all flagged variables have now been crossed out, the
           test has been passed, otherwise return to b.

Exercises IX 2

*1. Some of the steps below are correct. Others violate safeguard rules. Mark each correct or cite the specific violation.

a. ∀x∃yRxyz
    ∃yRzyz   UI

b. ∃yRzyz
    ∀x∃yRxyz   UGz

c. ∃yRzyz
    ∃x∃yRxyz   EG

d. ∃yRzyz
    Rzyz   EIy

e. ∀x(Rxy ⊃ Hxbyx)
    Ryy ⊃ Hybyx   UI

f. ∀x(∃y(Rzy v Rxz) ⊃ Px)
    ∃y(Rzy v Ryz) ⊃ Py   UI

g. Rxyz
    ∃zRzyz   EG

h. ∀x∀yRxy ⊃ Ryx
    ∀yRxy ⊃ Ryx   UI

i. ∃yRxz
    ∀x∃yRxz   UGxz

j. ∀xRxyz
    ∀w∀xRwyz   UGx

k. ∀x∀y(Rxy ⊃ Ryx)
    ∀x(Rxy ⊃ Ryx)   UI

l. ∃xRxb
    ∀y∃xRxy   UGb

m. ∃yRzyz
    Rzxz   EIyz

n. Ryz
    ∀xRxz   UGxz

2. Write deductions for:

a. ∀x∃y(Axy ⊃ Bx)
    ∃x ~Bx   /∃x∃y ~Axy

b. ∀x(Ax v Bx)   /∀xAx v ∃xBx

c. ∀x∃y(Sxz ⊃ Hyz)   /∃y∀x(Sxz ⊃ Hyz)

3. Write deductions for the following (degree of suggested predicates indicated by superscripts).

   *a. Some physicists like no dreamers
       <u>Some physicists are dreamers</u>
       Some physicists are not liked by all physicists (P^1, L^2, D^1)

   *b. Whoever admires himself is conceited
       <u>No one admires a conceited person</u>   (UD: People)
       No one is admired by everyone (A^2, C^1)

   c. Some Wittgensteinians read no Carnapians
      Whoever does not read someone misunderstands him in some respect
      <u>Bonfuss is a Carnapian</u>
      Bonfuss is misunderstood (by someone) (W^1, R^2, C^1, M^2, b)

   d. Whoever admires himself is conceited
      <u>Everyone admires a popular person</u>
      Every popular person is conceited (A^2, C^1, P^1)

   e. Whoever admires himself is conceited
      <u>No one admires a conceited person</u>
      No popular person is admired by everyone (A^2, C^1, P^1)

   f. <u>Everyone admires a popular person</u>
      Anyone who does not admire himself is not popular (A^2, P^1)

4. Prove

   No one loves himself unless he loves someone
   $\forall x(\sim Lxx \lor \exists y Lxy)$

3. Transitional Steps.

Our rules, symbols and safeguards for EI systematize an inferential step which has been used by skilled reasoners since very ancient times. The fact that introduction of a hypothetical individual is a transitional step is obvious from the outset. By contrast, UG, though equally old, is ordinarily not thought of as transitional. It typically represents a non-transitional conclusion of steps of reasoning about hypothetical individuals each of which represents anything in the universe of discourse - things which are <u>arbitrarily chosen</u>, so to speak. ("Arbitrary" means "dependent upon will or pleasure" - OED.) Nevertheless, it was earlier remarked that the safeguards of our particular deductive system permit a transitional use of UG. Indeed, the reader may already have made use of it on the strength of that assurance. Since such use is without natural precedent, and is not, in fact, shared by all other modern deductive systems, it will be well to examine more closely how its use is justified in the present system.

We have already remarked that, in extending the logic of connectives to inferences concerning hypothetical individuals, the principle $P \supset C$, of such an inference P/C, becomes an open clause (assuming P to be a finite class of premisses). If such a clause were of tautological form, it would be true for every possible combination of truth values for its components. Hence it would be true if its variables were taken to stand for <u>any</u> individuals, since each assignment of individuals to variables would at most change the combination of truth values, while the tautology is true for all combinations. Similarly, a change of assumed extensions of predicates also produces only a

3. Transitional Steps

change of truth value combinations, but with the overall result still being true.

In semantical terminology (given in the optional reading of the preceding chapter), an open clause of tautological form is true-for-a-under-i for any assignment, a, and any extensional interpretation, i.

Clearly, if a principle of tautological form is logically true, so is its universal quantification on any variable. In particular, we can form the universal closure of the principle by universally quantifying repeatedly with respect to every free variable that appears in it, and the result is logically true.

Now, the principle of a UI step from $\forall xFx$ to Fy is $\forall xFx \supset Fy$ (informally: If everything is F then any one thing (chosen from the UD) is F). It is obviously a logically true open clause. Therefore, since $\forall xFx \supset Fy$ is true for any y, and for any other free variables appearing, $\forall y(\forall xFx \supset Fy)$ is equally true logically (and so is its universal closure for other variables).

Similar considerations for EG permit us to transform the principle of an EG step, $Fy \supset \exists xFx$, into $\forall y(Fy \supset \exists xFx)$.

For UG, however, the principle, $Fy \supset \forall xFx$ (informally: If anything (in the UD) is F, everything is F), is clearly not true in general. Therefore, UG conceived unrestrictedly as any step from Fy to $\forall xFx$ (or from $C(w/u)$ to $\forall uC$) does not always constitute a valid inference, or, as we shall say, it is not <u>stepwise valid</u>.

It will prove important to note, however, that the principle is at least true for <u>some</u> assignment and interpretation. This is seen from the fact that (1) any interpretation of F which makes $\forall xFx$ true must make

3. Transitional Steps

Fy true, and (2) any interpretation which makes $\forall x Fx$ false makes $\exists x \sim Fx$ true. For the latter to be true, Fy must be false for some y, making the principle true. Therefore, we may at least prefix an existential quantifier to the UG principle and get $\exists y(Fy \supset \forall x Fx)$. The reader may recall this as one of the four forms marked "Principles of UI, EG, EI, and UG" at the bottom of the page of logically true forms at the end of section 3 of the previous chapter, and which we repeat here for convenience:

UI: $\forall y(\forall x Fx \supset Fy)$ EG: $\forall y(Fy \supset \exists x Fx)$

EI: $\exists y(\exists x Fx \supset Fy)$ UG: $\exists y(Fy \supset \forall x Fx)$

It will be noted that the principle for an EI step, EI, like UG, is prefixed by an existential quantifier. Since EI is easily felt as only transitional, it is no surprise that it does not represent a stepwise-valid step. But the similarity between EI and UG suggests that a line of reasoning which justifies EI as transitional may also serve to justify a transitional UG. This indeed proves to be the case.

Before beginning, however, let us assure ourselves that the existentially quantified EI principle above is indeed logically true, by the same sort of direct semantical consideration as applied to the UG principle.

Suppose $\exists x Fx$ to be false on some interpretation of F. Then $\exists x Fx \supset Fy$ will be true by having a false antecedent.

Suppose $\exists x Fx$ to be true on some interpretation. Then, Fx must be true for some assignment to x, i.e., Fy, for some y. Then $\exists x Fx \supset Fy$ is true by the truth of the consequent. Therefore, either way

3. Transitional Steps

$\exists x Fx \supset Fy$ is true for some assignment under some interpretation. This is all we require to ensure the logical truth of $\exists y(\exists x Fx \supset Fy)$.

Beside being convinced semantically of the logical truth of connective logic, and of QN, UI, EG, non-transitional UG, and the two weak principles for EI and UG, just discussed, we will also need to be convinced semantically of the logical truth of one of the rules of passage. What is needed is assurance as to the stepwise validity of moving from $\forall x(Fx \supset P)$ to $\exists x Fx \supset P$ (for blind P).

Suppose for an arbitrarily chosen interpretation and assignment that P is true. Then $\exists x Fx \supset P$ will be true by truth of the consequent; and $Fx \supset P$ will be true for any x, and so for every x. That is, $\forall x(Fx \supset P)$ will also be true.

Now suppose P is false on that interpretation and assignment, and recall that, by Mif, the two sentences $\forall x(Fx \supset P)$ and $\exists x Fx \supset P$ are equivalent to $\forall x(\sim Fx \vee P)$ and $\sim \exists x Fx \vee P$, respectively. When P is false, dropping it from a disjunction does not affect the truth value of the disjunction. Therefore, the values of $\forall x(\sim Fx \vee P)$ and $\sim \exists x Fx \vee P$ are like those of $\forall x \sim Fx$ and $\sim \exists x Fx$ respectively. But these are equivalent by QN. In either case, then, for an arbitrarily chosen assignment and interpretation, $\forall x(Fx \supset P)$ and $\exists x Fx \supset P$ must have the same truth value, and hence for _every_ assignment and interpretation, and hence the equivalence is a logically true equivalence.

With these matters established, Quine shows how any deduction for $P \vdash_Q C$ using transitional EI and UG may be shown to have a logically true principle (or $\vDash P \supset C$), provided the various safeguards already described are now violated. We will first decide the procedure in general terms and then show its operation in an example.

3. Transitional Steps

The procedure is as follows. By discharging the premisses by the SQ rule, to get $P_1 \supset (P_2 \supset \ldots C)$, and using importation, we can, in a few further lines, reach the line $P \supset C$, with no premiss-numbers of its own. $P \supset C$, of course, is the principle of the inference which we are to prove logically true. In order to do this we construct a related deduction in which all the transitional steps are segregated into one place, so to speak, and show their justification there. To do this, we begin by writing down the specific principle for each flagged step, together with the variables which were flagged and semi-flagged at that step. For example, suppose one UG step was as follows:

| 11 | $\exists x Ryxwyu$ | |
| 12 | $\forall z \exists x Rzxwzu$ | 11 UG ywu |

We would enter its principle in a column like the following:

flag-step principles	flaggings
$\exists x Ryxwyu \supset \forall z \exists x Rzxwzu$	ywu
. . . .	. . . .

Continuing in this way, until all the flag-step principles (and their flaggings) were recorded, we would now form a conjunction of them (in a certain order to be determined by the flag test). For brevity, we can represent each flagstep principle by an "S" followed by the variable that was flagged at the step in question. For the above sample step, whose flagged variable is y, the representation would be Sy. (Because of the restriction against multiple flagging, the flag variables provide a unique indexing.) The order of the conjuncts is chosen to be such that

3. Transitional Steps

if we represent the conjunction as $S_1 \cdot S_2 \cdot S_3 \ldots S_n$ and speak of the corresponding flagged variables as u_1, u_2, $u_3 \ldots u_n$, then u_1 would be the flagged variable which was the <u>last</u> to be crossed out, u_2 the next-to-last, and so on, with u_n being the <u>first</u> flagged variable to be crossed out. (Semi-flagged variables which never got flagged do not index any of the S's, of course.) Now we place the conjunction $S_1 \cdot S_2 \ldots S_n$ at the beginning of the deduction as line 0 (to avoid disturbing the original line numbers). We change the citation of <u>every flagged line in the deduction</u> to one which cites a combination of Drop and MP, of connective logic. The step could now be done by dropping the needed implication from line 0 and using MP. E.g., for our sample step we would write

```
P  |11   ∃xRyxwyu
P,0|12   ∀z∃xRzxwzu    11,0 Drop, MP
```

To repeat, we get Sy from line 0 by Drop. Then, since Sy is simply an if-clause with line 11 as antecedent and 12 as consequent, Sy, with 11, yields 12, by MP.

We can now discharge the new, conjunction supposition at line 0, and obtain as last line: $(S_1 \cdot S_2 \ldots S_n) \supset I$ (where I is used to abbreviate $P \supset C$, the principle of the original <u>Inference</u>). This is now the premissless last line of a Q-deduction in which no EI or UG enters. Since the revised deduction employs nothing but stepwise valid steps, each line is logically true. Consequently, by the rationale for non-transitional UG, we may write $\forall u_1 ((S_1 \cdot S_2 \ldots S_n) \supset I)$. This is equivalent to $\forall u_1 (S_1 \supset ((S_2 \cdot S_3 \ldots S_n) \supset I))$, by exportation. What we now do is facilitated by the order of the conjuncts determined by the flag test, which is such

3. Transitional Steps

that the flagged variable of any conjunct is free in no later conjunct.

Since the flagged variable of S_1, was the last to be crossed out, it does not appear free in any of the following S's. (If it did, it would have been semiflagged but not yet crossed out, so that the flagged variables of the following S's would never have been "lone"; but we have assumed that the flag test was passed, so they all became lone at some point and were crossed out.)

The form of the whole line at this point may therefore be represented as

(1) $\forall u_1(S_1(u_1) \supset P)$ where P abbreviates $((S_2.S_3...S_n) \supset I)$, which is blind to u_1. But (1) is logically equivalent to

(2) $\exists u_1 S_1(u_1) \supset P$, by the earlier established rule of passage.

Furthermore, $\exists u_1 S u_1$ must be a particular example of either the EI principle $\exists y(\exists x Fx \supset Fy)$ or of the UG principle $\exists y(Fy \supset \forall s Fx)$, from the way we have constructed $S_1.S_2...$. Both principles we showed to be logically true. Therefore, MP, applied to $\exists u_1 S u_1 \supset P$, yields P. And P must be logically true, because a logical truth can logically imply only logical truths.

Then the process can be repeated on P (i.e., $(S_2.S_3...) \supset I$) which contains u_2 free and is logically true, thereby allowing non-transitional UG to yield $\forall u_2(S_2(u_2) \supset ((S_3.S_4...) \supset I))$. The consequent, which may be called P, being blind to u_2 in virtue of the ordering of the conjuncts, as before, we have, by the rule of passage, $\exists u_2 S u_2 \supset P'$. The logical truth of $\exists u_2 S u_2$ (an EI or UG principle) yields the logical truth of the remainder P'.

3. Transitional Steps

Continuing to drop off the existentially generalized conjuncts of line 0 in this fashion, we are finally left with I (i.e., $P \supset C$) as logically true. This completes the description of the general procedure.

As a specific example, let us take the following deduction, which uses both EI and a transitional UG:

```
1|1   ∃x(∀yRyx ⊃ Px)      /∃x∃y(Ryx ⊃ Px)
1|2   ∀yRyz ⊃ Pz          1 EIz
3|3   Ryz                 S
3|4   ∀yRyz               3 UGyz (Transitional)
1,3|5 Pz                  2,4 MP
1|6   Ryz ⊃ Pz            3,5 SQ   The flag test is passed: lone z
1|7   ∃y(Ryz ⊃ Pz)        6 EG      is crossed out, then lone y.
1|8   ∃x y(Ryz ⊃ Px)      7 EG
```

For it to be valid, its principle $\exists x(\forall yRyx \supset Px) \supset \exists x\exists y(Ryx \supset Px)$ must be shown to be logically true. We proceed as follows:

First we write an extra supposition, putting it ahead of the rest of the inference at a special line 0. To form the new supposition we write a material implication corresponding to each EI or UG step. Corresponding to the UG step from 3 to 4 we form the material implication $Ryz \supset \forall yRyz$. For the EI step from 1 to 2 we form the material implication $\exists x(\forall yRyx \supset Px) \supset (\forall yRyz \supset Pz)$. The new supposition at line 0 is then formed as the conjunction of those two implications. The first member of the conjunction is chosen to be the one corresponding to the step whose flagged variable was crossed off last, i.e., to the UG which flagged y. Accordingly, our supposition is 0|0 $\underbrace{(Ryz \supset \forall yRyz)}_{S_y} \cdot \underbrace{(\exists x(\forall yRyz \supset Px) \supset \forall y(Ryz \supset Pz))}_{S_z}$ S. And we transform our original inference as follows:

3. Transitional Steps

And we transform our original inference as follows:

```
  0 | 0  (Ryz ⊃ ∀yRyz).(∃x(∀yRyx ⊃ Px) ⊃ ∀y(Ryz ⊃ Pz))    S
  1 | 1  ∃x(∀yRyx ⊃ Pz)                                    S
1,0 | 2  ∀yRyz ⊃ Pz                                        1,0 Drop, MP
  3 | 3  Ryz                                               S
3,0 | 4  ∀yRyz                                             3,0 Drop, MP
1,3,0| 5 Pz                                                2,4 MP
1,0 | 6  Ryz ⊃ Pz                                          3,5 SQ
1,0 | 7  ∃y(Ryz ⊃ Pz)                                      6 EG
1,0 | 8  ∃x∃y(Ryz ⊃ Pz)                                    7 EG
  0 | 9  ∃x(∀yRyz ⊃ Pz) ⊃ ∃x∃y(Ryz ⊃ Px)                   1,8 SQ
```

Line 9 is the principle of the original inference (which we henceforth abbreviate I). Though it has not yet been proven to be logically true, it has been deduced from the supposition at line 0 without use of EI or UG. The steps previously so labeled were here derived from 0 using only Drop and MP (both stepwise valid, of course). Therefore, if we now discharge supposition 0 (and abbreviate it by Sy.Sz — indexing each conjunct with the variable which was flagged at the step it corresponds to), the result is (Sy.Sz) ⊃ I. This, at least, is thus proven logically true by stepwise-valid steps. We now proceed to show that logically true (Sy.Sx) ⊃ I logically implies I, whereby I will also be shown to be logically true.

Exportation yields Sy ⊃ (Sx ⊃ I). Sy (which abbreviates Ryz ⊃ ∀yRyz) contains two free variables: z and y. Since the open clause Sy ⊃ (Sx ⊃ I) is logically true for any values of z and y we may universally generalize 6 by <u>non-transitional</u> UG, and obtain ∀y(Sy ⊃ (Sx ⊃ I)). Now y does not appear free in I (no flagged variable can appear free in the last line or its premisses). Furthermore, y does not appear free in Sx. We arranged the order of our conjunctions os that the one whose flag variable was

3. Transitional Steps

crossed off last came first. If it had appeared free in a later implicational conjunct, corresponding to another flagged variable, it would have been semiflagged in the original deduction, and not yet crossed out, so that the x in Sx could not have been "lone". But we saw that the original deduction passed the flag test, so that x was lone. Therefore, the consequent of ∀y(Sy ⊃ (Sx ⊃ I)) is blind to y. The rule of passage gives ∃ySy ⊃ (Sx ⊃ I), or ∃y(Ryz ⊃ ∀yRyz) ⊃ (Sx ⊃ I). The antecedent is of the form ∃y(Fy ⊃ ∀xFx) (relettering bound variables) which has already been established as logically true. A similar maneuver for Sx leaves us with I, which is (∃x∀yRyz ⊃ Px) ⊃ ∃x∃y(Ryx ⊃ P) in this case, established as logically true.

Since $\underline{I}$ was the principle of inference, the inference is thus shown valid. Thus, although the general method applied to an example is lengthy, it illustrates how a deduction using the not-stepwise-valid EI and UG steps can, when the safeguard rules have been obeyed, be shown to lead to a valid conclusion.

X

THEORIES

Quantificational logic serves as an essential starting point for developments in various directions.

Besides being used in, (1), the application to individual problems of inference, it can be used in, (2), the formulation and development of (elementary) theories, or in, (3), serving as a basis for stronger forms of logic (of which quantificational logic becomes a part, just as connective logic became part of quantificational logic). Stronger systems of logic are useful, in turn, for the same three ways – leading to yet stronger logics.

Behind such developments one glimpses the need for a theory about theories and their logics. This is the area of metatheory ("meta" is Greek for *over*) – another direction of inquiry and development.

We shall be taking steps in all of these directions. We will begin, in this chapter, by looking more closely at theories which use only quantificational logic. Such theories will be called Q-theories.

1. **Deductive Development from Axioms**

The student of quantificational logic is typically concerned, at first, with the use of logic in analyzing particular inferences. Given English sentences are symbolized, and when validity is proven, the readings given to predicate letters are forgotten.

It is sometimes important, however, to use a set of premisses not just for a single inference but for many. Such deductive developments from a single set of premisses may be just as transitory in interest as single inferences, or they may represent a serious theoretical investigation. Such investigations may range in scope from those involving only a single concept

1. Axioms

and a few premisses, to the development of an enormous deductive structure of central interest to science. An example of the former might be an investigation of a single two-place predicate R with the premisses $\forall x \sim Rxx$, $\forall x \exists y Rxy$, $\forall x \forall y (\exists z (Rxz.Rzy) \supset Rxy)$ - whose truth is found to require an infinite universe of discourse. A classical example of the latter is Euclidean (or a non-Euclidean) geometry.

In keeping with the geometric tradition, the initial premisses are often called <u>axioms</u> and the consequences deduced from them are called <u>theorems</u>. Traditionally, in geometry, the axioms were held to be "self-evidently true" and the theorems to have been proved true by being deduced from axioms. In modern technical usage, however, "axiom" and "theorem" refer merely to relative roles in a deductive development.

A set of axioms, together with all their deducible consequences, is called an <u>axiomatic theory</u>. The term "theory" alone, without "axiomatic", is used for a set of clauses which, without necessarily specifying any special set of axioms (or even assuming any to be finitely specifiable) is nevertheless <u>deductively closed</u>, in the sense that all its deductive consequences are "already" included in the set. Thus, all axiomatic theories are theories, but not all theories are axiomatic.

Since axiomatic theories are typically represented with the axioms listed first, axioms are also often called <u>primitive sentences</u> ("primitive" being understood merely as first in the deductive order, not as uncivilized). They are also called <u>basic sentences</u> (understood merely as deductively basic to the given system, not as unquestionable, or incapable of being further analyzed or defended). These various terms will be used synonymously. But one may be more appropriate than another in a given grammatical context.

In deducing a long sequence of conclusions from axioms, several practical needs arise. One is to be able to use the results of previous deductions in

1. Axioms

later deductions. Another is to reach agreements that will permit abbreviating long deductions. And another is to abbreviate recurrent long expressions by <u>defining</u> new symbols, in addition to those in the original premisses. Ways of meeting the first two needs are taken up in this chapter. Definitions are taken up in the next chapter.

The first of the needs, the use of previous results, is easy to meet, informally. But it requires a few words to fit into our deductive pattern.

In principle, one can visualize one very long deduction with line numbers steadily increasing. Earlier results could then be cited by line number. But, of course, not all previous lines are <u>results</u> in the deduction system we are using. A given line may depend not on the axioms alone, but on auxiliary suppositions. Or it may be only a transitional line. Furthermore, the increase of flagged variables would call for a steady influx of new variables (numbered when the supply of letters gives out, e.g., x_{191}, w_{201}, . . .) to avoid double flagging. All in all, it is easier to arrange for each result to be set aside, as in a file, along with its premiss numbers (now axiom-numbers), and indexed for later inference. A next new result can then be obtained by starting a fresh deduction with the agreement that, on any given line, a previous result can be used by citing its index, and placing its axiom-numbers in the premiss-number column. In other words, the system of "bookkeeping" we have been using is to be augmented. Similar augmentation will shortly be outlined for using, and keeping track of, the terms we define and of their definitions.

We need not be overformal in prescribing the additional bookkeeping, but merely agree that it will be convenient (in developing a theory, K) to use Latin numerals for the axioms of K and Arabic numerals for the theorems. To avoid confusing line numbers with theorem numbers one may use various devices. If one is dealing exclusively with one theory, one may cite an axiom merely by

1. Axioms

Roman numeral. A theorem number may be distinguished by an accompanying asterisk. But if one is developing several theories together, say K and M, the axioms and theorems of K may be cited as KIII, K2, etc., and those of M as MIV, M7, etc. In practice, names are often used - e.g., the <u>parallel axiom</u> of geometry, or the <u>Pythagoras</u> theorem.

In order to use an axiom or a previous result we may (1) simply reproduce it at a certain line (which may be an aid to the memory, of oneself or others), or (2) cite it as if it were at a previous line, together with a rule citation justifying the current line.

The first procedure, which we will call <u>invoking</u>, is similar to the P and S rules in that no previous line of a given deduction is cited nor any rule, but only the appropriate index. For example, axiom II of theory K may be written on a line with the citation KII. In the premiss-number column, also, one writes KII. (Often it is informally agreed that axiom-numbers are not to be shown in the premiss column, so that a conclusion with no premiss numbers is taken to be a result of theory - all logical truths being taken as results of every theory.)

The second procedure is already adequately characterized. An example of its use would be where theorem 19 of theory K, which stemmed from Axioms III and V, is "$\forall x(Px \supset \exists y Ryx)$". One could write a line "$Pb \supset \exists y Ryb$" with the citation: K19 UI. In the premiss-number column, one would enter KIII, KV (unless it had been agreed that a line with an empty premiss column was understood to be a result of the theory).

With these preliminaries, we turn to the next practical need, that of agreeing on ways to abbreviate long deductions.

2. Broadening Deductive Methods

Adding Rules. We have earlier seen that any deductive system, such as the Q-system, may add derived rules: after showing by schematic deduction that inferences of a certain form can always be carried out stepwise, one may enter it in a certain file and admit inferences of that form as single steps, with an appropriate new citation. Inference forms which can be carried out in both directions show logical equivalence, and so can be used to provide new equivalence rules (permitting replacement of part of an earlier line.)

Whether or not such moves are formally incorporated into a system, they may, of course, be used informally, in actual deductive work. Typical moves are those already used to convert a clause into prenex form, such as the rules of passage and of relettering bound variables. Advantage may also be taken of the fact that a sequence of equivalence transformations, being completely reversible, establishes the equivalence of the first and last clauses, without need for a deduction in each direction.

In writing deductions we shall not, in fact, use any of the above as line citations, except to admit the relettering of bound variables for which we will adopt the citation abbreviation: RBV. The RBV rule, restated for convenience, is that in any quantification QuC (which may be a proper part of a larger sentence) every occurrence of u may be replaced by an occurrence of another variable w, provided that w has no occurrence (already) in C. That the result of such replacement, QwC', is logically equivalent to QuC is obvious; but it should be noted that its actual proof, though not difficult, is not accomplished by any one schematic derivation of the type mentioned because of its generality. (The type of proof required may be postponed pending further examination of metatheoretic methods.)

2. Broadening Methods

<u>Combining Steps</u>. Steps may be combined, when obvious. We have already been combining double negation, (N), with other steps, e.g., by writing Elim(N) as citation for a step combining it with elimination. We shall now admit <u>any</u> truth-functionally valid step with a citation merely of "T", preceded by the line numbers of the lines directly involved. After all, truth-functional logic is assumed known at this point, and the validity of such a step can always be checked by truth-table, or other decision method, if not obvious. (We need not always avail ourselves of this freedom; it often aids clarity to spell out such steps, or even, when combined, to indicate the rules used, e.g., "Drop, Link".)

Quantificational steps may also be combined, but with more restraint. (A simple "Q" like the simple "T" above, is a bit too uncommunicative. Worse, there is no decision method for quantification theory, as there is for truth-functional logic, a fact established by Alonzo Church, and known as "Church's Theorem".)

QN steps are especially simple to combine, and we will admit as a single step, with citation QN, what would, in fact, require several single QN steps previously:

i $\quad \sim \forall x \exists y \forall z R x y z$
j $\quad \exists x \forall y \exists z \sim R x y z \qquad$ i QN (combining 3 QNs)

A second convenient occasion for combining steps is when a string of universal quantifiers is to be dropped by UI steps. Example:

i $\quad \forall x \forall y \forall z ((Rxy.Ryz) \supset Rxz)$
j $\quad (Rxy.Ryz) \supset Rxz \qquad$ i UI (3 steps combined)

Multiple UIs are especially unproblematic when quantifiers are merely dropped, as above, with no change of arguments. A change of arguments (which incurs the danger of variable capture) may be best indicated by a sequence of

2. Broadening Methods

substitution symbols:

    i $\forall x \forall y \forall z((Rxy.Ryz) \supset Rxz)$
    j $(Rzw.Rwz) \supset Rzz$ i UI $(z/x)(w/y)(z/z)$

Note that the following step, though valid, could not be correctly carried out by the UI sequence indicated below:

    i $\forall x \forall y \forall z((Rxy.Ryz) \supset Rxz)$
    j $(Ryx.Rxz) \supset Ryz$ UI $(y/x)(x/y)(z/z)$

The obstacle is that the instance indicated as the first step is not clear.

    i $\forall x \forall y \forall z((Rxy.Ryz) \supset Rxz)$
    j $\forall y \forall z((Ryy.Ryz) \supset Ryz)$ UI (y/x) [y captured]
                 ↑   ↑

A correct sequence of steps for that result, in the Q-system, can be made by making the first UI to a different variable, e.g., w, with a subsequent UG to prepare for a later UI to y, after the original occurrences of y have been changed:

    1 $\forall x \forall y \forall z((Rxy.Ryz) \supset Rxz)$
    2 $\forall y \forall z((Rwy.Ryz) \supset Rwz)$ 1 UI (w/x)
    3 $\forall z((Rwx.Rxz) \supset Rwz)$ 2 UI (x/y)
    4 $\forall u \forall z(Rux.Rxz) \supset Ruz)$ 3 UG wx
    5 $(Ryx.Rxz) \supset Ryz$ 4 UI $(y/u)(z/z)$

One can expedite matters, however, by using the RBV rule:

    1 $\forall x \forall y \forall z((Rxy.Ryz) \supset Rxz)$
    2 $\forall u \forall v \forall z(Rux.Rvz) \supset Ruz)$ 1 RBV twice
    3 $(Ryx.Rxz) \supset Ryz$ 2 $(y/u)(x/v)(z/z)$

Some writers adopt a rule of <u>simultaneous substitution</u>, applicable when a mere permutation of variables results (i.e., with no two positions, originally occupied by distinct variables becoming occupied by the same variable, and no two positions occupied by the same variable becoming occupied by distinct ones). Using such a rule requires an extended substitution symbolism, as in the following self-explanatory example:

2. Broadening Methods

1 $\forall x \forall y \forall z((Rxy \cdot Ryz) \supset Rxz)$
2 $(Ryx \cdot Rxz) \supset Ryz$ 1 UI $(\frac{x}{y} \frac{y}{x} \frac{z}{z})$

Simultaneous EI steps are often best avoided. But if used, the successive flaggings needed by single steps should be carefully recorded, and must satisfy the flag restrictions. Example:

i $\exists x \exists y \exists z Rxyz$
j $Ruyv$ i EI u, yu, vyu

UG steps at the end of a deduction are often of a routine, non-transitional nature, when double flagging is of no danger. A typical one-at-a-time pattern being:

:
17 $Rxwz$
18 $\forall z Rxwz$ 17 UGzwx   ⎛ zwx ⎞
19 $\forall y \forall z Rxyz$ 18 UGwx   ⎜ wx ⎬ — may be crossed off in the order: xwz
20 $\forall x \forall y \forall z Rxyz$ 19 UGx   ⎝ x   ⎠

Here, the cross-off test can obviously be passed (problems, if any, arising elsewhere in the deduction). Consequently, they may, informally, be combined into one, without bothering to write a flag list.

17 $Rxwz$
18 $\forall x \forall y \forall z Rxyz$ 17 UG

Combining _different_ quantifier steps, with a citation such as: EI, UI, EG, will be avoided.

Exercises X 1

In the following, a theory which may be called <u>the Heaviness Theory</u>, or H, is to be developed. The theorems shown below are to be deduced from the five axioms in the order indicated. Each deduction may (but need not) cite or invoke any theorem previously obtained. Steps may be combined, and other abbreviating methods of the foregoing section may be used.

<u>Basic Terms</u>. H,E (whose intended interpretation may be suggested by the readings:

Hxy: x is heavier than y;   Exy: x equals y in weight.

<u>Axioms</u>

HI.	$\forall x \forall y (Exy \supset Eyx)$
HII.	$\forall x \forall y \forall z ((Exy . Eyz) \supset Exz)$
HIII.	$\forall x \forall y \forall z ((Hxy . Hyz) \supset Hxz)$
HIV.	$\forall x \forall y (Hxy \equiv (\sim Hyx . \sim Exy))$
HV.	$\forall x \forall y (Exy \equiv (\sim Hxy . \sim Hyx))$

<u>Theorems</u>

*H1.	$\forall x \forall y (Exy \equiv Eyx)$
*H2.	$\forall x \forall y (Hxy \supset \sim Hyx)$
*H3.	$\forall x \sim Hxx$
H4.	$\forall x \forall y (Hxy \lor Exy \lor Hyx)$
H5.	$\forall x Exx$
H6.	$\forall x \forall y (Hxy \supset \forall z (Eyz \supset Hxz))$
H7.	$\forall x \forall y \forall z \forall w ((Hxy . Eyz . Hzw) \supset Hxw)$

3. Some Common Relational Properties

Several of the axioms and theorems in the preceding exercise section are of such common occurrence that a special terminology for them will be useful. The property that Axiom I ascribes to E (equalling in weight) is called symmetry. A statement of the same logical form will hold for many other predicates, for example: $\forall x \forall y (\text{Cousin}(x,y) \supset \text{Cousin}(y,x))$. All such predicates are said to designate symmetric relations.

The symmetry of a relation can be graphically represented by an arrow-diagram. In an arrow-diagram for a relation, R, individuals are shown as dots (or as name letters, e.g., a,b,c,...). If b has the relation R to c (i.e., Rbc), then one draws an arrow from b which points to c: b⌒c, and so on. If R is symmetric then every arrow is matched by a return arrow: b⇌c (or, equivalently, by a double-headed arrow: b↔c).

Statements of the form of Axiom III are statements of transitivity. Axiom III may thus be paraphrased by saying that being heavier than is a transitive relation, according to theory H. All comparative adjectives - bigger, wiser, older, ... are transitive, and so are many others: descendant of, part of, ...

In ordinary reasoning we are seldom conscious of using transitivity. We reason from Abe is taller than Bob and Bob is taller than Chuck to Abe is taller than Chuck as a matter of course. When a child is able to tell that Abe is taller than Chuck only from having seen Abe and Bob together and Bob and Chuck together, psychologists say he has attained the power of making indirect comparison. But neither child nor adult would infer from Abe is standing next to Bob and Bob is standing next to Chuck to Abe is standing next to Chuck. Yet, expressed with 2-place predicate symbols, the two inferences appear to have the same form:

$$\frac{\text{Tab}}{\text{Tbc}} \quad \frac{\text{Nab}}{\text{Nbc}}$$
$$\text{Tac} \quad \text{Nac}$$

3. Relational Properties

We may feel that the difference lies in the meanings of the predicates. This is reasonable. But to apply our logical symbolism, the difference must be spelled out. Adding $\forall x \forall y \forall z((Txy.Tyz) \supset Txz)$ to the premisses on the left would be true, and it makes the taller-than inference stepwise deducible.

On an arrow-diagram, a transitive relation, whenever it shows an arrow from a to b and b to c, will always show an arrow from a to c. More informally, we may say that in an arrow-diagram for a transitive relation, every pair of tail-gating arrows has a leapfrog arrow: a→b→c.

Theorem 2 may be paraphrased by saying that it asserts that H (heavier than) is asymmetric. The arrow-diagram of an asymmetric relation is characterized by a total absence of double-headed (or return) arrows. All comparative adjectives are asymmetric, and so are many other predicates such as mother-of.

The asymmetry of H contrasts with the symmetry of E. It will have been noticed that E is transitive, as well as H, according to Axiom II. But the contrast of symmetry properties is so distinctive that natural grammer has distinct expressions for each: The comparative, e.g., bigger-than, for transitive and asymmetric relations, and the as-big-as construction for transitive and symmetric relations.

Note that a relation need not be symmetric nor asymmetric. As lovers know, love is sometimes requited, sometimes not. I.e., in the arrow-diagram for Loves(x,y), some arrows are matched by a return arrow, some are not.

Theorems 3 and 5 show another difference between H and E. Theorem 3 can be paraphrased as saying that Heavier-than is irreflexive. Theorem 5 says that equalling in weight is reflexive. Nothing is heavier than itself, but everything equals itself in weight. In the arrow-diagram of a reflexive relation, every individual has an arrow from itself which points back to itself: a ↺ . Such an arrow will be called a self-arrow. An irreflexive relation will show no self-arrows at all. Again, there are relations which are neither reflexive nor irreflexive, such as admiration: Admires(x,y) .

Exercises X 2

Another important property (which is not exemplified in theory H) is that of being <u>intransitive</u>. A relation R is intransitive if its arrow-diagram shows <u>no</u> leapfrog arrows. In symbols, R is intransitive fif $\forall x \forall y \forall z((Rxy.Ryz) \supset \mathord{\sim} Rxz)$. Examples of intransitive relations are: mother, father, immediate successor (among natural numbers). Examples of relations which are neither transitive nor intransitive are: being acquainted with, being within ten feet of.

Exercises X 2

1. In the preceding discussion, the properties of symmetry, transitivity, and reflexivity have each been accompanied by the contrary properties of asymmetry, intransitivity, and irreflexity, with mention of relations which lack both the property and its contrary. We can, therefore, make a threefold classification of relations with respect to each property. For each relation in the table below put a 1, 0, or -1 in each column (at the relation's row) as follows: Put a 1 if the relation has the property listed at the top of the column (e.g., symmetry); put a -1 if it has the contrary property (e.g., asymmetry); put a 0 if the relation has neither the property nor its contrary.

		Sym.	Trans.	Reflex.
*a.	parent of			
b.	resembles exactly			
c.	(full) brother of			
*d.	outranks			
*e.	wife of			
f.	read a book by			
*g.	is formally introduced to			
h.	is within 2 of (UD: Natural Nos.)			

X 231
Exercises X 2

2. Proceed as in problem 1 for the relations whose arrow-diagram (in a three-membered universe) are shown below.

	Sym.	Trans.	Reflex
*a.			
*b.			
c.			
d.			
e.			
f.			
*g.			
*h.			

3. Prove that an asymmetric relation is irreflexive. I.e., write a deduction for ∀x∀y(Rxy ⊃ ~Ryx) /∀x~Rxx.

4. Prove that an intransitive relation is irreflexive. I.e., ∀x∀y∀z((Rxy.Ryz) ⊃ ~Rxz) /∀x~Rxx

Exercises X 2

5. Prove that a transitive, irreflexive relation is asymmetric. I.e., ∀x∀y∀z((Rxy.Ryz) ⊃ Rxz)
$$\frac{\forall x \sim Rxx}{\forall x \forall y (Rxy \supset \sim Ryx)}$$

6. Some relations, while not (totally) reflexive, have self-arrows for every dot on the arrow-diagram which has an arrow coming to, or going from it, i.e., ∀x∀y((Rxy v Ryx) ⊃ Rxx). Such relations may be called <u>field - reflexive</u>. Prove that a relation which is both transitive and symmetric must be field-reflexive. I.e., write a deduction for:

∀x∀y∀z((Rxy.Ryz) ⊃ Rxz)
$$\frac{\forall x \forall y (Rxy \supset Ryx)}{\forall x \forall y ((Rxy \vee Ryx) \supset Rxx)}$$

XI

DEFINITIONS

Definitions are necessary in explaining almost any subject. We have been defining words from the outset of this book. They are well enough understood for most practical purposes. But they often give rise to dispute in argument. Moreover, there have long been conflicting philosophical doctrines as to their purpose and basis. The use of definition in the deductive development of theories is less controversial, but it needs special consideration. Such consideration may, in turn, shed light on the use of definition in broader contexts, and on its logical and philosophical basis.

1. Definitions in Theory Development.

The role of definition in theory development may be thought of, at first, as merely that of abbreviation. Suppose that while developing a theory which uses a two-place predicate, P, we frequently need to use a clause of the form: $\exists z(Pzx.Pzy)$. Such clauses may occur with different variables, e.g., $\exists y(Pyx.Pyz)$, or $\exists x(Pxw.Pxz)$, or with names taking the places of the free variables of the clause, e.g., $\exists z(Pzb.Pzc)$. But in each case, the clause is saying the same thing about whatever the free variables, or names, may stand for. For example, if the reading for P was: Pxy: x is part of y, then $\exists z(Pzb.Pzc)$ would mean: Something is part of both b and c; $\exists x(Pxw.Pxz)$ would mean: Something is part of both w and z. If we define a new, two-place predicate to express this idea, simple predications may be used instead of occurrences of the longer, quantified compounds. For shortness, we might adopt an everyday word, such as 'overlap', which approximates the idea, and use it, in the context of the theory, as the official reading of the defined

1. Definitions in Theories

predicate. In other words, Oxy (x overlaps y) would be defined as an abbreviation for $\exists z(Pzy.Pzy)$.

The common way of writing such a definition of 'overlaps' would be:

$$Oxy \equiv \exists z(Pzx.Pzy) \qquad Df$$

In words: x overlaps y if and only if some z is part of both x and y. The open form of the equivalence reflects an older, but convenient, custom. It was intended as having the meaning of its universal closure, e.g., $\forall x \forall y (Oxy \equiv \exists z(Pzx.Pzy))$. Although we shall follow custom in using the shorter, open form, the universal intent must be born in mind. From the purely deductive point of view, the universal closure of a definition might be regarded as an added axiom. But the semantical treatment of definition, as its abbreviational role suggests, has the effect only of fixing the meaning of the defined predicate relative to the predicates in the definiens, instead of adding content to the theory. Moreover, treating definition deductively only as an added axiom would be cumbersome. To effect a definitional replacement by deductions from a "definitional premiss" would require many tedious steps. Instead, we shall adopt rules for direct definitional replacement.

First, let us take account of the conditions which a proper definition must fulfill. They were tacitly fulfilled by the 'overlaps' example. They can be made explicit by requiring it to be so that:

A <u>definition</u> of an n-place predicate, G, for a Q-theory, K, is a material equivalence of the form

$$G(u_1, u_2, \ldots u_n) \equiv G_D$$

where the lefthand member (of the equivalence) (called the <u>definiendum</u>) consists of a symbol, G, not belonging to K, followed by an n-place argument of n mutually distinct variables (called the definiendum variables), and

1. Definitions in Theories

the righthand member, G_D (called the definiens), is a clause of K which contains free occurrences only of the definiendum variables (though not necessarily all).

In the above, using a word-saving custom, references to theory K also serve as references to the language in which it is formulated.

The requirement that definiendum variables be mutually distinct permits a definition for $G(x,y)$, to say what it is for something, b, to have the relation G to itself, $G(b,b)$, when b is put for both variables, x and y, in the definiens. By contrast, definition for $G(x,x)$, telling what it is for any x to bear the relation G to itself, says nothing about what it is for something, b, to bear G to some other thing, c, $G(b,c)$.

The requirement that the definiens contain free occurrences only of definiendum variables ensures that the true application of a 2-place predicate to two individuals, for example, will not depend on something being true of a third individual, totally unspecified.

The requirement that G be a new predicate, not belonging to K ensures against circularity. But it may raise a question. In what language is the definition? The question can be answered by taking the definition to be in an enlarged language, called a <u>definitional extension</u> of K. Such an extended language can, in practice, be regarded as being defined simultaneously with the new predicate.

If K is an already definitionally extended language, all previously defined predicates belong to K and may appear in the definiens. When a language is successively extended by a sequence of definitions the requirement of newness for the definiendum ensures that a term can be defined only by previously defined terms.

1. Definitions in Theories

The largest part of the vocabularies of typical theories, such as geometry, will ordinarily be made up of defined terms, and the sequences of definitions of such theories play a central role, both in deductive development and in interrelating concepts.

The rules of definitional replacement will best be stated, in view of the foregoing, so as to apply to theories that are already definitional extensions. It will thus be understandable to refer in a rule to the sequence, D, of definitions, as it exists at the time the rule is applied.

Rules of Definitional Replacement

A step to a line j may be taken, citing an earlier line i, with citation i DfR G, for either of the steps as described below, provided that a definition, $G(u_1, u_2, \ldots, u_n) \equiv G_D$, is in the sequence, D. of definitions.

Eliminating a Defined Term

line j is obtained from i by replacing an occurrence of $G(r_1, r_2, \ldots, r_n)$ by an altered form of definiens, G_D, which is derived by

(1) relettering bound variables, if necessary, to ensure that they differ from each of $r_1, r_2, \ldots, r_n$, (remaining distinct from each other), and

(2) replacing each occurrence of $u_1, u_2, \ldots, u_n$, respectively, by $r_1, r_2, \ldots, r_n$.

Introducing a Defined Term

line j is obtained from line i by replacing an occurrence in line i of an altered form (as described above) of definiens, G_D, by $G(r_1, r_2, \ldots, r_n)$.

Writing steps in a deduction which eliminate or introduce a defined predicate by the given rules can be illustrated for our definition of O (overlaps) on the assumption that the definition is in the sequence of definitions of the language under consideration, as follows:

1. Definitions in Theories

Elimination Example 1

```
|8  ∀zOzz
|9  ∀z∃w(Pwz.Pwz)        8 DfR O
```

Here, the terms of the argument in the occurrence to be replaced are both z. Therefore, z replaces both x and y in ∃w(Pwx.Pwy). The latter expression is an altered form of the definiens, differing from it only by using the bound variable w instead of ~~x~~. Notice that the fact that the occurrence of z,z is inside the scope of ∀z makes no difference to definitional replacement. Since z is bound in line 8, it is proper that it be bound in the definitional equivalent line 9.

Elimination Example 2

```
|2  ∀w(Rwz ⊃ Oxz)
|3  ∀w(Rwz ⊃ ∃w(Pwx.Pwz))
```

Here it should be noticed that the occurrence of Oxz within the scope of ∀w does not prevent the choice of w for relettering the definiens, which must be distinct only from the argument terms x,z. The occurrences of w in the scope of the nested quantifier, ∃w, are bound by it, not by the external quantifier, ∀w.

Introduction Example

```
|5  ∀z(∃x(Pxz.Pxb) v ∃y(Pyz.Pyc))
|6  ∀z(Ozb v ∃y(Pyz.Pyc))           5 DfR O
|7  ∀z(Ozb v Ozc)                   6 DfR O
```

Here, one spots the two members of the universal disjunction of line 1 as proper alterations of the definiens of O replaceable, respectively, by predications Ozb and Ozc of the defined predicate O. Correlating the positions occupied by z,b in the first member, for example, with those of the definiendum variables, x,y, in the definiens ∃z(Pzx.Pzy). However,

1. Definitions in Theories

it should be noticed that in seeing that the conditions of the Introducing Rule are met, direct substitution can lead to problems. If the definiens, $\exists x(Pzx.Pzy)$, is altered by first relettering bound variable z as x we get $\exists x(Pxx.Pxy)$ so that when z,b replace x,y, we get $\exists z(Pzz.Pzy)$, which is not what is wanted. If z,b are first subsituted in for the definiendum variables x,y, we get unwanted $\exists z(Pzz.Pzb)$. To get the desired $\exists x(Pxz.Pxb)$ we must either use simultaneous substitution, or first reletter with a variable, such as w, distinct from the definiendum variables, then substitute z,b, for x,y, then reletter again, replacing w by x.

Exercises XI 1

*1. Assuming the definition 'Oxy $\equiv \exists z(Pzx.Pzy)$ Df' to be in the D-file, use DfR step(s) for each of the following.

    a. Eliminate (unabbreviate) the occurrence of 'O' in
       $\forall z(Pzw \supset \exists u(Fu.Ouz))$
    b. Abbreviate the following by introducing defined 'O'.
       $\forall w \forall z(\exists y(Pyz.Pyw) \supset \exists x(Pxw.Pxz))$

2. Suppose it is desired to reformulate the 'Heaviness' Theory (H) of Exercises I 1 by using Axiom HV as a definition of E.

    *a. Write the definition in proper Df form.
    *b. Using DfR step(s), express Axiom HI in primitive (unabbreviated) terms.
    c. Do the same for Axioms HII and HIV.

For the following problems we shall refer to a 'Kinship Theory', K, (adapted from an example given by Rudolf Carnap). It will illustrate, among otner things, that definition need not always be for the purpose of abbreviation. It may be (as here, in part) to exhibit interrelationships among previously understood terms. (But difference in purpose does not affect the logical treatment of a definition.)

Theory K. UD: Humans

Primitive Terms: Ma (Male), Fe (Female), Par (Parent)

Primitive Sentences (Axioms):

    I $\forall x(Ma(z) \vee Fe(x))$
    II $\forall x \sim(Ma(x).Fe(x))$
    III $\forall x \forall y(Par(x,y) \supset \sim Par(y,x))$
    IV $\forall x \forall y \forall z((Par(x,y).Par(y,z)) \supset \sim Par(x,z))$

Definitions (Beginning D sequence):

    D1 $Ch(x,y) \equiv Par(y,x)$ Df
    D2 $Mo(x,y) \equiv (Fe(x).Par(x,y))$ Df
    D3 $Fa(x,y) \equiv (Ma(x).Par(x,y))$ Df

3. What properties do Axioms III and IV ascribe to the relation of being a parent of?

Exercises XI 1

*4. Express Axioms I and II in normal English.

*5. Define: Daughter, Son, Grandparent, Grandmother, Grandson. (Symbols: Dau, Son, Gpar, Gmo, Gson).

*6 Prove, from the axioms and definitions, that any parent of someone is a father or mother of that person. I.e:
$\forall x \forall y (Par(x,y) \supset (Fa(x,y) \vee Mo(x,y)))$

7. Using your definitions from #5, with axioms, etc., prove that

   a. One's grandparents are never one's parents.
   b. No one is a son of his grandmother.

XII

IDENTITY AND NUMBER

1. <u>Identity</u>

The concept of identity is used in the reasonings of every human, from childhood onward. But it is not definable by simple quantificational logic alone. To handle it, quantification theory must be supplemented by a special symbol for it and appropriate rules. Quantification theory when so supplemented is sometimes referred to as the theory of quantification-with-identity, and a Q-language incorporating it may be called a QI language. (Often a theory couched in such a language is said simply to be in standard notation.)

Identity is represented by a two-place predicate. The "official" reading we shall adopt for it will be "x is identical with y". The symbolization of such a clause in our format would be I(x,y). However, by long tradition, it is usually represented as x=y. In the following we shall often follow tradition in this respect, even in stating its rules. However, to avoid complicating all the other rules UI, EI, etc., we shall regard "x=y" or "(x=y)" only as an informal way of writing Ixy or "=(x,y)".

Beside the "official reading" mentioned, other readings may be used. Mathematical usage suggests "x equals y". This will sometimes be convenient, especially in mathematical applications (in spite of the fact that it stems from a view of the foundation of mathematics that is no longer current). On the other hand, some everyday usage suggests simply "x is y". This is best avoided. Everyday usage also admits "John is hungry", but not in a sense which would be symbolized as "John = hungry" or "John = hunger", in symbolic logic. (The ambiguities of "is" have caused considerable

1. Identity

misdirected effort in the development of logic and philosophy.) Other renditions might be "x is the same as y" or "x is the same thing as y". But "identical" and "same" are about equally ambiguous, as are other possibilities. The full meaning of "=", as we shall use it, will become progressively clearer in working with the rules for it. (The meaning of "v" was not determined by the reading "or", after all.)

We shall be using just two basic rules for identity. They will be called the <u>Rule of Identity</u> (with citation I) and <u>Identity Replacement</u> (with citation IR).

<u>Rule of Identity</u> (I)

r=r (r being any term) may be entered at any line, without premiss numbers, with citation: I.

<u>Identity Replacement</u> (IR)

From preceding lines, i, j, whose clauses, in either order, are C and either r=s or s=r (r and s both terms), a clause, C', at line k, may be justified by the citation: i, j IR, <u>provided</u>:

a. C' is obtained from C by replacing all, some, or none of the free occurrences of r in C by s;
b. None of the free occurrences of r, where replacement is made, are within the scope of an operator on s (where s would be captured).

The need for the identity concept (which students - and philosophers - have sometimes questioned) is most quickly seen in trying to symbolize sentences such as

1. Identity

"John loves Cynthia and someone _else_."

"Everyone _except_ George was happy."

"Zero is smaller than every non-negative integer _but_ it_self_."

"Whoever helps an_other_ is benevolent."

Words like "else", "except", "but", "other" suggest negation and indefinite reference. In symbolizing them, one may therefore expect to use a negation sign and a variable. Identity does not appear involved until we realize that being other-than is simply _not_ being identical-with.

To symbolize the first sentence we may begin by paraphrasing it at greater length - without the tricks of English that are used to avoid repeating words (often a wise step in symbolizing). In the longer paraphrase we have:

John loves Cynthia and John loves someone else.

This is a conjunction whose first component may be expressed: Ljc. If the second component were merely "John loves someone", it could be symbolized: ∃xLjx. But it would add no information since it simply follows from the first component by EG. The felt negation and generality in "else" may be made explicit by paraphrasing the second component even more explicitly as:

John loves someone who is not identical with Cynthia.

The symbolization of the complete original sentence is now obvious as:

Ljc.∃x(Ljx.∼x=c)

As a first simple application of I, we may prove a truth of logic: the _law of identity_, that everything is identical with itself: ∀x(x=x).

```
1  w=w
2  ∀x(x=x)      1 UG w
```

1. Identity

This proof is not intended to prove the law from something <u>more</u> certain, of course. The law is taken as true in virtue of the meaning we intend "=" to have. I.e., if someone were to claim that some individual b constituted an exception, i.e., $\sim b=b$, he would simply be said to have confused the meaning of "=" with some other relation. In English we might try to explain identity simply as <u>the</u> relation which everything has to itself and to nothing else. But this would be circular because identity would be needed to explain "-self" and "else", as we shall see. For the moment, we merely note that the "proof" is a formal exercise of the system, showing only that the formulation of I within the system is adequate to prove the law. (It may also be noted that the variable w may be so chosen as not to conflict with any other needed flagging.)

Other deductive systems take the law itself as basic. In a broader sense, its history might be claimed to be roughly as long as that of logic itself. The law of identity and the laws of excluded middle and (non-)contradiction constituted the three "laws of thought" of traditional logic. (Although the most prevalent formulation of the traditional law of identity is "A is A", the ambiguities of "is", and of varying discussions of the law's meaning, must caution against overconfident identification of the traditional law with ours.)

The "official" reading of the second component is, of course:

There is an x such that John loves x and it is not the case that x is identical with Cynthia.

Taking up the second sentence, "Everyone except George was happy", we may, for simplicity, assume that the tacit universe of discourse is limited to guests at a certain party. We would symbolize "Everyone was happy"

1. Identity

for that small UD as $\forall x Hx$. Paraphrasing "except" with the help of negation and identity, we might hit upon "Everyone who was not identical with George was happy." Experience with elementary symbolization would now yield: $\forall x(\sim x=g \supset Hx)$. This would be satisfactory for many purposes. However, it would not logically imply that George was __not__ happy, it merely excludes his case from the statement. To get a symbolization which __would__ imply that George was not happy (which many would feel __was__ implied by the original English) we could replace the if-then symbol by the stronger if-and-only-if (or fif) symbol and get:

$\forall x(\sim x=g \equiv Hx)$

To see how this implies that George is not happy, consider the deduction:

```
1|1   ∀x(~ x=g ≡ Hx)      /Hg
1|2   ~g=g ≡ Hg            1 UI
1|3   Hg ⊃ ~g=g            2 T (Eqi, Drop)
 |4   g=g                  I
1|5   ~Hg                  3,4 T (MT(N))
```

The English most closely corresponding to the first symbolization, $\forall x(\sim x=g \supset Hx)$, would seem to be something like: "Everyone, with the possible exception of George, was happy", although no (modal) concept of possibility is actually involved. But note that George's unhappiness could be expressed by simply adding it explicitly to this weaker version, e.g., as

$\forall x(\sim x=g \supset Hx) \cdot \sim Hg$

We shall return to the pros and cons of such variant symbolizations presently. The basic points have been made. Symbolizations of the remaining examples may now simply be given as additional illustration. In doing so, however, we will abbreviate $\sim x=y$ as $x \neq y$, informally.

1. Identity

Zero is smaller than every non-negative integer but itself.

$\forall x((Nx . x \neq 0) \supset 0 < x)$ (The traditional "<" being also used.)

Whoever helps another is benevolent.

$\forall x \forall y((Hxy . x \neq y) \supset Bx)$

With these examples, the reader should have no difficulty with the following exercise in symbolization.

Exercises XII 1

Symbolize in QI notation (Subject-matter symbols are often suggested. UD: A tacitly understood group of people, possibly different for different problems.)

*1. Brooks distrusts everyone but himself.
    (b: Brooks, Dxy: x distrusts y)

*2. Brooks admires only himself. (Axy: x admires y)

*3. Trapp and someone else had the combination.
    (t: Trapp, Cx: x had the combination)

*4. No one other than Fitch could have escaped.
    (f: Fitch, Ex: x could have escaped)

*5. Tully and Cicero were one and the same individual.

*6. One's brother is never identical with oneself.

 7. If George is not seeing Mavis, he is seeing someone else.

 8. If George is not seeing Mavis, someone else is.

 9. Of any two people, one is more fortunate than the other.
    (Fxy: x is more fortunate than y)

10. At least two distinct individuals had the combination.

11. Phil outruns anyone else on the team but Don.
    (p: Phil, Oxy: x outruns y, Tx: x is on the team, d: Don)

12. Different individuals sometimes have every ancestor in common.
    (Axy: x is an ancestor of y)

13. None but the fox, Reynard, is as sly as Reynard. (F,r,S)

14. Between any two distinct points, there is a point which is
    distinct from either. (UD: Points, Bxyz: x is between y and
    z (though possibly identical with y,z, or both))

Exercises XII 1

2. <u>QI Deduction</u>.

Employing I and IR in QI deductions is quickly mastered. We have already seen one example for I. The rationale of IR is so universally understood that we can convey it by the fragmentary but familiar phrase: "Putting equals for equals." Simple examples of correct IR steps are the following:

```
i  Fa              i  x=a              i  x=y
j  b=a             j  Rax              j  x=z
k  Fb    i,j IR    k  Raa   i,j IR     k  y=z   i,j IR
```

In the third example, both lines i and j contain identity clauses. To see that it nevertheless conforms to the IR format, we may take i as the <u>required</u> identity clause, and j as the clause containing a free occurrence of x. The free occurrence of x is then replaced by y to obtain line k.

A slightly more complex example:

```
i  ∀x(Hyxy ⊃ ∃yRxy)
j  z=y
k  ∀x(Hzxy ⊃ ∃yRxy)    i,j IR
```

This example shows z replacing y at y's first free occurrence, but not at its second. This partial replacement is permitted by IR, in contrast to rules which are expressed with the help of the C(r/u) notation. (The substitution notation, it will be recalled, requires substitution of r for u at <u>every</u> free occurrence of u.) Despite the greater flexibility of IR, however, capture of a variable is still prohibited - by the proviso of the IR rule. An example of a violation of the proviso would be:

```
i  ∃yGyx
j  x=y
k  ∃yGyy    i,j IR (improper)
```

Exercises XII 1

Here, the last line is obtained by replacing a free occurrence of x in line i by y. But the free occurrence of x is within the scope of a quantifier on y, which captures the new replacement. Interpreting Gyx as: y is a greater number than x, the last line is obviously false. But the preceding lines could be arrived at from obviously true premisses, e.g., as lines 4 and 5 below:

```
1|1   ∀x∃yGyx        P
2|2   ∀x∃y(x=y)      P
2|3   ∃y(x=y)        2 UI
1|4   ∃yGyx          1 UI
2|5   x=y            3 EI yx
```

With these few examples of proper and improper IR steps, the reader should be able to do the deductions and proofs of the following exercise section with little or no aid from the answer section.

Exercises XII 2

In the first three of the following problems the inferences are first formulated in English, as illustrative of inferences involving identity. But symbolizations are given, since the focus of the exercises is on the construction of deductions.

*1. Tully was not Cicero's brother because Tully was the same individual as Cicero, and no one is his own brother.

    1 t=c
    2 ∀x∼Bxx   / ∼Btc

*2. George does not like Mavis, but someone does
    Someone other than George likes Mavis

    1 ∼Lgm.∃xLxm   / ∃x(Lxm.x≠g)

*3. Someone sent flowers
    Whoever sent flowers had not heard
    Only Clare had not heard
    Clare sent flowers

    1 ∃xSx
    2 ∀x(Sx ⊃ ∼Hx)
    3 ∀x(∼Hx ⊃ x=c)   / Sc

4. Someone who knew the combination took the formula
   If anyone knew the combination it was Trapp or Simms
   Trapp or Simms took the formula

   ∃x(Cx.Fx)
   ∀x(Cx ⊃ (x=t v x=s))
   Ft v Fs

5. Every student except (possibly) John was prepared
   Of any two students one or the other was prepared

   ∀x((Sx.x≠j) ⊃ Px)
   ∀x∀y((Sx.Sy.x≠y) ⊃ (Px v Py))

Prove the following as logically true forms in QI logic:

*6. (x=y) ⊃ (y=x)   11. Fx ⊃ ∀y(x=y ⊃ Fy)

*7. (x=y.y=z) ⊃ x=z   12. x=y ⊃ (Fx ⊃ Fy)

*8. ∃x(Fx.x=y) ⊃ Fy   13. x=y ⊃ (Fx ≡ Fy)

*9. Fy ⊃ ∃x(Fx.x=y)   14. (x=y.z=w) ⊃ (Hxz ⊃ Hyw)

*10. ∀x(x=y ⊃ Fy) ⊃ Fy   15. (Hxy.∼Hxz) ⊃ y≠z

3. <u>Number</u>

The importance of adding identity and its rules to purely quantificational logic may be appreciated when we notice that a Q-language (using quantificational logic alone) can not be more specific about number than <u>some</u> and <u>all</u>. To be sure, a Q-language can speak <u>about</u> numbers. That is, it can take numbers as its UD with '1', '2', ... as proper names and with 'Odd', 'Even', 'Divisible by', 'Greater than', etc., as predicates. But a mere Q-language can not use such 'proper-name' numbers to express answers about <u>how many</u> (even about numbers). The step from <u>at-least-one</u> to <u>at-least-two</u> seems small, but it can not be taken explicitly in a Q-language. Essential to the concept of number, or even of plurality, is <u>distinctness</u>. Things must be 'told apart' if they are to be counted.

Of course, things, a and b, can be told apart if something is true of a which is not true of b, e.g., Aa.∼Ab. But we need to be able to conclude <u>explicitly</u> that a and b are distinct. We can not count simply by accumulating statements like Aa.∼Ab. In a QI language distinctness can be made explicit. It is simply non-identity. And with identity logic we can conclude from Aa, ∼Ab that a≠b. The deduction is:

```
  1   | 1  Aa
  2   | 2  ∼Ab       /a≠b
  3   | 3  a=b        S
 2,3  | 4  ∼Aa        2,3 IR
 1,2  | 5  a≠b        3,1,4 SA
```

Distinctness can be defined, instead of writing x≠y as an informal alternative to ∼ x=y. That is, we can give the following definition of Jxy (x is distinct from y) in terms of Ixy:
    Jxy ≡ ∼Ixy Df L
But for the present, to avoid lengthening deductions with too many DfR steps, we will take the informal attitude. (The 'L' in 'Df L', above, is intended to suggest a definition belonging to <u>Logic</u>, as opposed to any specific Q-language. Such definitions could be treated in several different ways — as belonging to a specific definitional extension of QI logic or of a specific QI language, etc.)

3. Number

Adding identity and its logic, we can, in the resulting QI-languages, symbolize, and reason with, sentences about at-least-two, at-most-three, exactly two, etc. Examples of such sentences: 'Anyone who is married to at least two people is a bigamist', 'Everyone has two parents', 'Everyone has exactly one mother', 'Some people have more than five children.' We can, in fact, <u>use numerical quantifiers</u>, as defined below. A numerical quantifier will be written by inserting a numeral between an existential quantifier symbol and the variable being quantified. Underlining the numeral will mean 'at least'; an overstroke will mean 'at most'; and a numeral with neither underline nor overstroke will mean 'exactly'. For example: ∃3xPx(∃3̄xPx,∃3xPx) would, on a certain reading for P, be read, respectively, There are at least (at most, exactly) three little pigs.

With a numerical quantifier, the 'bigamist' sentence, mentioned above, can be symbolized (for a UD of persons) as ∀x(∃2yMxy ⊃ Bx). The 'official' reading: For every x, if there are at least two y such that x is married to y, then x is a bigamist.

Definitions for the numerical quantifiers differ from those of Chapter II, but they are easy to understand and use. Because of the difference, they will be marked with 's'. Their use will be made clear, and their 's' status explained, after giving them.

'At-least' quantifiers (DfsL)

∃1xFx ≡ ∃xFx
∃2xFx ≡ ∃x∃y(Fx.Fy.x≠y)
∃3xFx ≡ ∃x∃y∃z(Fx.Fy.Fz.x≠y.x≠z.y≠z)

'At-most' quantifiers (DfsL)

∃1̄xFx ≡ ∀x∀y((Fx.Fy) ⊃ x=y)   ≡ ~∃2xFx
∃2̄xFx ≡ ∀x∀y∀z((Fx.Fy.Fz) ⊃ (x=y v x=z v y=z))   ≡ ~∃3xFx
etc.   etc.

3. Number

'Exactly'Quantifiers (DfsL)

		or
∃0xFx	~∃1xFx	~∃xFx
∃1xFx	∃1xFx.~∃2xFx	∃1xFx.∃1̄xFx
∃2xFx	∃2xFx.~∃3xFx	∃2xFx.∃2̄xFx
etc.		etc.

The reader will notice that each of the numerical quantifiers above requires a separate definition. Successive definitions follow obvious patterns, however, so that the defining process can go as far as desired. The fact that they can be given at all (and will yield simple arithmetical truths by identity logic) supports a well-known claim (called <u>logicism</u>) that mathematics is based on logic alone. (The defining expressions, when purged of defined signs, contain only the signs of QI logic (aside from predicate F, which plays only a general role.)) More powerful methods are needed in further developments of mathematics (even to define 'number', as opposed to individual numerical quantifiers), and the extent to which these more powerful methods can be regarded as 'logic alone' is still controversial. In any case, it is important to become familiar with the numerical reasoning possible in QI.

To use the above definitions, they must be understood as <u>schematic</u> definitions (Df<u>s</u>) in which Fx can stand for any of infinite number of clauses,

(1) letting 'Fx' stand for any clause in which there is a free occurrence of some variable, here represented as x, and perhaps of other free variables as well, and

(2) letting the 'y' which is bound in the definiens stand for some variable which is <u>not</u> free in Fx.

Let us apply this sort of definition to unabbreviate the bigamist sentence, which we had symbolized: ∀x(∃2yMxy ⊃ Bx). Here y is the bound variable corresponding to x in ∃2xFx, so that we must seek a 'definiens' for ∃2yFy. Here, Fy must stand for the clause Mxy, so that x is an 'other free variable' in Fy, in the sense of (1), above. Therefore, the second bound variable of the 'definiens' must be chosen to be different from both x and y. Choosing it to be z, we can write:

$\exists 2yFy \equiv \exists y \exists z(Fy.Fz.y \neq z)$ and since Fy is to stand for Mxy, we obtain the following definitional equivalence for the definitional replacement:

$\exists 2yMxy \equiv \exists y \exists z(Mxy.Mxz.y \neq z)$. We can now unabbreviate $\forall x(\exists 2yMxy \supset Bx)$ by replacement as:

$\forall x(\exists y \exists z(Mxy.Mxz.y \neq z) \supset Bx)$.

This is logically equivalent to $\forall x \forall y \forall z((Mxy.Mxz.y \neq z) \supset Bx)$ by a familiar 'Rule of Passage'. Both symbolizations can be read informally as 'Any x who is married to a y and a z, y distinct from z, is a bigamist'.

The existence of various logical equivalents is a familiar phenomenon. But in connection with unabbreviating numerical quantifiers, certain ones are of special interest. For example, the exactly-one quantifier has the following among its logical equivalents:

$\exists 1xFx$ $(\exists 1xFx . \sim \exists 2xFx)$
a. $\exists xFx . \forall x \forall y((Fx.Fy) \supset x=y)$
b. $\exists x(Fx . \forall y(Fy \supset y=x))$
c. $\exists x \forall y(Fy \equiv y=x)$

Each of these three, progressively more compact, formulations proves useful in certain circumstances, and it is worthwhile to become familiar with each one. Proving that they are equivalent, moreover, is an instructive exercise in QI logic (assigned in the coming exercise section.) Each may be used, informally, to unabbreviate the quantifier.

For example, everyone has exactly one mother, symbolized with numerical quantifier as $\forall x \exists 1yMyx$, may be symbolized in undefined QI terms in the three, corresponding ways:

Exercises XII 3

a. $\forall x(\exists y Myx.\forall y \forall z((Myx.Mzx) \supset y=z))$
b. $\forall x(\exists y(Myx.\forall z(Mzx \supset z=y)))$
c. $\forall x \exists y \forall z(Mzx \equiv z=y)$

Moreover, corresponding equivalents exist for each 'exactly' quantifier. Thus:

$\exists 2xFx$, i.e., $\exists 2xFx . \sim \exists 3xFx$

a. $\exists x \exists y (Fx.Fy.x \neq y).\forall x \forall y \forall z((Fx.Fy.Fz) \supset (x=y \lor x=z \lor y=z))$
b. $\exists x \exists y (Fx.Fy.x \neq y.\forall z(Fz \supset (z=x \lor z=y)))$
c. $\exists x \exists y (x \neq y.\forall z(Fz \equiv (z=x \lor z=y)))$

Opportunities for following out these suggested lines of thought will be found not only in the following exercise section, but also in later applications.

(It should be noted that the exactly-one quantifier is of special importance. Some authors symbolize it as E!x, and use no other numerical quantifier.)

Exercises XII 3

*1. Symbolize 'Everyone has exactly two parents' in three ways: using the numerical quantifier, and the two more compact forms b, and c. (UD: People. Pxy: x is a parent of y)

2. Write QI deductions for

a. $\exists x \forall y (Fy \equiv y=x)$ / $\exists x(Fx.\forall y(Fy \supset y=x))$
b. $\exists x(Fx.\forall y(Fy \supset y=x))$ / $\exists x \forall y(Fy \equiv y=x)$
c. $\exists x Fx . \forall x \forall y ((Fx.Fy) \supset x=y)$ / $\exists x(Fx.\forall y(Fy \supset y=x))$

3. Write the three 'progressively more compact forms' a, b, c, for $\exists 3xFx$ and $\exists 4xFx$.

4. Formulating the Kinship Theory, begun in E II 1, as a QI theory, we may add two new axioms to the effect that everyone has exactly one mother and one father:

V $\forall x \exists y \forall z((Fe(z).Par(z,x)) \equiv z=y)$
VI $\forall x \exists y \forall z((Ma(z).Par(z,x)) \equiv z=y)$

From the new, enlarged set of axioms, prove the theorem that everyone has exactly two parents. (Use any of the symbolizations you gave in problem 1.)

XIII

QI Theories

With the addition of identity and its logic to quantification theory, the range of theories that can be formulated becomes broader. Indeed, so much can be done without proceeding to a stronger logic that many logicians refer to QI language as 'standard notation'.

1. <u>QI Axioms on Relations</u>

Axioms on relations in QI theories, like those in Q-theories, exhibit recurring forms (beside those in Q-theories) for which it is also convenient to have names. The first group we shall consider are single-axiom forms. Then we shall note ways in which combinations of axiom forms characterize certain basic kinds of <u>ordering</u>. Some of the concepts will be exemplified in addition to the Kinship Theory, begun earlier. Others will be important later.

In the following, headings will give the term to be applied to a relation, R, obeying the symbolized sentence which follows it.

<u>One-Many (1:M)</u>

$\forall x \forall y \forall z ((Rxz . Ryz) \supset x=y)$

In words, R is a one-many relation fif x and y can bear the relation R to any z only if x and y are identical. In other words, no two distinct things x, y can bear R to the same z. (Equivalently, $\forall x \forall y (x \neq y \supset \sim \exists z (Rxz . Ryz))$) Example: Mother. (No one has more than one mother.) In an arrow-diagram of a one-many relation, no dot has more than one arrow pointing at it. But a dot may have several arrows pointing away, e.g., from mother to children. In the reverse case, where a dot may have several approaching arrows but not more than one departing, a relation is

1. QI Axioms on Relations

Many-One (M:1)

$\forall x \forall y \forall z ((Rzx.Rzy) \supset x=y)$

One-One (1:1)

$\forall x \forall y \forall z (((Rxz.Ryz) \vee (Rzx.Rzy)) \supset x=y)$

Examples: Twin, Husband (in monogamous societies), immediate predecessor (among natural numbers). A one-one relation is both one-many and many-one. An arrow-diagram has, at most, one arrow approaching, and one leaving, each dot.

Sample Arrow Diagrams (1:1)

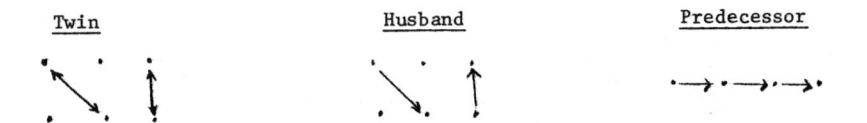

Twin   Husband   Predecessor

The foregoing forms, which prescribe essentially numerical properties for the relations which obey them, can be extended in many ways. One-two relations (1:2) can be defined. An arrow diagram might look like this

Two-many relations (such as parent), may also be characterized; using methods similar to those for defining the numerical quantifiers. But we need not pursue those directions here.

Beside the foregoing 'numerical' use of identity, identity is also important in modifying some of the properties we have already encountered. For example, we may wish to express the fact that a certain relation, R, is ordinarily asymmetric, i.e., $Rxy \supset \sim Ryx$, <u>except</u> if $x=y$. We could then write $\forall x \forall y (x \neq y \supset (Rxy \supset \sim Ryx))$. Such a relation is called

Exercises XIII 1

<u>Antisymmetric</u>

$\forall x \forall y ((Rxy . Ryx) \supset x=y)$

The formulation above is equivalent to the preceding version (use contraposition). An asymmetric relation is also antisymmetric. But many important relations are antisymmetric but not asymmetric. Example: $\leq$ (less-than-or-equal-to).

Making a distinctness condition such as $x \neq y$ is sometimes indicated by use of the prefix 'alio-' (Latin for <u>other</u>). For example:

<u>Aliotransitive</u>

$\forall x \forall y \forall z ((Rxy . Ryz . x \neq z) \supset Rxz)$

Relations such as <u>brother</u>, <u>sister</u>, are aliotransitive. No one is his own brother, or own sister, but with that exception, a brother of a brother is always a brother. Similarly for sister, etc.

Exercises XIII 1

*1. Define the following concepts of Kinship Theory so that they will be aliotransitive and asymmetric, if appropriate:

   a. Sibling (Sib); b. Brother (Bro); c. Sister (Sis); d. Cousin (Co)

2. Order

There are various sorts of order. We say that things have been put in order when they are arranged so as to have certain kinds of relation to one another. The kinds of relation themselves may be called kinds of order, or orderings.

A familiar sort of order is exhibited by the natural number: 1, 2, 3, ... or the alphabet: a, b, c, ... In the case of the natural numbers, we may take the ordering relation to be <. 1<2, 2<3, 1<3, etc. In our notation (L:less), this would be: L12, L23, L13, etc. For the alphabet, we commonly say 'a comes before b', 'b comes before c', 'a comes before c', etc. Using 'precedes' instead of 'comes before', we could say (using each letter as a name of itself) Pab, Pbc, Pac, etc.

In the terminology for relations, we recognize both L and P as asymmetric and transitive. But they share another important property: they are, so to speak, in 'single-file'. No two numbers (or letters) are 'neck-and-neck'; of any two (distinct) numbers one precedes the other. Restricting the universe of discourse just to natural numbers, we can express this for less-than as follows:

Connexity

$$\forall x \forall y (x \neq y \supset (Lxy \vee Lyx))$$

As earlier, the caption, 'connexity', names the property to be ascribed to any relation obeying a law of the form which follows. Accordingly, alphabetic precedence, P, would be said to be connected (or connex) in a UD consisting of just the letters of the alphabet fif $\forall x \forall y (x \neq y \supset (Pxy \vee Pyx))$.

A relation which is asymmetric, transitive, and connected is said to be a strict linear order. That is, we define (in English - supplemented by the

2. Order

abbreviation 'R'):

R is a __strict linear order__ fif R is asymmetric, transitive, and connected   Df

   (The 'Df', written at the right, is in analogy with the Df citation written as part of the deductive development of a specific theory. Though imprecise, in a natural language context, definition in natural language is, after all, the prototype which the formalized step attempts to make more precise.)

   The adjective 'strict' is used to distinguish it from another sort of relation, which numbers and letters also bear to one another and which imposes the same linear arrangement. In the case of numbers, we have $\leq$. We normally think of this as a composite concept (less-than-or-equal-to) though there is no logical reason why less-than should not be the composite (with the condition 'and distinct-from conjoined to $\leq$). In any case, $\leq$ is connected and transitive. This, coupled with antisymmetry ($\leq$ is reflexive), is sufficient to yield the linear arrangement. Mathematicians have, in fact, found it simpler to work with, in various applications, and have come to call it:

Simple (linear) Order

   R is a __simple (linear) order__ fif R is antisymmetric, reflexive, connected, and transitive.   Df

   There is yet another sort of relation which also yields a linear arrangement, and which is at least equally familiar. It is the relation of __immediately preceding__ (being immediately followed, or succeeded, by, or having as next successor). It is the relation we have in mind in counting. Though actually tacit, we might think of it as 1 __then__ 2, __then__ 3, etc. In order to have a single word for it, let us call it the __then__-relation and express it (ungrammatically) as Then(x,y) to be read 'x then y'. As abbreviation, we may follow the Greeks

2. Order

in using their single letter, θ, for 'Th', and write θxy. As before, we can write θ12, θ23, ... But not θ13. θ is intransitive. Each number is immediately followed by only one number. The arrow diagram of θ is 1 ⟶ 2 ⟶ 3 ⟶ 4 ⟶ ... . By contrast, the arrow diagram of less-than begins 1 ⇒ 2 ⇒ 3 ⇒ 4 —.., with all possible leapfrog arrows; while the arrow diagram of ≤ has self-arrows, into the bargain.

θ gets its Indian-file effect from the fact that it is one-one. Furthermore, within the UD of numbers, its arrow diagram has a kind of indirect connectedness, even though it is obviously false that ∀x∀y(x≠y ⊃ (θxy v θyx)). The kind of connectedness which θ has can be simply defined, but only in a stronger logic than QI, as we shall later see. In the meantime, we may observe that it has a certain close relation with <, or less-than, expressed as:

∀x∀y(Lxy ≡ (θxy v ∃z(Lxz.θzy)))

From this, it follows that

   a. ∀x∀y(θxy ⊃ Lxy)

   b. ∀x∀y∀z((θxy.θzy) ⊃ Lxz)

   c. ∀x∀y∀z∀w((θxy.θyz.θzw) ⊃ Lxw)

      etc.

In other words, any number we start from, counting (by θ) is less-than any number we arrive at. And less-than is connected. Pending more exact treatment, we shall call a one-one relation, such as θ, a succession. A succession, then, must be carefully distinguished from both strict and simple linear orderings, even though they are closely related. The two orderings are transitive, while a succession is intransitive. Mathematical usage now restricts 'order' to transitive relations of various kinds, so that a succession is not an ordering, in the technical sense, even though it is closely related to orderings.

2. Order

Another concept which it is well to distinguish from orderings at the outset, is that of a <u>sequence</u>. Sequences must also be distinguished from successions. The following list of letters, can be regarded as a sequence but not as a succession: c, d, h, d, e. Consider a relation whose arrow-diagram for these letters we might be inclined to draw: c →d →h →d →e. We would notice that we had not followed the usual practice in writing arrow diagrams, in that we had written 'd' twice. In the usual practice, a dot or name representing a member of the universe of discourse appears only once. Therefore, we might amend it as: c → d ⇄ h. But since arrows go from d to both h and e, the diagram is not that of a succession, which must be one-one. For similar reasons, any attempt at an ordering would result in a breach in connexity. What we can do, is say that the list is related, in a certain way, to a succession. That is, since there is a first, second, etc., we can take the <u>succession</u> 1, 2, 3, 4, 5 and correlate members of the list to members of the succession (as if they were regarded as 'positions'). The correlation might be indicated as follows:

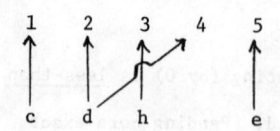

```
1   2   3   4   5
↑   ↑   ↗↑   ↑
c   d   h   e
```

This diagram itself might be regarded an arrow diagram of a relation Pxy, which could be read: x is at position y. I.e., c is at position 1, d is at position 2, d is <u>also at position 4</u>, h is at position 3, etc. For future reference, we may note that P is one-many.

We shall return to successions and sequences presently. Our concern for the moment is with transitive relations.

2. Order

The type of order which is exemplified by heavier-than is similar to that of strict linear order in being transitive and asymmetric. But it is not connected, in the sense defined. One of any pair of distinct individuals will not always outweigh the other. Distinct individuals may be equal in weight. Ordering things by weight will not, in general, produce a linear arrangement of things, but of groups of things (having equal weight). The things might be said to be ranked by weight. The groups, or ranks, would be linearly ordered, but not the things. Heavier-than is an instance of what we shall accordingly call a strict ranking relation.

Before giving a more exact characterization of ranking relations, let us reexamine the Heaviness Theory. It will be recalled that in problem 2, in Exercises XI 1, it was suggested that we might reformulate the H-theory of Chapter X in terms of H alone by changing the status of the axiom, HV, to that of being a definition of E in terms of H. Such a change is not a mere formality, to be sure. If E had a distinct meaning of its own in the original theory then Axiom V had definite factual content, and to define E in terms of H not only changes the meaning of E, but lessens the factual content of the theory as a whole, making it non-committal about the original E. In fact, to avoid confusion, it might be well to choose a different letter for the defined concept, e.g., Bxy, to be read x (exactly) balances y. Now, for the original axioms to be true, the original E would have to have the same extension as the new, defined B. That is, it would have to be true of any x, y of which $\sim$Hxy. $\sim$Hyx was true. This, together with the transitivity of the original E (Axiom II) would require (as seen in problem 2) that $\forall x \forall y \forall z ((\sim Hxy . \sim Hyx . \sim Hyz . \sim Hzy) \supset (\sim Hxz . \sim Hzx))$. Furthermore, eliminating defined E in Axiom IV (in problem 2) yielded an expression which is provably equivalent to the asymmetry of H (originally theorem H2). Thus, we see that a characterization of H requires just three axioms:

(1) $\forall x \forall y \forall z ((Hxy . Hyz) \supset Hxz)$ (transitivity)

(2) $\forall x \forall y (Hxy \supset \sim Hyx)$ (asymmetry)

(3) $\forall x \forall y \forall z ((\sim Hxy . \sim Hyx . \sim Hyz . \sim Hzy) \supset (\sim Hxz . \sim Hzx))$

The last sentence may be said to express the transitivity of H-balance (defined E), or the <u>balance-transitivity</u> of H. The clutter of negation signs can be avoided by contraposing and applying Nand:

$\forall x \forall y \forall z ((Hxz \vee Hzx) \supset (Hxy \vee Hyx \vee Hyz \vee Hzy))$

Neither of the latter formulations are especially convenient, however, and other axioms will serve. For example, the following, more useful, formulation is not logically equivalent by itself; but with the help of the other axioms, the transitivity of H-balance can be proved:

$\forall x \forall y ((\sim Hxy . \sim Hyx) \supset \forall z ((Hxz \supset Hyz) . (Hzx \supset Hzy)))$

Informally: If x and y are in balance, then any z which is outweighed by one is outweighed by the other; and if z is heavier than one, it is heavier than the other. More informally yet, we might say that if x and y are in balance all heaviness relations are <u>transfered</u> from one to the other. Accordingly, any relation having this property may be called <u>transferent-on-balance</u>.

In these terms, we can now define:

<u>Strict Rank Order</u> (or Strict Ranking).

R is a <u>strict ranking</u> fif R is transitive, asymmetrical, and transferent-on-balance (or balance-transitive).

2. Order

H-theory (with E defined) can now be simply summarized by saying that H is a strict ranking. Any theorem of H theory holds also for all other strict rankings. Conversely, we can regard ourselves as developing the theory of all strict rankings, by withholding any interpretation of H, and proceeding by purely syntactic (synonymously: formal, or proof-theoretic) deductive development from the three axioms for transitivity, asymmetry, and transference-on-balance (or an equivalent axiom set). It is in this abstract sense, in fact, that most theories are now developed, not only in logic and mathematics, but in such areas as game theory, information theory, economics, etc. The theories involved may be far more complex than that of strict rankings, of course. Geometry, and its various varieties, have so often been developed abstractly, that its original, spatio-temporal interpretation is sometimes lost sight of, with the result that geometry may be spoken of as if necessarily abstract!

A further effect of the abstract approach is that many logicians would regard the transition from the original H-theory to that in which Axiom V was taken as a definition of E as purely one of expedience. As earlier remarked, definitions are deductively like added axioms (of the characteristic definition-like form). As it happens, converting Axiom HV to a definition was not, in fact, inappropriate because being equal-in-weight does not ordinarily mean more than a weight-balance not tipping in either direction. But for other ranking relations, equality might mean something more.

Just as we earlier defined two linear orders: strict and simple, so we can define two rank orders. Having defined strict ranking, we now define:

2. Order

Simple Rank Order

R is a <u>simple ranking</u> fif R is transitive and strongly connected. Strong connexity is simply connexity without the distinctness condition: $\forall x \forall y (Rxy \vee Ryx)$.

    The simplicity of the two conditions for simple ranking is one illustration of why modern logicians often prefer to take simple rather than strict orderings as basic, even though the strict relations have greater appeal to common sense. (This is reflected in the fact that natural languages form strict-order comparatives like 'heavier than' more readily than the corresponding simple-order expressions such as "at least as heavy as".) Though less 'natural', the deductive utility of simple orders may be seen from the fact that our previous version of Heaviness Theory can be equivalently replaced by:

S Theory (At Least as Heavy)

Primitive:

    S (Sxy: x is at least as heavy as y)

Axioms:

    SI. $\forall x \forall y (Sxy \vee Syx)$
    SII. $\forall x \forall y \forall z ((Sxy \cdot Syz) \supset Sxz)$

Definitions:

    D1 $Exy \equiv (Sxy \cdot Syz)$ Df
    D2 $Hxy \equiv (Sxy \cdot \sim Syx)$ Df

From S theory, all the previous results are also deducible. The symmetry and transitivity of E, the asymmetry of H, the various trichotomies, the transference-on-balance of H, etc. Conversely, we can deduce the two axioms of S-Theory from the three strict-ranking axioms if we define Sxy as $\sim$Hyx. Some of these will be suggested for deductive practice in the next exercise section.

2. Order

Before passing to the next class of orderings, let us notice a certain kinship between linear and rank orders. As earlier remarked, rank orders produce a linear order of **ranks** (i.e., groups of individuals such that no individual of a given group 'outranks' any other members of the group). The role played by the equality, or balance, of the rank order (i.e., $\sim$Rxy.$\sim$Ryx for a strict ranking or Rxy.Ryx for a simple ranking) in producing this linear order of ranks corresponds to the role played by identity in linear orderings of individuals. Comparison of roles will be easier if we symbolize the rank equality, strict or simple, by E and identity by I.

Comparing simple orders first, notice that a simple linear order beside transitivity, and strong connexity, is antisymmetric. Expressed with I, this is:

Antisymmetry: $\forall x \forall y ((Rxy.Ryx) \supset Ixy)$

This property, with E replacing I, is had also by simple rankings when E is replaced by its definition for simple rankings, i.e.:

'Rank antisymmetry': $\forall x \forall y ((Rxy.Ryx) \supset Exy)$

becomes $\forall x \forall y ((Rxy.Ryx) \supset (Rxy.Ryx))$—a logical truth!

In other words, we might say that a simple linear order is antisymmetric **with respect to I**, while a simple rank order is (trivially) anti-symmetric **with respect to E**.

E, like I, is transitive, reflexive, and symmetric. Such a relation is called an **equivalence** relation. Such a relation segregates individuals into mutually exclusive "equivalence classes". It is these classes that are put in linear order by the ranking relation.

Strict linear order bears a like relation to strict rank order. That is, besides transitivity and asymmetry, a strict linear order is connected.

3. Partial Order

Now while a rank order is transitive and asymmetric, it is not connected in the usual sense with respect to I, but it is "connected-with-respect-to-E" when E is replaced by its definition for strict-rankings. That is, the difference between linear and rank orders may be displayed as follows:

Strict Linear Order Connexity

$\forall x \forall y (\sim Ixy \supset (Rxy \vee Ryx))$

Strict Rank Order Connexity

$\forall x \forall y (\sim Exy \supset (Rxy \vee Ryx))$

The latter is seen to be a logical truth when E is replaced by its definition for strict ranking:

$\forall x \forall y (\sim (\sim Rxy . \sim Ryx) \supset (Rxy \vee Ryx))$, i.e.,

$\forall x \forall y ((Rxy \vee Ryx) \supset (Rxy \vee Ryx))$.

In this case, as for simple ranking, the essential thing in producing the linear orderings of ranks (equivalence classes) is the transitivity of E (since its reflexivity and symmetry follow from its definition together with the asymmetry of the strict ranking.) For strict rankings, this similarity of E and I (transitivity) requires that the relation obey an additional axiom such as the 'transitivity of balance' or 'transference on balance'. Relations that do exhibit this additional property for defined E may be thought of as exhibiting a kind of connexity which is not trivial like that above. Such relations will be called quasi-connected (following H. Hendry).

3. Partial Order

Some important relations, such as Part, fall short of the connectedness properties discussed in the previous section. More exactly, let Pxy, which

3. Partial Order

we read: x is part of y in Chapter II, be meant in the broad sense which could be read: x is part <u>or all</u> of y. And let Pxy be meant in the narrower sense which could be read: x is part, <u>but not all</u>, of y. The line through 'P' may be thought of as suggesting a 'minus' - (something short of the whole). This latter concept is often called 'proper part' by logicians. To be sure, etymology and usage give "part" primarily the latter meaning, so that the first meaning would seem to deserve being called 'improper part'. But for reasons not unlike those which have led logicians to use simple orderings in place of strict ones, the broader, 'simple' part has come to inherit the simpler term. In any case, we can say that P is like a simple order, in that it is transitive, antisymmetric, and reflexive, it is not connected strongly or otherwise. (Neither one of a given pair of things need be part of the other.) Similarly, P̶ is like a strict order in that it is transitive and asymmetric, but it is not only not connected, but it is not quasi-connected. That is, an E defined as $\sim$P̶xy.$\sim$P̶yx is not transitive. This may be graphically seen by picturing an object a as a proper part of object c, and an object b separate from both a and c:

We see that $(\sim\text{Pab}.\sim\text{Pba}).(\sim\text{Pbc}.\sim\text{Pcb})$
$\quad\quad\quad\quad\quad\quad\underbrace{\quad\quad\quad\quad}_{\text{Eab}}\;\underbrace{\quad\quad\quad\quad}_{\text{Ebc}}$

So transitivity of E would require $\sim$Pac.$\sim$Pca, but, on the contrary,
$$\underbrace{\quad\quad\quad\quad\quad\quad}_{\text{Eac}}$$
we see that P̶ac.

To accommodate Part, and other relations, logicians define partial orders without requiring connexity. Although "partial order" was originally applied to the strict (irreflexive) case (by Hausdorff in 1914, according to Church), it has become more commonly applied to the weaker, reflexive case. Accordingly, we will define:

3. Partial Order

Partial Order

A relation R is a __partial order__ fif it is transitive, antisymmetric, and reflexive.

The strict counterpart (merely transitive and asymmetric) is called __strict partial ordering__ by Suppes. But terminology varies.

It should be noted that these latter concepts do not exclude connectivity, but simply do not require it. Therefore, the term 'partial order' covers simple linear orderings and rankings, as well as relations (like part) which are neither.

The foregoing only broaches the subject of order. Many important distinctions remain to be drawn — such as that between discrete and dense orderings, the latter being exemplified, for the asymmetric case, by $<$ among the fractions: Between any two there is another, i.e., $\forall x \forall y (x < y \supset \exists z (x < z . z < y))$. But the reader will at least have formed an idea of some very commonly occurring notions arising in QI theories.

Exercises XIII 2

1. Can a one-one relation be*transitive? *intransitive? symmetric? asymmetric? reflexive? irreflexive? Give examples or counter-examples when possible to support your answers, either by words for relations, or by arrow diagrams. Otherwise proceed deductively.

2. Apply as many as you can of the relation-property terms below to each of the relations listed:

    Relation-property terms:

    One-one, one-many, strict linear order, simple linear order, strict ranking, simple ranking, partial order, equivalence.

    Relations:

    =, ≠, > (among natural numbers), brother-of, at-least-as-heavy-as, oldest-son-of, husband, ancestor, neighbor, not-lighter−than, unbeatable-by (in a certain UD of contestants), mother, parent, proper-part-of, overlaps.

3. A more compact set of axioms (due to Herbert Hendry) for a strict ranking (such as heavier-than) is given below. Show them equivalent to those given in this section by

    (a) deducing the present axiom A III from the originally given set;

    (b) deducing the third (transferent-on-balance) axiom from the present axioms.

    AI. $\forall x \forall y \forall z((Hxy \cdot Hyz) \supset Hxz)$

    AII. $\forall x \sim Hxx$

    AIII. $\forall x \forall y (Hxy \lor Hyx \lor \forall z(Hxz \equiv Hyz))$

XIV

FUNCTIONS

1. Functions and Functional Relations

Many theories, especially those involving numbers, would, if axiomatized in a QI language, require axiomatizing what we shall call functional relations (defined below). While QI logic is adequate in principle for such theories, it proves more convenient to extend both logic and language by introducing a new category of symbols called function-symbols, which combine with names and variables to form a broader class of 'terms', which include not only names and variables, but also what will be called function-terms. (An expression such as 3(4x + 2), familiar in elementary algebra, is, in effect, such a function-term.) Q-languages, extended to include identity and function symbols, will be called QIF languages, and the logic for them will be called QIF logic. The alterations to be made to a QI system are minor, but the added convenience is great.

Although QIF logic is used to avoid the need for axiomatizing function relations, to understand how it does so, we must understand functional relations. A two-place functional relation is a one-many relation with an additional existential feature. It will be recalled that to say that there was at most one x such that Fx, i.e., $\exists 1xFx$, we could use the QI sentence: $\forall x \forall y ((Fx.Fy) \supset x=y)$. Recalling also that a relation F was said to be a one-many relation fif $\forall x \forall y \forall z ((Fxz.Fyz) \supset x=y)$, we see that the assertion that F is one-many could be also symbolized: $\forall x \exists 1yFyx$. In words: For every x there is at most one y such that Fyx. The additional existential feature that makes a relation F a functional

1. Functions

relation is the circumstance that for every x there is <u>at least one</u> y such that Fyx, i.e., $\forall x \exists y Fyx$. Combining the two features, we can define

F is a <u>two-place functional relation</u> fif for every x there is exactly one y such that Fyx, i.e., $\forall x \exists 1y Fyx$.

The fact that for any given x there is one and only one y such that Fyx is taken advantage of by introducing a function symbol, f, and taking fx to stand for that particular y. In other words, we shall say that y is identical with fx fif Fyx. The QIF logic to be used will allow us to prove both the uniqueness of fx, for given x, (corresponding to the one-many-ness of F), and the existence of fx for every x, corresponding to the existential feature of F. Therefore, if we take the functional-symbol, f, as basic, F need not appear at all.

The same idea can be extended to relations of higher degree. Thus, a three-place relation, G, will be said to be a functional relation fif $\forall x \forall y \exists 1z G(z,x,y)$ and we can introduce a two-place function-symbol, g, and take g(x,y) to stand for the one and only z which bears G to x,y. For example, we might symbolize the statement that 7 is the sum of 4 and 3 by a three-place relation: S(7,4,3), or by using a two-place function symbol, s, and writing 7 = s(4,3). Of course, we would more customarily write 7 = 4+3. But just as we adopted a standard format for predication, with predicate first, so we will assume a standard format for function-terms, with function-symbol first. Using a standard format will permit us to formulate our rules in a general way. But in informal practice we will often write such expressions in customary ways, e.g., 4+3, just as we have been writing x=y, x≠y, x>y instead of Ixy, ∼Ixy, and Gxy.

Specification of the syntax and deductive rules for a QIF language differs little from that of a Q-language, as given in the Introduction.

2. QIF Logic

First, the change from a Q language to a QI language requires the inclusion of I (or =) among the two-place predicates (but as a logical sign common to QI languages, not as a subject-matter sign belonging to any particular theory.) Moreover, QI logic extends the concept of deducibility so that a QI deduction may have I and IR steps, as we have seen.

The change from a QI language to a QIF language, requires that one does the following:

(1) Supplement the vocabulary by adding (after the lists of subject-matter predicates of various degrees) lists of function-symbols (1-place, 2-place, etc., as needed). Usually, when speaking generally, we shall use small letters (f,g,...) for function symbols. But for specific theories we may use strings of letters, beginning with a small letter, e.g., such as sq (for square of), sm (for sum), or we may informally use +, x, etc.

(2) Add the following definition, e.g., after that of 'predication':

A function-term is an n-place function symbol followed by an n-place argument, the argument being enclosed in parentheses.

(3) Change the definition of 'term' by adding 'or a function-term' so that it reads:

A _term_ is a name, a variable, or a function-term.

'Function-term', here, is meant as the single expression defined separately above, in which "-term" may be regarded as part of the spelling, rather than as a reference to _term_, just as the 'red' in 'predicate' does not refer to a color. This definition, is therefore not circular. But it is recursive. Since 'term' appears in the definition of 'n-place argument', a function-term may have other function-terms as terms in _its_ argument. In other words, function-terms can be built up from function-terms in the same way that clauses can be compounded from clauses.

2. QI Logic

(4) Change the definition of <u>free in C</u> to read:

An occurrence of a term r in C (where r may now be not only a name or variable, but a function-term, hence a sequence of symbols) is <u>free in C</u> fif <u>no variable</u> in r (or r itself) is bound in C.

(5) Change the definition of clear instance to read as follows:

An instance of a clause C obtained by substituting a term r for every free occurrence of a variable u in C is a <u>clear</u> instance fif no such occurrence is within the scope of a quantifier on <u>any variable in r</u>, in the sense above (where that variable would be 'captured').

(6) Change proviso b. of the IR rule to read:

None of the free occurrences of r, where replacement is made, are within the scope of a quantifier on <u>any variable in s</u> (where that variable would be captured).

With these adjustments made, all other rules work as before. But the resulting QIF logic will be found to permit many useful new types of reasoning. Asterisked problems in the following exercise section illustrate their use.

3. Defining Function-Symbols

Defining a function-symbol in the course of developing a QIF theory can take place in two ways. If the new function-symbol is to abbreviate a recurring function-term, then the definition can be written as an identity clause, with provisos and procedure similar to those used in defining predicates. Such a definition will be called an <u>identity-form definition</u>. For example, if we wished to define a 2-place function symbol f to abbreviate a certain function-term built out of two 2-place function symbols i and c we might write:

$f(x,y)=c(i(x,y),i(y,x))$ Df

f(x,y) would be said to be the definiendum, and the right-hand term of the identity would be the definiens. As before, the language would be definitionally extended so that the above identity clause would be a clause of the extended language, and the definition itself would be henceforth regarded as being in the D-file of the extended language and theory, and 'DfR f' steps would now be meaningful and acceptable in deductions of the theory. (Note that the underlying logic of the DfR step would be simpler than previously. It would be simply that of an IR step, i.e., an identity replacement.)

To state the Df conditions, explicitly, in a general way, little more need be done than to generalize from the example. (The example might be read as a definition of the material-equivalence truth-function (reading f(x,y) as the 'fifalence' of x,y) as the conjunction (c) of two material implications (i), or in more familiar notation: The truth value of $A \equiv B$ is identical with that of $((A \supset B).(B \supset A))$, where A and B are regarded as variables.

XIV 277
3. Defining Function-Symbols

Making an Identity-Form Definition of a Function-Symbol

An identity-form definition of an n-place function-symbol, g, for a QIF theory, K, is made by writing an open, identity clause, marked 'Df' of the form

$g(x_1,...x_n) = g_D$ Df

where the definiendum, g, is not in K, the n definiendum-variables $x_1,...x_n$ are mutually distinct, the definiens, g_D, is a term of K containing no variables other than the definiendum variables (but need not contain all of them).

A different form and procedure is required if it is desired to define a function symbol otherwise than by a function term. Suppose that a theory is able to prove a theorem concerning a certain clause C which contains n+1 free variables to the effect that for any values of n of them, there exists exactly one value of the remaining variable which makes the clause true. Whatever the variables or their manner of occurrence in C, we can represent it as $C(y,x_1,...x_n)$ where y is the variable whose value exists and is fixed uniquely by the others. Our supposition, then, is that the theory can prove that

$\forall x_1 \forall x_2 ... \forall x_n \exists 1 y\, C(y, x_1,...x_n)$.

In other words, if a relation G were defined with its variables in the indicated order, e.g., as

$G(y,x_1,...x_n) \equiv C(y_1,x_1,...x_n)$ Df

G would be a functional relation. But this is precisely the circumstance in which deductions are facilitated in QIF logic by use of a function-symbol instead of a relation symbol. Therefore it is obviously desirable to define a function-symbol, g, instead of the relation symbol G, in terms

3. Defining Function-Symbols

of clause C. Obviously, neither a QI nor a QIF language would permit either an identity or a material equivalence to appear directly between a term and a clause. However, the defining clause, C, can be definitionally asserted to be materially equivalent to the clause $y=g(x_1...x_n)$. 'Defining' this entire clause will enable us to use IR to introduce or eliminate occurrences of the defined function-symbol.

Accordingly, we may specify the second method of defining function-symbols as follows:

<u>Making an Equivalence Form Definition of a Function-Symbol</u>

An equivalence form definition for an n-place function-symbol, g, for a QIF theory K is made by writing an open equivalence clause, marked 'Df', of the form:

$$y=g(x_2 x_3 ... x_n) \equiv C \qquad Df$$

where the definiendum, g, is not in K, the variables $y_1 x_2, ... x_n$ are mutually distinct, and where the definiens C is a clause of K containing no free variable other than $y_1 x_2, ... x_n$, and where $\forall x_1 \forall x_2 ... \forall x_n \exists 1y\, C$ is a theorem of K.

The theorem mentioned is called the <u>justifying theorem</u> of the definition, and it is customary, in axiomatic development, to record it, and its proof, before making the definition it justifies.

Obviously, if C were a clause for which the theorem did not hold, such a definition could imply more than one distinct value for g, which IR would erroneously identify.

4. The Problem of Partial Functions

It will probably have occurred to the reader that many of the functions commonly used in mathematics do not fully meet the requirements mentioned as necessary, either to formulate a QIF theory or to introduce them by an equivalence-form definition. Such functions are commonly said not to be 'defined' over the whole universe of discourse. For example, division is commonly said not to be defined for 0 (in various UDs of numbers). That is, if we had a 3-place relation Dzxy: z is x divided by y, it could not be proved that $\forall x \forall y \exists 1 z Dzxy$, but only the qualified theorem $\forall x \forall y (y \neq 0 \supset \exists 1 z Dzxy)$. Consequently, a typical procedure is to give a so-called conditional, or qualified definition, as follows:

$y \neq 0 \supset (z = d(x,y) \equiv D(z,x,y))$ Df

or, in more familiar form, in terms of multiplication (*):

$y \neq 0$ $(z = x/y$ $x = (z * y)$ Df

This sort of definition, though important in mathematical practice, does not lend itself to straightforward treatment in QIF theories, and so such 'functions' will not be included in the present discussion.

Exercises XIV 1

*1. Using the readings: E(x); x is even; s(x): the square of x; d(x); the double of x, (UD: Natural Numbers). Translate the following symbolized sentences into normal English:

a. $\forall x(E(x) \supset E(s(x)))$

b. $\forall x E(d(x))$

c. $\forall x E(s(d(x)))$

*2. Write the QIF deduction for:

$\forall x(Ex \supset E(sx))$ (omitting unnecessary parentheses)

$\forall x E(dx)$ /$\forall x E(s(dx))$

*3. Prove: $\forall x \exists y \ y=fx$

*4. Prove: $\forall x \forall y \forall z((y=fx . z=fx) \supset y=z)$

5. Prove: $\forall x \forall y \exists z \ z=g(x,y)$

6. Prove: $\forall x \forall y \forall z \forall w((z=g(x,y) . w=g(x,y)) \supset z=w)$

*7. Write the QIF deduction for:

$x=3$ / $s(x) = s(3)$ (Squaring both sides of an equation)

8. Write the QIF deduction for

$2x = 3+y$ / $2x + z^2 = 3+y+z^2$ (adding to both sides of an equation)

Exercises XIV 1

Translate *9 – 17 into normal English using the readings
UD: sentences):

Ixy: x logically implies y

Exy: x is logically equivalent to y

Lx: x is logically true

Cx: x is self-contradictory (logically false)

Tx: x is true

Fx: x is false

nx: the negation of x

ixy: the implication with antecedent x and consequent y

dxy: the disjunction with components x,y

cxy: the conjunction with components x,y

*9. ∀x∀yI(x,dxy)

*10. ∀x(Cx ⊃ ∀yIxy)

*11. ∀x∀y I(c(x,ixy),y)

*12. ∀x∀y((Tx.Ixy) ⊃ Ty)

*13. ∀x∀y∀zE(d(c(nx,y),x),dyx)

14. ∀x(Cx ⊃ ∀yCcxy)

15. ~∀x∀y((Tx.Ty) ⊃ Exy)

16. ∀x∀y(Tixy ≡ Ti(ny,nx))

17. ∀x∀y E(ixy,i(ny,nx))

XV

TOWARD HIGHER LOGIC

1. Quantifying Predicate Variables

An important gain in the power of quantificational logic is made by extending the use of "every" and "some" beyond that of elementary logic. In the elementary logic of quantifiers, "every" and "some" are used only in connection with "individuals" belonging to some given universe of discourse. But often the premises or conclusions of our inferences are formulated in ways that indicate quantification not only over individuals but also over their properties, characteristics, acts, states, and relationships. For example, we may encounter existential sentences such as "There are diseases which are contagious but which no Londoner has ever had", or universal statements such as "Every teachable ability needed for this job is provided by a high-school education."

Just as elementary (or <u>first-order</u>) quantification theory introduces variables for individuals, so second-order (and higher) logic introduces variables also for properties of individuals. Since properties of individuals are attributed to them by <u>predicates</u>, variables for properties may appear in higher logic where predicates with fixed meanings appear in first-order logic. For example, where elementary logic may have a sentence such as Measles (bobby), or the open clause Measles(x), higher logic admits clauses such as X(bobby) and X(x). But such variables need not appear only in predicate position. They may also appear in argument position. And so may the words for the properties themselves, e.g.,

XV 283
1. Predicate Variables

Contagious (X) and Contagious (Measles). This corresponds to the fact that it is often natural to predicate something of properties. They may be said to be contagious, teachable, hereditary, or to be abilities, shortcomings, diseases, etc. The extension of quantification to non-individual variables is straightforward and the familiar steps of quantificational logic still hold good (with appropriate modifications). We can, in fact, immediately inspect the following example of a simple deduction using quantification and predication extended in this way:

1 Bobby has measles and measles is a contagious disease
2 Every one who has a contagious disease is quarantinable
   Bobby is quarantinable

Using b for Bobby, M for having measles, C for being a contagious disease and Q for being quarantinable, the inference is shown below. It uses only UI (universal instantiation), extended to property variables and the logic of connectives:

Premiss Numbers	Line Numbers		Citations
1	1	M(b).C(M)	P
2	2	∀x∀Y((Y(x).C(Y)) ⊃ Q(x))	P
2	3	∀Y((Y(b).C(Y)) ⊃ Q(b))	2 UI (b/x)
2	4	(M(b).C(M)) ⊃ Q(b)	3 UI (M/Y)
1,2	5	Q(b)	1,4 MP

The inference is straightforward and the symbolism is clear. (Here, and often in the following, parentheses are kept around arguments, both predicate and individual-term.) However, the observant reader will have noticed a change from elementary logic in indicating the interpretations of the symbols. In elementary logic, it is customary to indicate the interpretation of a predicate letter with the help of variables, e..g, M(x): x has measles, V(x,y): x visits y, etc. In the above example, however, M was said simply to

1. Predicate Variables

be for <u>having measles</u>. This was done to facilitate the reading of C(M), where M appears unaccompanied by an argument of its own. If we had indicated the interpretation as M(x): x has measles, i.e., HasMeasles(x), it might have prompted C(M) to be read as "Has measles is contagious." English grammar would reject this as a nonsentence. But it would accept "Having measles is contagious." At the same time, reading M(b) as "Having measles (Bobby)" or "Bobby (is) having measles" is not too forced. However, the use of higher logic to symbolize corresponding English sentences often calls for greater deviations from surface English.

It is a deeply ingrained feature of English, and other natural languages, that when a property is predicated of an individual, the expression used for the property is often different from that used for the property when something is said about <u>it</u>, i.e., when the property is the subject of a predication. Compare the variety of phrasing differences when a property word is in the subject position with that used when the same property is referred to in the predicate position:

	Property word in <u>predicate position</u>	Property word in <u>subject position</u>
<u>Verb</u>	Bobby sleeps. Bobby breathes.	Sleeping is restful. Respiration is sometimes audible.
<u>Adj</u>	Bobby is brave. Bobby is hungry. Bobby is awkward.	Bravery is a virtue. Hunger may be felt as pangs. Awkwardness is usually outgrown.
<u>Noun</u>	Bobby is a student. Bobby is an expert.	Studenthood can be trying. Expertise can be acquired.

The striking shifts in expression illustrated above are connected with the grammatical distinction between subject and predicate and

1. Predicate Variables

with the philosophical debates that have revolved around it.

We shall have more to say about these matters, but for the present we shall merely make a practical suggestion about the informal reading of the symbolism and, then some remarks about the terminology of higher logic.

The practical suggestion is that in order to sidestep the complicated shifts between predicate-form and subject-form that occur in natural language, the reader may often adopt a simplified, "cave-man" reading of the symbolism, e.g.,

Predicate position		Subject-position	
$M(b)$	Bobby measles	$C(M)$	Measles contagious
$S(b)$	Bobby sleep	$R(S)$	Sleep restful
$B(b)$	Bobby brave	$V(B)$	Brave virtue.

The point of this sort of reading is that a property word, such as "brave", retains the same form in both positions. This can be done also, of course, by using the subject-form in both positions. The important thing is that in either position the word is to stand for the same property. (A nineteenth century grammarian (H. Sweet) put the matter clearly when he said "The change of white into whiteness is a purely formal device to enable us to place an attribute-word as the subject of a proposition. . . . Whiteness is correctly described as an "abstract" name, signifying an attribute without reference to the things that possess the attribute. The truth is, of course, that white is as much an abstract name as whiteness is, the two being absolutely identical in meaning."

Of course, this suggestion does not help in translating from English into symbols, except in clarifying the target.

1. Predicate Variables

Turning now to the terminology of higher logic, the grammatical subject-predicate distinction is represented by relative position and parentheses, but the term "predicate" itself is commonly retained for the property word even when it is not in predicate position. Thus "Virtue (Brave)" is said to be the application of a predicate to a predicate. And in "Virtue(X)" the predicate "virtue" is applied to a predicate variable. This is mildly confusing usage. But it is widely used, and for a reason: English does not have a very convenient alternative. It is possible, of course, to speak of property words and property variables (as x, y, . . are called individual variables). But elementary logic's predicates also stand for relations, which higher logic also wishes to quantify over; so higher logic would need to speak of property-or-relation variables. Rather than this, presentations of higher logic customarily fall back on the not strictly appropriate, but understandable, use of "predicate variable," and "predicate (constant)" for non-individual signs, even in subject position. We will follow suit.

With these preliminaries the reader can try his skill on the following, first exercises in higher logic. The first few are especially simple. Many are marked with asterisks. That means that answers are given in the Answer Section, for help in self-testing. Although the exercises require only deduction in symbols, each inference is stated first in English. The premisses and conclusion of each is then given in symbolic form, together with an interpretation of the symbols. Thus each problem can serve as an example of how the symbolism of higher quantification is used to represent given sentences in English. After

Exercises XV 1

the first few, the reader may wish to try his own hand at symbolization, covering the symbolization given, at first. (If your symbolization is different from that shown, it is not necessarily incorrect. It may be logically equivalent.)

Exercises XV 1

*1. Ann have every virtue   V: being a virtue
    Honesty is a virtue   H: being honest
    Ann is honest   a: Ann

   1 $\forall Z(V(Z) \supset Z(a))$
   2 $V(H)$ /H(a)

*2. Burt smokes   S: smoking
    Smoking is a bad habit   H: bad habit
    Burt has a bad habit   b: Burt

   1 $S(b)$
   2 $H(S)$ /$\exists X(H(X).X(b))$

*3. Bernice has every ability Jerry has   A: ability
    Jerry has every ability Carl has   b,j,c
    Bernice has every ability Carl has

   1 $\forall Z((A(Z).Z(j)) \supset Z(b))$
   2 $\forall Y((A(Y).Y(c)) \supset Y(j))$ /$\forall X((A(X).X(c)) \supset X(b))$

*4. Some acquired tastes are had by all men of refinement
    Some poets have no acquired tastes
    Some poets are not men of refinement

    A: acquired taste, M: man of refinement, P: poet

   1 $\exists Z(A(Z).\forall x(M(x) \supset Z(x)))$
   2 $\exists x(P(x).\forall Y(A(Y) \supset \sim Y(x)))$ /$\exists x(P(x).\sim M(x))$

Exercises XV 1

*5. Frederick and Sybil both gamble
Gambling is a vice
Anyone who has a vice in common with someone is suited to that person
Frederick and Sybil are suited to each other

(Symbolization similar to previous examples)

1 G(f).G(s)
2 V(G)
3 ∀x∀y(∃Z(V(Z).Z(x).Z(y)) ⊃ S(x,y))
   S(f,s).S(s,f)

*6. There is a certain quality such that Ann loves everyone who possesses it, but which is had by some who are not very ambitious
If you love a person, you respect that person
Some who are not very ambitious are respected (by someone)

Lxy: x loves y, Ax: x is very ambitious, Rxy: x respects y, a: Ann

1 ∃Y(∀x(Y(x) ⊃ L(a,x)).∃z(Y(z).~A(z)))
2 ∀x∀y(L(x,y) ⊃ R(x,y))
   ∃x∃y(~A(x).Ryx)

7. Every teachable ability required for the job is provided by a high school education
Twelfth grade reading is a teachable ability
Some high school graduates do not have twelfth grade reading ability
Twelfth grade reading ability is not required for the job

T: teachable ability; J: required for the job
H(x): x is a high-school graduate, R(x): x has twelfth grade reading ability

1 ∀Z((T(Z).J(Z)) ⊃ ∀x(H(x) ⊃ Z(x)))
2 T(R)
3 ∃x(H(x).~R(x))
   ~J(R)

2. Abstraction

One need not explore into the possibilities of higher quantification very far before realizing that something more is needed. Although we easily symbolize and construct the deduction for:

Ann has every virtue, honesty is a virtue
Ann is honest

we hit a snag for

Ann has every virtue, Not smoking is a virtue
Ann does not smoke

We were able to instantiate to honest as if it were a proper name, but we have no single word for not smoking. We could have, of course, just as we have "teetotaling" for not drinking; and we could coin one for not smoking. And for loving one's neighbors, etc. But logic should hardly require creative lexicography. What is needed is a general way to symbolize complex properties. It should be possible to tie together whatever is said about an individual into one unit. Such a unit could then play a role like the one played by names in elementary universal instantiation, etc. The described need is filled by introducing an abstraction operator. Given any clause about an individual, b, a complex property that it ascribes to b can be abstracted by replacing some occurrence of b by some variable u and prefixing the clause by λu which we may call an abstraction operator on u. (Or a lambda operator on u, since the abstraction symbol used, "λ", is the Greek letter lambda.) For example, given the closed clause $\sim$Smoke(ann), an expression for the property of not smoking, which is being ascribed to Ann, may be symbolized by choosing a variable, say x, and writing $\lambda x \sim$Smoke(x). This may be read

2. Abstraction

as "the property of x such that x does not smoke" or as "the property that (any) x has, when x does not smoke", or more briefly, of course, as the property of not smoking.

The abstracted expression for a property may, in higher logic, appear in predicate position as a <u>grammatical</u> predicate, or in argument position as a "predicate" only in the sense of standing for a property. For example, just as "Ann is honest and honesty is a virtue" may be symbolized as Honest(ann).Virtue(Honest), so "Ann does not smoke and not smoking is a virtue" may be symbolized in both of the following ways:

(1) $\sim$ Smoke(a). Virtue($\lambda x \sim$ Smoke(x))

(2) $[\lambda x \sim$Smoke(z)](a).Virtue($\lambda x \sim$ Smoke(x))

The square brackets in (2) are not necessary but are helpful to the eye in grouping the whole expression as a predicate for the argument (a). — We will continue to use brackets informally in this way — for the predicate position only. An expression $\lambda u C$ will be called a <u>1-place lambda predicate expression</u>, with u <u>bound</u> in C, the <u>scope</u> of λu, being C.

We are now in a position to obtain something like the quantificational facility we need. If we apply UI (appropriately modified) with respect to this new expression for not smoking we can make the deduction:

1	1	∀Z(Virtue(Z) ⊃ Z(a))	P
2	2	Virtue($\lambda x \sim$ Smoke(x))	P
1	3	Virtue($\lambda x \sim$ Smoke(x)) ⊃ [$\lambda x \sim$ Smoke(x)](a)	1 UI
1,2	4	[$\lambda x \sim$ Smoke(x)](a)	2,3 MP

The conclusion provides the intended information, but in a cumbersome form. To get the simpler, equivalent conclusion, $\sim$ Smoke (a), we require a new rule which permits us to drop the abstraction operator on x and

2. Abstraction

substitute a for every (free) occurrence of x. We may state a first simplified version of such a rule as follows:

Lambda Predicate^1 Reduction (Citation: LPR^1)

A line may be justified by LPR^1 as obtained from an earlier line when the earlier line contains an occurrence of [λuC](r) as part, or all, of its clause (where u is a variable, C a clause, and r a term) and the line is obtained by replacing that occurrence of [λuC](r) by C(r/u) (i.e., the result of substituting r for u at every free occurrence of u in C), provided C(r/u) is a clear instance of C (i.e., no occurrence of u, free in C, is within the scope of a quantifier or operator on r within C.)

By using and citing this rule, we can add the desired, simpler last line:

1,2 | 5   ~ Smoke(a)   4 LPR^1

As a slightly more complex example, consider the inference:

Ann has every virtue
<u>Being courteous to everyone is a virtue</u>
Ann is courteous to Bob

Using C(x,y) for x is courteous to y, b for Bob, V for being a virtue, and a for Ann, the deduction would be as follows:

1	1	∀Z(V(Z) ⊃ Z(a))	P
2	2	V(λx∀yC(x,y))	P
1	3	V(λx∀yC(x,y)) ⊃ [λx∀yC(x,y)](a)	1 UI
1,2	4	[λx∀yC(x,y)](a)	2,3 MP
1,2	5	∀yC(a,y)	4 LPR^1
1,2	6	C(a,b)	5 UI

A closely related rule, <u>Lambda Predicate^1 Abstraction</u> (LPA^1), the reverse of LPR^1, has already been indicated at the beginning of this chapter. Tacitly understanding it to have the same terminology as LPR^1, we can state it more briefly as follows:

Lambda Predicate^1 Abstraction (LPA^1)

C(r/u) may be replaced by [λuC](r), provided C(r/u) is a clear instance of C.

2. Abstraction

LPA[1] permits us to extend existential generalization (EG) to complex properties. Consider the inference:

> Bob snubs everyone poorer than himself
> Snubbing everyone poorer than oneself is a defect
> <u>Jane is courteous to Bob</u>
> Jane is courteous to some who have defects

Using previous symbols, and j for Jane, P for being poorer than, S for snubbing, and D for being a defect, and omitting parentheses around individual arguments, the inference is:

1	1	$\forall x(Pxb \supset Sbx)$	P
2	2	$D(\lambda y \forall x(Pxy \supset Syx))$	P
3	3	Cjb	P
1	4	$[\lambda y \forall x(Pxy \supset Syx)](b)$	1 LPA[1]
1,2,3	5	$Cjb.D(\lambda y \forall x(Pxy \supset Syx)).[\lambda y \forall x(Pxy \supset Syx)](b)$	2,3,4 Join
1,2,3	6	$\exists Z(Cjb.D(Z).Z(b))$	5 EG
1,2,3	7	$\exists x \exists Z(Cjx.D(Z).Z(x))$	6 EG

The lambda operator does not directly affect the EI and UG rules, since these rules do not act on designations of particular properties, complex or otherwise, but only on <u>variables.</u> I.e., EI introduces a new (flagged) predicate variable on the strength of a preceding existential line, while UG produces a universally quantified line from a preceding line which contains a free predicate variable, which is then flagged.

The following list of sample lambda steps should be studied to acquire familiarity with various correct steps, and also with incorrect ones, and ones which are blocked, i.e., require an RBV step before completing. Parentheses are omitted around all arguments, as will sometimes be done in the following, especially when all are made up of individual terms.

2. Abstraction

Examples of lambda steps

1. Pa
    $[\lambda xPx]a$ LPA   (Since a is P, a has the property of x such that x is P.)

2. $[\lambda xPx]a$
    Pa   LPR   (Since a has the property of x such that x is P, a is P.)

3. Rbc
    $[\lambda yRby]c$ LPA   (Since b has R to c, c has the property of b's having R to it.)

4. $[\lambda yRby]c$
    Rbc   LPR   (Since c has the property of y such that by has R to y, b has R to c.)

5. b=b
    $[\lambda x(x=x)]b$ LPA   (Since b is identical with itself, b has the property of x such that x is self-identical, i.e., the property of self-identity.)

6. b=b
    $[\lambda x(b=x)]b$ LPA   (Since b is identical with b, b has the property of b's being identical with it, i.e., b has the property that x has when b is identical with x.)

7. b=b
    $[\lambda x(x=b)]b$ LPA   (LPA can replace all or any b's in b=b, in 5,6,7.)

8. $[\lambda y \exists xRyxy]z$
    $\exists xRzxz$ LPR   (correct)

9. $[\lambda y \exists xRyxy]y$
    $\exists xRyxy$ LPR   (correct)

10. $[\lambda y \exists xRyxy]z$
    $\exists xRzxy$ LPR   (Incorrect. LPR requires substitution for each lambda variable which is free in the lambda scope.)

11. $[\lambda y \exists xRxyz]x$
    $\exists xRxxz$ LPR   (Incorrect. $\exists xRxxz$ is unclear, x having been captured.)

12. $[\lambda y \exists xRxyz]x$
    $[\lambda y \exists wRwyz]x$ RBV
    $\exists wRwxz$ LPR   (Direct LPR blocked; substituted x would be captured by $\exists x$) (The RBV step yields a logically equivalent lambda expressions, in which x would not be captured, permitting correct LPR.)

13. $[\lambda y \exists xRxyz]z$
    $\exists xRxzz$ LPR   (Correct, since LPR requires only a clear, not necessarily distinct instance.)

2. Abstraction

As the examples so far given suggest, the rules for quantificational steps in deductions are not greatly changed. Pending a more detailed statement after further enlargements, little more needs to be said about the changes than that they are the obvious ones. The only warning which merits mention at this point concerns universally instantiating to a lambda expression, or existentially generalizing from one. Lambda expressions present an added threat of variable capture. Care must consequently be taken to see that a lambda expression, in such contexts, contains no free occurrence of a variable which would be captured. As an illustration for UI, consider the sentence

(1) $\forall Z \forall y (\forall x Z x \supset Z y)$

A UI step instantiating to $\lambda z E z x$ for Z would be barred because it contains a free occurrence of x which would be captured by $\forall x$ when substitution was made for Z in the antecedent of the implication. To see why it should be barred, let Exy mean x is equal to y, in the universe of discourse of numbers. $\forall x E x x$ is clearly true, and so is our beginning sentence, (1), which says that for every property Z and number y, if Z holds for every number, it holds for y. Now consider the following steps from these two truths:

```
1  ∀xExx                              P
2  ∀Z∀y(∀xZx ⊃ Zy)                    P
3  ∀y(∀x[λzEzx]x ⊃ [λzEzx]y)          2 UI (λzEzx/Z)
4  ∀y(∀xExx ⊃ [λzEzx]y)               3 LPR
5  ∀xExx ⊃ [λzEzx]2                   4 UI (2/y)
6  [λzEzx]2                           1,5 MP
7  E2x                                6 LPR
8  ∀xE2x                              7 UG x
```

Exercises XV 2

A conclusion from the two truths would appear to be that two equals every number. The fault lies in line 3, where the improper UI from line 2 results in a non-clear instance of the scope of ∀Z in line 2.

Exercises XV 2

*1. From each of the lines below, carry out step(s) of the sort indicated. (It may be that a step is not possible directly, but that an RBV step may be inserted to yield a logically equivalent step. If several different steps are possible (as may happen with LPA), indicate several of them.

    a. LPR: [λz∀x(Rzx ⊃ Ryz)]w

    b. LPR: [λz∀x(Rzx ⊃ Ryz)]y

    c. LPR: [λz∀x(Rzx ⊃ Ryz)]x

    d. LPA: ∀x(Rzx ⊃ Ryz)

    e. LPR: [λz∀x∃y(Rzx ⊃ Ryz)]y

    f. LPA: ∃x(Bxc.Rcyc)

2. Write deductions (with LPA or LPR steps if necessary):

    *a. To forgive (someone) is divine
        Brooks forgives all who are wealthy
        Whoever has a divine quality is a saint
        <u>Brooks is wealthy</u>
        Brooks is a saint

        Fxy: x forgives y; D(Z): Z is divine; Wx: x is wealthy
        Sx: x is a saint; b: Brooks

    D(λx∃yFxy)
    ∀x(Wx ⊃ Fbx)
    ∀x∀Z((D(Z).Zx) ⊃ Sx)
    <u>Wb</u>
    Sb

Exercises XV 2

*b. Every visionary is able to deceive himself
Being glib and able to deceive someone is a commercially valuable characteristic
Every glib visionary has a commercially valuable characteristic

∀x(Vx ⊃ Dxx)
C(λx(Gx.∃yDxy))
∀x((Gx.Vx) ⊃ ∃Y(C(Y).Yx))

c. No one who has had all the advantages would be guilty of larceny
Stealing a car is larceny
Reggie stole his private tutor's Buick
Having a private tutor is an advantage
A Buick is a car
Reggie did not have all the advantages

A(X):X is an advantage; L(X):X is larceny; Sxyz:x steals y from z; Cx:x is a car; Oxy:x owns y; Txy:x is a private tutor of y; Bx:x is a Buick; r:Reggie

∀x∀Y((∀Z(A(Z) ⊃ Zx).L(Y)) ⊃ ~Yx)
L(λx∃y∃z(Cy.Ozy.Sxyz)), ∃x∃y(Bx.Oxy.Tyr.Srxy)
A(λx∃yTyx)
∀x(Bx ⊃ Cx)
~∀Z(A(Z) ⊃ Zr)   Hint: Use Absurdity

*3. Symbolize:

  a. Everything has some property.

  b. There is some property which everything has.

  c. Not all properties have instances.

  d. There is some property which nothing has.

  e. Every two things (not necessarily distinct) have a property in common.

  f. For every two distinct things there is a property which the first has but the second lacks.

*4. Prove each of the sentences of 3 to be truths of (higher) logic.

XVI

EXTENSIONALITY

1. Extensions

In the foregoing discussions of higher logic, predicates have been taken to stand for properties. However, many assertions, and inferences using them, depend only upon what each predicate applies to, rather than upon what specifc property is predicated. That is, they depend only on the extensions of predicates, not their intensions, or meanings. The extension of a 1-place predicate, it may be recalled, was the class of things of which the predicate was true, while the extension of an n-place predicate was the class of ordered n-tuples of things of which it was true. The frequent dependence upon extensions is reflected in the fact that simple predications in English can be paraphrased using a reference both to a property and to a class. Examples:

    Fido is a dog
    Fido has the property of being a dog
    Fido is a member of the class of dogs

    The moon is spherical
    The moon has the property of being spherical
    The moon is a member of the class of spherical things

Similar paraphrases are often possible also when the predication is not of individuals. For example, in the sentence "Emus are numerous", the predicate "numerous", not applying to any individual emu, can be paraphrased:

    The property of being an emu has numerous instances
    The class of emus has numerous members

1. Extensions

Taking advantage of the widespread dependence of assertions and inferences only on extensions, the system of higher logic to be developed here will incorporate what will be called <u>rules of extensionality</u>, making it what is called a <u>system of extensional higher logic</u>. Although it will be limited to inferences which depend only upon extensions, those are important. They include those of mathematics and, indeed, of most sciences.

One effect of dealing with extensions only will be to make it appropriate to read a lambda expression such as λxPx, not only as "The property of x such that x is P", but also as "The class of x's such that x is P". The reader may have encountered a symbolism used by mathematicians with just such a reading. A widely used one is [x:Px]. However, the mathematician's symbol is used not in connection with LPA and LPR but with rules belonging to set theory, of which a bit more will be said later on. On the other hand, in view of the parallels noticed, it will continue to be appropriate to symbolize most sentences containing words like "property", "trait", etc., as we have been doing.

<u>Preliminary Extensionality Rule for Predicates</u>

Our first extensionality rule, PX^1, like LPR^1 and LPA^1, applies to 1-place predicates, lambda predicate expressions, and variables. (So far no other sort of predicate variable has been used.) The rule will be generalized presently.

XVI 299
1. Extensions

Predicate[1] Extensionality (PX^1)

A line j F=G may be justified by the citation i PX^1 as obtained from an earlier line i whose entire clause is ∀u(Fu ≡ Gu), where u is a variable and F and G are each a 1-place predicate, lambda expression, or predicate variable. The premiss number line j is i.

Some sample correct applications of PX^1 are:

i ∀x(Xx ≡ Yx)
j X=Y   i PX^1

i ∀x(Zx ≡ [λy(Py v Qy)](x))
j Z=λy(Py v Qy)   i PX^1

i ∀y([λx∃zRzx](y) ≡ [λw(Pz v Qw)](y))
j λx∃zRzx = λw(Pz v Qw)   i PX^1

PX^1 is often used in combination with the rules of identity and abstraction.

Consider the inference:

Being an emu is a property with numerous instances
Every bird which is related to the ostrich and native to Australia
  is an emu, and vice-versa
──
Being a bird which is related to the ostrich and native to Australia
  is a property with numerous instances.

A correct deduction is shown below, with symbols interpreted as follows: E: being an emu, N: having numerous instances, B: being a bird related to the ostrich, A: being native to Australia.

```
1 |1   N(E)
2 |2   ∀x((Bx.Ax) ≡ Ex)       /N(λy(By.Ay))
2 |3   ∀x([λy(By.Ay)](x) ≡ Ex)        2 LPA
2 |4   λy(By.Ay)=E                    3 PX (leaving superscript aside)
1,2|5  N(λy(By.Ay))                   1,4 IR
```

Since the inference depends only on extensions, it can be expressed equally well in terms of classes instead of properties:

The class of emus is numerous
Every bird which is related to the ostrich and is native to Australia
  is an emu, and vice-versa
──
The class of (all) birds which are related to the ostrich and are
  native to Australia is numerous

More simply, of course, both properties and classes can be left aside, as in "Emus are numerous", and "Birds related to the ostrich and native to Australia are numerous".

Although the foregoing inference is an example of the value of extensionality in facilitating an unobjectional IR step, one may well feel that the identity $\lambda y(By.Ay)=E$ does not lend itself well to a reading in terms of properties. Identity between differently characterized properties does indeed raise questions. One may wish to read it with the extensional interpretation made explicit in some such way as "The property of being a bird related to the ostrich and native to Australia is extensionally identical to the property of being an emu".

Exercises XVI 1

*1. Write a deduction for:

<u>Bigamy is the property of being married to more than one person</u>
All bigamists are married

$$\frac{B=\lambda x \exists y \exists z (y \neq z . Mxy . Mxz)}{\forall x(Bx \supset \exists y Mxy)}$$

Hint: The deduction, though phrased in property language, requires only the extensional conception (rephrase the premiss in class language); nevertheless it requires no PX step, but only IR.

*2. Prove $F=\lambda xFx$ Hint: Use PX

*3. Prove $\forall x(Fx \equiv Gx) \equiv (F=\lambda xGx)$ Hint: Use PX and invoke result of 2.

*4. Prove $x=y \equiv \forall F(Fx \supset Fy)$ Hint: Requires LPR, IR, but not PX.

2. The Theory of Classes

Since extensionality rules are to be adopted, and paraphrases in terms of classes are to be fully acceptable, it becomes of interest to relate extensional higher logic to the theory of classes.

Under the assumption of extensionality, predicate variables may be equally well spoken of as class variables. However, the theory of classes is commonly formulated not in the symbolism of higher logic, but only as a QI theory with the universe of discourse taken to be classes. In such a theory, no mention can be made of members of the classes, but only of the classes as wholes. The QI theory uses a primitive vocabulary which, depending on formulation, may include two names, three function symbols, perhaps a 2-place relation symbol, and identity.

The primitive terms of the QI theory of classes can be defined in extensional higher logic, as shown below, when the universe of individuals is no longer taken to be classes. In doing so, however, it makes explicit the class interpretation, so that it preempts the theoretically interesting study of different interpretations of the primitives of the QI theory. The definitions below, being in higher logic, use class variables, where individual variables would be used in the QI theory. In the commonly used notation shown for the function symbols and 2-place predicate, they appear, as in $x=y$, between the arguments.

2. Theory of Classes

The <u>union</u> of X and Y

$(X \cup Y) = \lambda x(Xx \vee Yx)$ Df

The <u>intersection</u> of X and Y

$(X \cap Y) = \lambda x(Xx . Yx)$ Df

The <u>complement</u> of X

$-X = \lambda x \sim Xx$ Df

Inclusion

$(X \subset Y) \equiv \forall x(Xx \supset Yx)$ Df

Null Class

$\Lambda = \lambda x(x \neq x)$ Df

Universal Class

$V = \lambda x(x=x)$ Df

In the QI theory, the inclusion symbol acted like an ordinary 2-place predicate. In the definition, it appears as a second-level predicate. Similarly, the symbols for union, intersection, and complement are now second-level function symbols, the first we have thus far encountered.

"$(X \cup Y)$", "$(X \cap Y)$, and "$-X$" are defined so as to be replaceable (by IR) by lambda predicates, and vice versa. Therefore, "Smith is a rich broker" could be symbolized in the following ways:

Rs.Bs
$[\lambda x(Rx.Bx)]s$
$[(R \cap B)]s$

In other words, class expressions formed with "cup" ($\cup$), "cap" ($\cap$), and $-$, can serve as compound predicates. This has some convenience. However in such use, as well as in using logic to prove theorems in the theory of classes, one must quickly develop shortcuts to avoid use of the definitions given with the help of lambda. For example, suppose one wishes to prove a law of associativity for union, i.e.,

$((X \cup Y) \cup Z) = (X \cup (Y \cup Z))$

2. Theory of Classes

The proof would be as follows:

```
1  ((Xx v Yx) v Zx) ≡ (Xx v (Yx v Zx))           Assoc
2  ([λx(Xx v Yx)]x v Zx) ≡ (Xx v [λxYx v Zx]x)   LPA twice
3  ([X ∪ Y]x v Zx) ≡ (Xx v [Y ∪ Z]x)             DfR twice
4  [λx([X ∪ Y]x v Zx)]x ≡ [λx(Xx v [Y ∪ Z]x)]x   LPA twice
5  [(X ∪ Y) ∪ Z]x ≡ [(X ∪ (Y ∪ Z))]x             DfR twice
6  ∀x([(X ∪ Y) ∪ Z]x ≡ [(X ∪ (Y ∪ Z))]x)         UG
7  ((X ∪ Y) ∪ Z) = (X ∪ (Y ∪ Z))                 PX
```

But one would ordinarily be satisfied by line 1.

Some useful equivalences are the following

$A = V$	$\forall x Ax$	$A \cap -B = \Lambda$	$\forall x (Ax \supset Bx)$
$A \neq \Lambda$	$\exists x Ax$	$A = A \cap B$	$\forall x (Ax \supset Bx)$
$A \cap B \neq \Lambda$	$\exists x (Ax . Bx)$	$A = B$	$\forall x (Ax \equiv Bx)$

One form of the theory of classes, has the following nine axioms (shown with class variables):

$X \cup \Lambda = X$ $\qquad\qquad$ $X \cap V = X$

$X \cup Y = Y \cup X$ $\qquad\qquad$ $X \cap Y = Y \cap X$

$X \cup (Y \cap Z) = (X \cup Y) \cap (X \cup Z)$ $\qquad$ $X \cap (Y \cap Z) = (X \cap Y) \cup (X \cap Z)$

$X \cup -X = V$ $\qquad\qquad$ $X \cap -X = \Lambda$

$$\Lambda \neq V$$

The axioms, apart from interpretation, are said to characterize a Boolean Algebra. The axioms and theorems become truths of logic under the class definitions given. However, a quicker way of finding an equivalent to a given "equation" of Boolean Algebra than using the definitions is to transform each Boolean term by replacing each letter

X,Y,... by Xx, Yx, Zx..., each occurrence of V by $x=x$, Λ by $x \neq x$ and, recursively, replacing each term $(A \cup B)$ by $(Ax \vee Bx)$, $(A \cap B)$ by $(Ax . Bx)$, $-A$ by $\sim Ax$. Then replace the single identity or disidentity in the Boolean sentence, as follows: $A = B$ by $\forall x(Ax \equiv Bx)$

$$A \neq B \text{ by } \sim \forall x(Ax \equiv Bx)$$

Exercises XVI 2

*1. Using predicates as class names, and only identity and the defined symbols for union, intersection, complement, inclusion, universal class and null class, symbolize the sentences below.

a. There are no dragons (D)

b. Some artists are rich (A,R)

c. Every rich artist is happy (R,A,H)

d. No rich artist is happy (R,A,H)

e. Every member is a Republican or a Democrat (M,R,D)

f. Horses and cows are mammals (H,C,M)

XVII

A SYSTEM OF HIGHER LOGIC

1. The System

The methods of the preceding two chapters will now be extended and incorporated in a formulation of a system of higher logic applicable to what will be called HQIF (for Higher QIF) languages. Lambda and extensionality rules will be given for n-place predicates in general and also for function terms. The rules of quantifiers will be extended to variables and terms of new types. (The variety of types will be classified with the help of special type symbols.) The system will first be concisely presented with the help of metalinguistic notation. Then examples and discussions will be given to aid understanding.

Type symbols will be used both metalinguistically and, as part (subscript) of object language symbols. (However, in practice such subscripts will be abbreviated or omitted.) The types are characterized recursively by the following.

0 is a type

(t) is a type, if t is a type

t_1, t_2 is a type, if t_1 and t_2 are types

$(t_1:t_2)$ is a type, if t_1 and t_2 are types

The type of various kinds of expression is determined recursively by the definitions to follow.

Metalinguistic symbols will be used much as earlier, but with certain additions and amendments. More precisely, combining old with new, metalinguistic symbols will be used as follows:

1. The System

B,C   will stand for clauses

r,s   will stand for terms of any type

u,w   will stand for variables of any type

ρ will stand for an argument, $r_1, r_2, \ldots r_n$, for some n

σ will stand for an argument, $u_1, u_2, \ldots u_n$, for some n consisting only of variables

$\forall\sigma$ will be an abbreviation for $\forall u_1, \forall u_2, \ldots \forall u_n$

C(r/u) will stand for the result of substituting r for each free occurrence of u in C, provided r,u have the same type.

C(ρ/σ) will stand for the result of substituting each term, r_i, in r for every free occurrence of the corresponding variable, u_i, of σ in C (or s), provided that each r_i, u_i have same type, and ρ, σ are n-place arguments of same n.

The definition of <u>clear instance</u>, amended for HQIF:

C(r/u) is a <u>clear instance</u> of C fif no free occurrence of u in C is within the scope of a quantifier or operator on r, or on any variable in r.

C(ρ/σ)⎫ is a <u>clear instance</u> of C (or s) fif no free occurrence of a
s(ρ/σ)⎭ variable of σ in C (or s) is within the scope of a quantifier or operator on any term r of ρ, or on any variable free in any such r.

The definition of <u>distinct instance</u> is unchanged from that for Q-languages.

1. <u>Name</u>, with type 0: (E.g., a, b, c, ...)

2. <u>Predicate</u>, each of some type (t): (E.g., P, Q, R, ...)

3. <u>Function Symbol</u>, each of some type $(t_1:t_2)$: (E.g., s, d, ...)

4. <u>Individual Variables</u>, with type 0: x, y, z, ...x_1, y_1, z_1,

5. <u>Predicate Variable</u>, of type (t) for each type t: X, Y, Z, F, G, ...$X_1, Y_1, \ldots$

6. <u>Function Variable</u>, of type $(t_1:t_2)$ for each of the types t_1, t_2 : f, g, ... $f_1, g_1, \ldots$

7. <u>Logical Signs</u>: $\sim$, v, ., $\supset$, $\equiv$, =, $\forall$, $\exists$, λ, (,)

1. The System

(Formational Syntax of HQIF Language -)

8. A <u>term</u> of type t is an individual expression, a predicate expression, or a function expression of type t.

9. An <u>individual expression</u>, of type 0, is
    a. a name or an individual variable, or
    b. a function-application of type 0.

10. An <u>n-place argument</u>, of type t is a sequence of term, $r_1, r_2, \ldots r_n$ (separated by commas, if n>1), and t is the sequence $t_1, t_2, \ldots t_n$ of the respective types of the terms.

11. An n-place argument is <u>pure</u> fif it contains n distinct variables.

12. A <u>predicate expression of type (t)</u> is
    a. predicate constant or predicate variable of type (t), <u>or</u>
    b. a (lambda predicate) expression, $\lambda\sigma C$, where σ is a pure argument of type t, and C is a clause, <u>or</u>
    c. a function application of type (t).

13. A <u>function expression of type $(t_a:t_v)$</u> [i.e., $(t_a$ of arg.:t_v of value)] is
    a. a function constant or function variable whose type-symbol consists of two type symbols, t_a and t_v, (t_v being the type of a <u>term</u>), separated by a colon and enclosed in parentheses, <u>or</u>
    b. a (lambda function) expression, $\lambda\sigma(r)$, where σ is a pure argument of type t_a and r is a term of type t_v, <u>or</u>
    c. a function application of type $(t_a:t_v)$.

14. A <u>function application of type t</u> is a function expression of type $(t_a:t)$ followed by a parenthesis-enclosed argument of type t_a.

15. A <u>predication</u> is a predicate expression of type (t) followed by a parenthesis-enclosed argument of type t.

16. A <u>clause</u> is
    a. a predication, <u>or</u>
    b. r=s where r and s are both terms and of the same type, <u>or</u>
    c. any expression of one of the following forms: $\sim C$, $(B.C)$, $(B \vee C)$, $(B \supset C)$, $(B \equiv C)$, $\forall u C$, $\exists u C$.

1. The System

17. a. In an occurrence of QuC, Qu is a <u>quantifier on</u> u, and C is its <u>scope</u>, and all occurrences of u in QuC are <u>bound</u> in that occurrence of QuC by Qu.
    b. In an occurrence of λσC, or λσ(r), λσ is a (lambda) <u>operator on</u> each variable in σ, and clause C (or term r) is its scope, and each occurrence of each variable of σ in λσC or λσ(r) is <u>bound</u> in that occurrence by λσ.

18. An occurrence of a term r in an occurrence of a clause or term is <u>free in</u> that occurrence fif no variable in r (or r itself) is bound by a quantifier or operator in C.

19. A clause, predicate expression, function expression, or function application is <u>open</u> if some variable has a free occurrence in it, otherwise, <u>closed</u>.

20. A <u>sentence</u> is a closed clause.

The deductive rules will be given schematically, and will assume the rules of connective logic, without repeating them.

Quantifier Negation (QN) Replacement

~∀uC :: ∃u~C
~∃uC :: ∀u~C

Universal Instantiation (UI)

i ∀uC
j C(r/u)   i UI   (<u>clear</u> instance of C, r same type as u)

Existential Generalization (EG)

i C(r/u)
j ∃uC   i EG   (<u>clear</u> instance, r same type as u)

Existential Instantiation (EI)

i ∃uC
j C(w/u)   i EI_w+ semiflag   (<u>distinct</u> instance, w same type as u)

1. The System

Universal Generalization (UG)

i C(w/u)
j ∀uC   I UG w + semiflag   (<u>distinct</u> instance, w same type as u)

Identity (I)

i r=r   I   (r a term)

Identity Replacement (IR)

i r=s   (or s=r)   (r,s terms of same type)
j C
k C'   i,j IR   (C' obtained from C by replacing some or all free occurrences of r by s, none captured)

Predicate Extensionality (PX)

i ∀σ(Hσ ≡ Kσ)
j H = K   i PX   (Where H,K are predicate expressions of same type and appropriate for σ)

Function Extensionality (FX)

i ∀σ(hσ = kσ)
j h=k   i FX   (Where h,k are function expressions of same type and appropriate for σ)

Lambda	Abstraction	Reduction
$C(\rho/\sigma) :: [\lambda\sigma C](\rho)$	LPA →	← LPR
Where $C(\rho/\sigma)$ is a clear instance of C		
$s(\rho/\sigma) :: [\lambda\sigma(s)](\rho)$	LFA →	←LFR
Where $s(\rho/\sigma)$ is a clear instance of s		

Relettering Bound Variables (RBV) Replacement

QuC :: QwC'

    Where u and w are variables of the same type, and w is distinct from every variable in C, and QwC' is obtained by replacing every occurrence of u in QuC by w.

In the following RBV equivalences, σ and σ' are pure n-place arguments (for the same n), and each variable of σ', is the same as the corresponding variable in σ, except for a variable, w_i, of σ', which is of the same type as the corresponding variable, u_i, of σ; then

$\lambda\sigma C$ :: $\lambda\sigma'C'$

    (Where C' is obtained by replacing each occurrence of u_i in C by w_i.

$\lambda\sigma(r)$ :: $\lambda\sigma'(r')$

    (Where r' is obtained by replacing each occurrence of u_i, in r by w_i.

Safeguards

With the broadenings of terminology and notation given, the statement of the safeguards is exactly as in previous systems.

1. The System

Types

To become familiar with the system of types, we may begin by noting that names (if there are any in the given language) are of type 0, according to definition 1. Each of an infinite number of individual variables are also of type 0, by definition 4. Since 0 is a type, so is (0). According to definitions 2 and 5, (0) may be the type of some predicates, and will be the type of infinitely many predicate variables. According to definition 15, a predication is a predicate expression of type (t) followed by a parenthesis-enclosed argument of type t. The predicate expression may be a predicate of type (t), according to definition 15a, hence of type (0). Therefore, if "Honest" is given as a predicate of type (0), and "ann" is a name, then "Honest(ann)" is a predication. In other words, (0) is the type of 1-place predicates of individuals. Similarly, a predicate "Hits", of type (0,0) followed by an argument "Mary, Ben" (type 0,0) in parenthesis, i.e., "Hits(Mary,Ben)", is also a predication. Therefore, (0,0) is seen as the type of 2-place predicates of individuals; and similarly (0,0,0) is the type of 3-place predicates of individuals, and so on. Definition 5 requires an infinite number of predicate variables of each of these types in the vocabulary of a HQIF language.

The preceding discussion should give an idea of the way in which the definitions assign types to various expressions recursively, beginning with the types specified for the special, non-logical vocabulary of a particular HQIF language. And we may continue with increasing informality.

1. The System

Levels

For 'Honesty is a virtue" to be symbolized as V(H), where H is a predicate of type (0), V must be of type ((0)), according to definition 15, and must have been assigned that type in specifying the vocabulary of the HQIF under discussion. Such a predicate is said to be of second level.

Other expressions, terms and variables, can be assigned levels as well, beginning with names and individual variables on level 0. A term or variable whose type is $(t_1, t_2, \ldots t_n)$ or $(t_1:t_2)$ is assigned a level which is one higher than the highest level assigned to an expression of any of the types $t_1, t_2, \ldots t_n$.

Some sample terms which might appear on levels 0, 1, and 2, are the following:

Level 2	virtue	shape	color	disease
Level 1	honest	spherical	blue	measles
Level 0	Ann	the earth	the Pacific	Bobby

In each case, level-2 words are meaningful predicates for the level-1 words but not for the level-0 words. Thus, it is meaningful to say 'Ann is honest", and "Honest(y) is a virtue', but not 'Ann is a virtue'; 'The earth is spherical', 'sphericity is a shape', but not 'The earth is a shape'; 'Bobby has measles', 'Measles is a disease', but not 'Bobby is a disease'. One might object that the second-level predicates can be meaningfully applied to the names by using 'has', as in "Ann has a virtue", "The earth has a shape", "The Pacific has a color", and "Bobby has a disease". However, having a color is not the same thing as being

1. The System

a color, and would require a different predicate. If V meant having a virtue, it could not be predicated meaningfully of H. That is, it would not be meaningful to say that honesty has a virtue, or that measles had a disease. "Ann has a virtue" could be symbolized with the second level predicate as $X(V(X).X(a))$ or with a distinct first level predicate meaning virtuous.

According to the method which was described for assigning levels, predicate M (for mother), of type (0,0), is on level one. To symbolize a sentence saying that the relation of being a mother-of is irreflexive, a predicate symbol, Ir, would have to be of type ((0,0)). It would be a one-place predicate of binary relations (i.e., a relation designated by a two-place predicate). On the other hand, the relation of being a subclass of, (inclusion) would be a binary relation of properties, so that its symbol (C' in the previous chapter) would be of type ((0),(0)). Both Ir and C would be of second level. (An easy way to tell the level from the type symbol is to count the largest number of unpaired left (or right) parentheses separating any zero from the region outside the symbol.)

Also on level one would be functions of individuals which had individuals as values. If the universe of discourse of an HQIF language were natural numbers, then s(square), d(double) would have type (0:0), while the type of sum and product would be (0,0:0), and all would be on level one. On the other hand, $-, \cup, \cap$, for complement, union, and intersection applied to classes of individuals would have the types, ((0):(0)) for complement, and ((0):(0)) for the others, all being on level two.

1. The System

Keeping track of types, and hence of what terms can meaningfully form predications, or function-applications, with what other terms is important for clarity, and consistency. One way of keeping track would be to use the type symbols as subscripts for each primitive term and each variable of the language. However, while it will be sometimes useful in principle to suppose this done, more limited, and less detailed, indications will usually suffice in practice. For example, different type-fonts have already been used to distinguish between individual variables, predicate variables, and function variables. It often suffices to keep track of degree (the n, in 'n-place predicate') by adding a numeral as right superscript, or of level, by left superscript, or both.

Definition 12b: Extending Lambda Predicate Expressions

Previously, lambda expressions have been used to form complex 1-place predicates from clauses. They are extended, in definition 12b, to form 2-place predicates, for example, by allowing the lambda operator to bind two variables. Thus, $\lambda xy(x<y \vee x=y)$ could be the relation which x bears to y such that x is less than y or x is equal to y. When in predicate position, brackets are useful as before. Argument pairs are treated as before, sometimes informally omitting their parentheses and commas. Thus $[\lambda xy(x<y \vee x=y)](3,5)$ is true. In argument position, this lambda predicate could appear, e.g., in 'Reflexive$(\lambda xy(x<y \vee x=y))$', or in '$\leq = \lambda xy(x<y \vee x=y)$'. Similarly, lambda predicates expressions of higher degree are formed with lambda on correspondingly more variables.

Definition 12c: Predicate Expressions which are Function Applications

An example of a predicate expression formed from a function application, consider "Senior ∪ Junior". It is a function application of the class-union function having two classes as arguments and a class as value. That is, ∪ is of type ((0),(0):(0)). The application, standing for the value the union, the class of upperclassmen, is of type (0), and can act as a predicate for individual expressions, e.g., [Senior ∪ Junior](ann).

Definition 13b: Lambda Function Expressions

Lambda can be used similarly to form expressions for complex functions. For example, in a universe of discourse of natural numbers, $2^n + 1$ is often said to be function. But that is to take it as the function that might be "defined" as $f(n) = 2^n + 1$. Lambda provides an expression to stand for the function without introducing a new symbol to be defined. By a process similar to LPA, which will be called lambda function abstraction (LFA), we could express $2^n + 1$ or $2^3 + 1$ as, respectively, $[\lambda x(2^x + 1)]n$, or $[\lambda x(2^x + 1)]3$. Here, "$\lambda x(2^x + 1)$" symbolizes the function, and may be read as "the function of x whose value is $2^x + 1$".

Definitions 13c and 14: Function Applications

If f is a function of two arguments, type (0,0:0), then $\lambda y(fxy)$ is a function expression of type (0:0). An application, e.g., $[\lambda y(fxy)]z$, yields an individual term of type 0, fxz, obtainable by a step of lambda

1. The System

function reduction (LFR). $\lambda x(\lambda y(fxy))$ is a function expression whose values are functions. Its type is (0:(0:0)). An application, e.g., $[\lambda x(\lambda y(fxy))]w$, yields (by LFR) a function expression, $\lambda y(fwy)$, of type (0:0).

<u>Definitions 17-19</u> slightly reworded to cover the new sorts of terms.

The only deduction rules which need further explanation at this point are the lambda rules. Here, the metalinguistic symbolism has been used to show them as equivalence replacements, with abstraction steps, LPA, LFA, differing from reduction steps, LPR, LFR only in direction. The abstraction steps are shown introducing (going in the direction of) an occurrence of lambda, and the reduction steps eliminating (going away from) an occurrence of lambda.

The process is not quite as straightforward as the symbolism might suggest, however. Consider first the case of LPA. The clause that gets replaced in favor of $[\lambda\sigma C]\rho$ is $C(\rho/\sigma)$, that is, it is a clause which must be seen to be obtainable from C by substituting each occurrence of a term of ρ in C for the corresponding variable of σ. There may be several different C clauses from which the same clause $C(\rho/\sigma)$ can be obtained, some involving different ρ and σ. Thus, in the early example, L(b,b) (Bobby loves himself), using b,b as ρ and x,y as σ, L(b,b) can be obtained by substituting corresponding members of b,b for x,y in L(x,y). That is, $C(\rho/\sigma)$ is L(x,y)(b,b/x,y), which is Lbb. So LPA can replace Lbb by $[\lambda xyL(x,y)](b,b)$. But L(b,b) can also be obtained by substituting b for z in either L(b,z) or L(z,b). So LPA can also replace L(b,b) by $[\lambda zL(b,z)](b)$ or by $[\lambda zL(z,b)](b)$. A more complicated example is the

1. The System

following (in which commas have been omitted, as they already have been in writing the variables immediately following lambda, and omitting also the parentheses around arguments). ∀t(Hxyzt v Syzy) can be obtained by various substitutions in various clauses, including the ones shown below. In other words it can be represented in the metalinguistic notation by any of the formulas on the left, and be replaced by the corresponding lambda predications on the right.

$$\forall t(Hxyzt \; v \; Syzy)$$

may be represented as	may be replaced by
∀t(Hxwvt v Swvw)(zy/vw)	[λvw∀t(Hxwvt v Swvw)]zy
∀t(Hswvt v Swvw)(xyz/swv)	[λswv∀t(Hswvt v Swvw)]xyz
∀t(Hswzt v Syvw)(xyz/swv)	[λswv∀t(Hswzt v Syvw)]xyz

On the other hand, in all cases in which an occurrence of lambda is to be eliminated by LPR, the result is always unique since the substitution to be used is spelled out in the lambda expression.

Lambda steps for functions are similar. For example, take s and p to be the sum and product functions in a universe of discourse of natural numbers. Both are of type (0,0:0). $2x + x^2$, i.e., (2x + x·x), can be written s(p(2,x),p(x,x)). An LFA step could replace it by various lambda expressions, including:

[λz(s(p(2,x),p(z,x)))]x,

[λyz(s(p(z,y),p(x,y)))]x2

Exercises XVII 1

*1. Prove $f=g \supset \forall x(fx=gx)$ where f and g are function variables of type (0:0).

*2. What types would f and g have to have in order that $f=g \supset \forall x \forall y \forall z (fxyz=gxyz)$ be a clause?

*3. Prove that $f=g \supset \forall x \forall y \forall z (fxyz=gxyz)$.

*4. Prove that $\forall F \exists G \forall x (Gx \equiv Fx)$

*5. Prove that $\sim \forall F \exists y \forall x (Rxy \equiv Fx)$

XVIII

HIGHER LOGIC AND SET THEORY

1. Logic and Mathematics

An HQIF system is of interest not only because of its deductive power. It is of at least equal importance because of the complexity of the ideas it can formulate -- what might be called its expressive power or articulateness. For example, it can be developed like an axiomatic theory with definitions and theorems, even though it has been formulated without axioms. We have already seen how numerical quantifiers can be defined. In HQIF, such definitions can be converted into definitions of '0', '1', '2',... etc., as second-level predicates of classes of indivdiuals type ((0)) . But more impressive steps are soon forthcoming. HQIF logic, or rather an older form of which HQIF is a simplified version, was developed in Principia Mathematica (three volumes, 1910-1913) by B. Russell and A. N. Whitehead as a systematic basis for mathematics. They succeeded in defining (in at least one reasonable way) the key concepts of mathematics, as known at the time, including not only the particular finite natural cardinal numbers 0, 1, 2, ..., etc. but also a predicate meaning cardinal number, so that it could be said, and proved, for example, that N(5). (Instead of 'N', they used a different symbol.) Since '5' was on level two, 'N' had to be on level three.

At level three, and successively higher, levels, they were able to define the other familiar kinds of numbers, signed integers, fractions, real numbers, complex numbers, and less familiar things such as relation numbers. For proof of needed laws, the logic system had to be supplemented by two axioms, called the axiom of infinity and the axiom of choice. But these could at least be formulated in purely logical terms. The reader may thus glimpse in even these brief remarks, something of the expressive power and deductive capability of such a system of higher logic.

However, there are significant alternative directions which may be taken, and it will provide a better understanding of certain features of the system to look into an important underlying issue.

2. Russell's Paradox

As we have seen, the system of types in our logic for HQIF languages imposes tight restrictions on what kinds of expressions may be predicated of what. Various ways of relaxing these restrictions have been put forward. But first let us see how total relaxation (suspension of all type restrictions) would lead to trouble. This most extreme relaxation would allow any sort of expression to be predicated of anything. To see that this would not do, consider a law of comprehension, $\forall F \exists G \forall X (G(X) \equiv F(X))$. This is similar to what was proved as exercise *4 of the preceding exercise section, except that here 'X' is used with the intended typelessness. This very general 'comprehension law' would appear as provable as was that of *4. But it leads us to a contradiction, as follows:

2. Russell's Paradox

1. $\forall F \exists G \forall X (G(X) \equiv F(X))$
2. $\exists G \forall X (G(X) \equiv [\lambda F \sim F(F)](X))$ 1 UI
3. $\forall X (G(X) \equiv [\lambda F \sim F(F)](X))$ 2 EI G
4. $\forall X (G(X) \equiv \sim X(X))$ 3 LPR
5. $G(G) \equiv \sim G(G)$ 4 UI

As another way of viewing this difficulty, the property $\lambda F \sim F(F)$ may be thought of as the property of not being true of itself. Suppose we were to define such a property, calling it Impredicability, symbolized Imp, i.e.,

$Imp(F) \equiv \sim F(F)$ Df.

We would be in trouble if we inquired whether impredicability was impredicable. The definition would yield $Imp(Imp) \equiv \sim Imp(Imp)$. That is, if impredicability was impredicable then it was not impredicable, and if it was not impredicable, then it was, etc.

It would seem that whatever restriction we place on predication, it should (like the HQIF system) at least prohibit predication of anything to itself, (positively or negatively). Certainly, ruling such assertions meaningless seems a satisfying solution to the puzzles of ancient philosophers who used to argue about such things as whether beauty was itself beautiful (symbolizable in HQIF as B(B) only violating type restrictions). But the absoluteness of such a ruling can be argued when it comes to predicates at higher levels in the type system -- especially under the extensional interpretation. To see the problem, recall that the extensional interpretation, a (one-place) predicate stands for a class, the class of entities of which the predicate, with its meaning, is true. And a predicate variable stands for a class, pure and simple. Thus, higher level (one-place) predicates stand for

2. Russell's Paradox

classes of classes of, etc. Now many predicates seem meaningful for classes of any level, for example, Empty, Non-empty, Having-more-than-one-member, Having-exactly-one-member, and so on. Each of these predicates would have as its extension the class of all those classes to which it applied. But since these extensions would themselves be classes, it would appear meaningful to ask, with respect to such predicates, whether they were true of their own extensions. Such questions would most often have obvious answers. For example, the class of non-empty classes would itself be non-empty; the classes of classes having more than one member would have more than one member, and so be a member of itself; and similarly for more-than two, three, etc. If we designate such classes of classes, respectively, as $\underline{1}$, $\underline{2}$, $\underline{3}$, etc., it would appear both meaningful and true to assert $\underline{1}(\underline{1})$, $\underline{2}(\underline{2})$, $\underline{3}(\underline{3})$, etc. On the other hand, the class of empty classes would not be a member of itself, since it would not be empty. It would contain the one empty class (all empty predicates being extensionally the same). Likewise, the class of classes having at most one member would have more than one member, and so not be a member of itself. Similarly for for the class of classes having at most two members, or three, etc. Designating each of these latter class of classes, respectively, $\overline{1}$, $\overline{2}$, $\overline{3}$, etc., it would seem correct to assert: $\sim \overline{1}(\overline{1}), \sim \overline{2}(\overline{2}), \sim \overline{3}(\overline{3})$, etc. It seems reasonable, therefore, to say that some classes belong to themselves and some do not, even though type restrictions would forbid it in HQIF. But then it seems also reasonable at first, to speak of the class of all those classes which do not belong to themselves.

2. Russell's Paradox

And we are led to ask whether that class itself is a member of itself, and are confronted by the same paradox as before.

This is the famous <u>Russell Paradox</u> (concerning the class of classes which are not members of themselves). Bertrand Russell found it possible (1902) to construct this paradox within the system of Gottlob Frege (1893), showing it to be inconsistent. (Frege's was the first system of higher logic ever formulated exactly; it also provided the first formulation of the logic of quantifiers. For this and other achievements, Frege is rightly regarded as one of the greatest pioneers of modern logic.) Frege's powerful system was obviously of great value and it seemed that it should be possible to amend it in some way that would preserve its value and banish inconsistencies.

In 1908, Russell published a first version of the system of types. The system avoided paradoxes by ruling out such expressions as $F(F)$ and $\sim F(F)$ as meaningless. It was, in fact, more complex and restrictive than that of the HQIF system. Russell's original system was called the <u>ramified</u>, or branched, system of types (while that of the HQIF system is a version of what is called the <u>simple</u> system of types). The simple theory of types stems from suggestions of F. P. Ramsey in the nineteen twenties, and the form given it here is based on that of Rudolf Carnap (see his <u>Introduction to Symbolic Logic and its Applications</u> (1958). The deductive system of HQIF, however, was adapted, and extended to higher logic from that of Willard van Orman Quine (see his <u>Methods of Logic</u>, second edition, 1959).

Variations in type systems are not followed up here. They must be contrasted instead with a very different approach -- that associated with the important development known as <u>set theory</u>. Set theory as an altnernative to type theory began to form just about simultaneously with type theory. Although set theory had already received great development (e.g., by Georg Cantor), its development as an alternative to type theory came when Ernst Zermelo (1908) took special precautions to formulate it so as to ensure it against the same paradoxes that beset Frege.

3. <u>Set Theory</u>

Without developing set theory in any detail, we can get an idea of its basic conceptual framework, and then focus on the steps taken to avoid paradox.

In its most basic form, set theory uses a single universe of discourse which contains not only indivdiuals (in whatever sense), but also sets. (A <u>set</u> is essentially what we have been calling a class — at least as a common sense approximation.) In saying the UD contains sets, it is meant to imply that it also contains not only sets of sets of every level, but also sets with members from various levels, (i.e., 'heterogeneous' sets, which are not admitted in type theory.) This has the advantage that it allows the extension of a predicate of classes to include far more than just classes on level lower in the type system, and to avoid, for example, the need to suppose a separate prediate for 5, for class of each type.

3. Set Theory

The term which is basic to set theory is a two-place predicate which might be read as (is a) member of. It is represented in set theory by the Greek letter epsilon, ϵ. ϵ is used in infix, rather than prefix position. That is, one writes $x \epsilon y$, instead of $\epsilon(x,y)$, as we wrote $x=y$ and $x<y$. Since there is only one universe of discourse, the logic needed is only first-order, and the variables, $x,y,z,\ldots$, range over individuals, sets of them, sets of sets, etc., without type restrictions. In place of an abstraction operator λx (creating a predicate, when prefixed to a clause) there is a similar device, often written as $[x:C]$, which creates an "individual" expression, for a set: The set of x such that C. Now it will be recalled that Russell's paradox could be obtained from our comprehension law, $\forall R \exists G \forall X (G(X) \equiv F(X))$, when we dropped type restrictions. It is time to examine a possible set theory analogue to the comprehension law. Since set theory is first order, we must first drop the quantifier $\forall F$ and consider instead the laws that could have been obtained, one for every clause with one free variable which we might have obtained by higher UI to a lambda expression followed by LPR. Then, since set theory quantifies over sets, we can replace predicate variables, G and X, by "individual" variables, y and x, and write "$\exists y \forall x (x \epsilon y \equiv \ldots x \ldots)$" as a schematic form where "$\ldots x \ldots$" takes the place of Fx. Since each such law was what could have been obtained in higher logic by universally instantiating from $\forall F \exists y \forall x (x \epsilon y \equiv Fx)$ to a lambda predicate and applying LPR, we can read these comprehension laws as collectively asserting that every property which the language can attribute to some x, i.e., by asserting '$\ldots x \ldots$', has an extension, y. From our earlier discussion

of the intensions and extensions, this seems like an obvious logical truth. Its higher level correlates are provable also in HQIF, as was the comprehension law of problem *4. However, this proves not to be clear sailing for set theory. One of the 'comprehension laws' of the prescribed form would have, in the place occupied by '...x...', the clause '$\sim x \in x$'. It could have been obtained from the higher logic form $\forall F \exists y \forall x (x \in y \equiv Fx)$ by universally instantiating to the lambda predicate: $\lambda x \sim x \in x$, meaning the property of a class x of not being a member of itself, or, extensionally, the class of classes which are not members of themselves! Russell's paradox looms. The contradiction is explicitly derivable for the contemplated comprehension law as follows:

1. $\exists y \forall x (x \in y \equiv \sim x \in x)$
2. $\forall x (x \in y \equiv \sim x \in x)$ 1 EI y
3. $y \in y \equiv \sim y \in y$ 2 UI

(Compare this with problem *5 in the previous exercise section, reading 'R" as the predicate, epsilon.)

This was the situation which Zermelo remedied by modifying the comprehension laws. Such modification could take place directly, because set theory was formulated as an axiomatic theory within a first-order logical frame, and what were deduced comprehension laws in HQIF were to be among the axioms of set theory.

The remedy chosen by Zermelo was to weaken the axioms so as to say, in effect that <u>within any given set</u> a property would pick out a subset of things within that set which had the property. This amendment may be represented as follows: $\forall z \exists y \forall x (x \in y \equiv (x \in z . Fx))$ (where 'Fx' is

3. Set Theory

used informally instead of '...x...'). Thus, x is a member of a y whose existence is asserted only if x is simultaneously in a pregiven set z (which might be called a safety set) and has property F. Zermelo called such a modified axiom an Aussonderungsaxiom which meant an axiom of separating out (a certain subset of z). In English, it is accordingly often called an axiom of separation or an axiom of subset formation. Before inquiring into the motivations and consequences of this modification, it may be well to see exactly how the modification does block the Russell paradox. Following the steps that previously led to disaster, we arrive at the line $y \in y \equiv (y \in z . \sim y \in y)$. By connective logic, this is equivalent to
$(y \in y \supset (y \in z . \sim y \in y)) . ((y \in z . \sim y \in y) \supset y \in y)$. The first member of the conjunction becomes $\sim y \in y \vee (y \in z . \sim y \in y)$ by Mif. This in turn simplifies to $\sim y \in y$ by the dominance rule (the same-sign, 3/2 rule). The second member of the conjunction, by Mif, Nand, and N, becomes $(\sim y \in z) \vee (y \in y) \vee (y \in y)$, which by Red and Mif becomes $y \in z \supset y \in y$. The whole conjunction, then, is $\sim y \in y . (y \in z \supset y \in y)$ which simplifies finally to $\sim y \in y . \sim y \in z$. This is clearly no contradiction. It simply means that from any given set z, the 'Russell property' $[\lambda x \sim x \in x]$ selects a subset y of z which is not a member of z nor of itself. It may be thought at first that Zermelo's Aussonderung axioms contrast unfavorably with the comprehension laws of HQIF which seem to say unqualifiedly that every property has an extension. However, there are built-in limitations in the HQIF laws. What they say is that every property of a given type has an extension limited by type. There is,

3. Set Theory

therefore, a certain kinship between the way paradoxes are avoided by type theory and by set theory. The kinship is one which concerns practical effects only, however. The underlying points of view are very different. For Russell, and the type-theoretic approach in general, it is a question of limiting the range of <u>meaningfulness</u> of expression. For Zermelo it was a question of limiting what sets could be proved to exist. It remained meaningful to ask of any set whether it was or was not a member of itself. One may ask whether or not the set of all sets which are not members of themselves is a member of itself. If one tries to prove that the set-of-all-sets-which-are-not-members-of-themselves is (or is not) a member of itself, one would first have to prove that there was such a set. But to prove this, one needs to have proved the existence of some set of which it could be a subset. One might think of the set of all sets, but the existence of this in turn can not be proved.

The foregoing may suffice to indicate the practical value of the theory of types in avoiding paradox, and the very different attitude underlying set theory's avoidance of paradox. But it remains to be made clear how set theory can be viewed as "an alternative direction for higher logic".

For this we need to look briefly at other features of set theory, the nature of some of its other axioms, definitions, and results.

First of all, let us recall that although set theory uses only first order logic, its universe of discourse includes the sets that were the extensions, or values, of every one-place predicate, or variable, that could appear in a type-theoretic system of logic, and many more besides (e.g., heterogeneous sets).

3. Set Theory

Second, relations and functions seem lacking in set theory, at first glance, but it proves possible to construe certain sets in such a way that they could take the place of relations. A two-place relation could be regarded as a class of ordered couples. An ordered couple, <b,c>, in turn, could be taken to be a (heterogeneous) set containing both b and the set containing just b and c ({b,{b,c}} in set theory notation). Functions, in turn, were left as special kinds of relations (recall the functional-relations of Chapter XIV). The expression [x:C], for the set of x such that C, proved definable, and usable in much the way that λxC is used in type-theory, affording something like higher UI.

Actual deductions in the two systems are often quite different, of course, though the first-order logic is the same. But, it must be conceded that whatever type theory can do, set theory can do. It is for this reason that set theory has been spoken of as an alternative direction in higher logic. On the other hand, type theory has been called (by Quine) "set-theory-in-disguise". Quine maintains that only first-order logic is true logic, and that set theory is a branch of mathematics. Without debating the question here, it may at least be remarked that Frege, Russell, and many others have regarded quantification over predicates as a completely natural extension of pure logic, whatever precautionary restrictions are used to avoid inconsistency. In any case, the fact remains that by extending our familiar methods of quantification beyond a single, first-order domain, we are able to do, in a direct and transparently clear way, what set theory can do only by use of many accumulated theorems, from an imposing set of axioms.

3. Set Theory

Both set theory and logic are in a state of rapid development, and it is difficult to foresee how the future will view them. At the moment, the areas of frontier exploration for set theory and for logic seem in many ways quite different. Set theory is at present much occupied with problems arising in connection with its most powerful axioms, and with realms of enormously infinite sets. Logic, on the other hand, though using set theory in its semantic metatheory, is much concerned with extending logic into non-extensional areas (where set theory seems least applicable). Whatever future developments there may be in these areas, an understanding of a system of extensional, type-theoretic logic, such as the HQIF system, offers a significant vantage point.

A 331

ANSWERS SECTION

Answers to Exercises I 1

1. <u>True or False</u>

　*a.　Logic is based on the psychology of human thought.

　　　　<u>False</u>. (What distinguishes valid from invalid reasoning does not lie in the thought <u>process</u>.) p. 1

　*b.　Any deductive inference whose premisses and conclusion are all true is valid.

　　　　<u>False</u>. (Consider this [invalid] inference: Salt is not an element/Salt is a compound of sodium and chlorine.) pp. 1,2,7-10

　*c.　A deductive inference can not be said to be true or false but only valid or invalid.

　　　　<u>True</u>. (Only the sentences involved can be true or false.) pp. 1,2

　*d.　A deductive inference whose conclusion is false and whose premisses are all true may nevertheless be valid.

　　　　<u>False</u>. ("Valid inference" means one for which that is impossible.) pp. 1,2

　*e.　Logic overlooks shades of gray between true and false, and so, strictly, should be replaced by probability theory.

　　　　<u>False</u>. (Reread page 5)

　*f.　According to logic, a sentence for which there is no evidence for or against is neither true nor false.

　　　　<u>False</u>. (If true, it would be impossible for there to be any unknown truth!) pp. 3-5

Answers to E II 1

*1
1	1	P
2	2	P
3	3	P
1,2	4	1,2
3	5	3
1,3	6	1,5
1,2,3	7	4,6

*2
1	1	P
2	2	P
3	3	P
1,2	4	1,2
1,2,3	5	3,4
1,2,3	6	2,5

Answers to E II 2

*1
1	1	$\sim A \supset B$	P
2	2	$\sim C \lor \sim A$	P
3	3	C	P /B ← optional reminder of the desired conclusion
2,3	4	$\sim A$	2,3 Elim(N) (combining the step to $\sim \sim C$)
1,2,3	5	B	1,4 MP

*2
1	1	$A \lor \sim B \lor C$	P
2	2	$\sim C$	P
3	3	B	P /A
1,2	4	$A \lor \sim B$	1,2 Elim
1,2,2	5	A	3,4 Elim(N)

*3
1	1	$B \supset \sim A$	P
2	2	$C \supset \sim D$	P
3	3	$\sim B \supset C$	P
4	4	A	P /$\sim D$
1,4	5	$\sim B$	1,4 MT(N)
1,3,4	6	C	3,5 MP
1,2,3,4	7	$\sim D$	2,6 MP

ANSWER SECTION

Answers to E II 3

*1.
```
     1│1  A ⊃ B        P
     2│2  B ⊃ C        /A ⊃ C ("P" omitted)
     3│3  A            S
   1,3│4  B            1,3 MP
 1,2,3│5  C            2,4 MP
   1,2│6  A ⊃ C        3,5 SQ
```

*2.
```
     1│1  A ⊃ B        P
     2│2  ~B v C       /~C ⊃ ~A
     3│3  ~C           S
   2,3│4  ~B           2,3 Elim
 1,2,3│5  ~A           1,4 MT
   1,2│6  ~C ⊃ ~A      3,5 SQ
```

*3.
```
     1│1  A ⊃ ~B       P
     2│2  A ⊃ ~C       P
     3│3  B v C        /~A
     4│4  A            S
   1,4│5  ~B           1,4 MP
 1,3,4│6  C            3,5 Elim
   2,4│7  ~C           2,4 MP
 1,2,3│8  ~A           4,6,7 SA
```

Answers to E II 4

*1.
```
     1│1  (B v C) ⊃ A  P
     2│2  B            P /A
     2│3  B v C        2 Add
   1,2│4  A            1,3 MP
```

*4.
```
     1│1  A.B              P
     2│2  ~C               P
     3│3  (~C.A) ⊃ D       P /D
     1│4  A                1 Drop
   1,2│5  ~C.A             2,4 Join
 1,2,3│6  D                3,5 MP
```

*5.
```
     1│1  A ⊃ (B.C)    P
     2│2  C ⊃ D        P /A ⊃ D
     3│3  A            S
   1,3│4  B.C          1,3 MP
   1,3│5  C            4 Drop
 1,2,3│6  D            2,5 MP
   1,2│7  A ⊃ D        3,6 SQ
```

Answers to E III 1

1. $\underline{A\ B}$ *d. $\underline{\sim A.B}$ *e. $\sim(A.B)$ *f. $\sim A\ v\ \sim B$
   F T   F T   F T   T   F
                T   F   T
                T   T

       *g. $\sim(A\ v\ B)$ *h. $\sim B \supset A$ *i. $\sim(B \supset A)$
              F   T   T   F   T   F
                T   F   F
                F   T   T

*2. $\underline{A\ B\ C}$ a. $(A.C) \supset B$ b. $(A\ v\ B) \supset (B \equiv \sim C)$
   T F T   T T   F   T   F   F   T
                  T   T   F
                    F   T

       c. $(\sim B\ v\ \sim C) \supset (A.\sim C)$
             T   F   T F
                 T   F
                      F

Answers to E III 2

                     ⌒ Premisses ⌒ Concl.

1. *c.   A B | $\sim A$ | $A \supset B$ $\sim A \supset B$ /B
          T T | F | T   T   T ⎤
          F T | T | T   T   T ⎦ cases in which both premisses
          T F | F | F   T   F   are true.
          F F | T | T   F   F   VALID

2. *d.   A B | $\sim A$ | $\sim B$ | $A \supset \sim B$ /$B \supset \sim A$
          T T | F | F | F   F
          F T | T | F | T   T ⎤ cases in which premiss
          T F | F | T | T   T ⎦ is true.
          F F | T | T | T   T   VALID

    *e.   A B | $\sim B$ | A $A\ v\ B$ /$\sim B$
           T T | F | T   T   F ⎤ loophole: both premisses
           F T | F | F   T   F   true, but conclusion false.
           T F | T | T   T   T   INVALID
           F F | T | F   F   T

Answers to E III 2 (continued)

3. In giving the answer to this one, the extremely condensed method is shown. Display values appear beneath first occurrence of letter. Column of each partial sentence appears under main connective of that partial sentence. Furthermore, multiple occurrences of a T or F in a column are represented by drawing their "tails" longer.

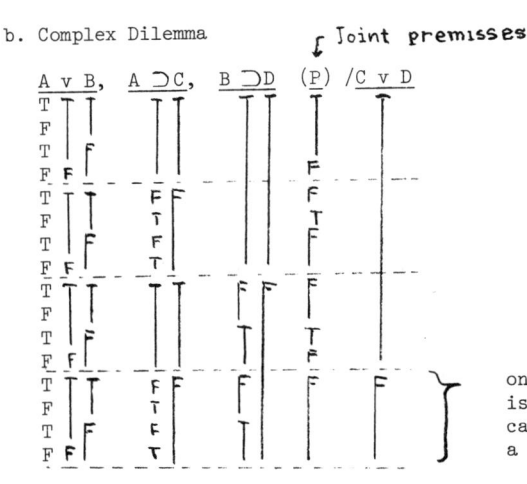

b. Complex Dilemma   ⟵ Joint premisses

A v B, A ⊃ C, B ⊃ D (P) / C v D

only cases where conclusion is false are included in cases were (P) column has a F. **Valid.**

Cases were all premisses are true may be conveniently summarized in joint premiss (P) column. Note use of guide lines (dashed).

Answers to E III 3

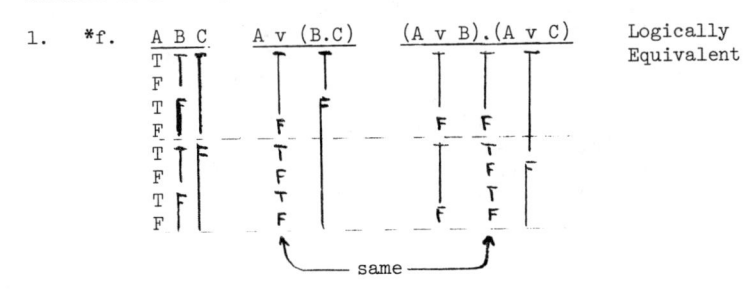

1. *f.   A B C   A v (B.C)   (A v B).(A v C)   Logically Equivalent

⟵ same ⟶

Answers to E III 3 (continued)

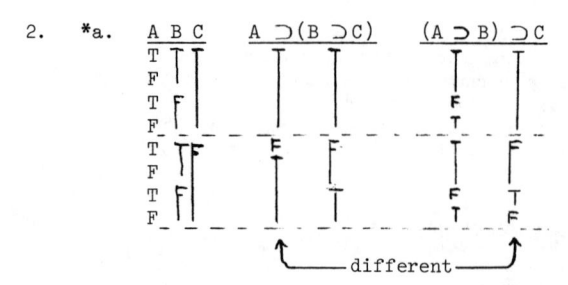

2. *a. Truth-table comparison of A ⊃ (B ⊃ C) and (A ⊃ B) ⊃ C — **Not Logically Equivalent** (different).

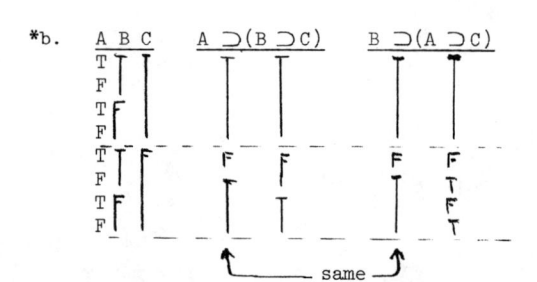

   *b. Truth-table comparison of A ⊃ (B ⊃ C) and B ⊃ (A ⊃ C) — **Logically Equivalent** "The commutation (of antecedents) law" (same).

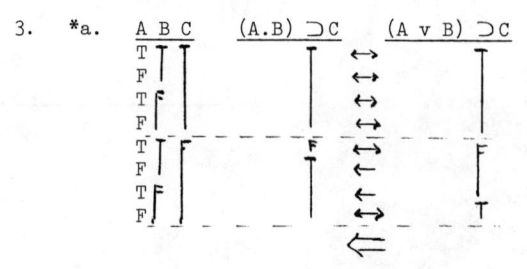

3. *a. Truth-table comparison of (A·B) ⊃ C and (A v B) ⊃ C.

The comparison may be carried out line by line. Mark a double-headed arrow for TT and FF. Mark → for FT and ← for TF. If all lines get double-headed arrows the two sentences are logically equivalent. If any two lines get arrows pointing in opposite directions, neither logically implies the other. If all arrows which are not double-headed point in one direction, that direction is the direction of logical implication (in this case, right to left).

Answers to E III 3 (continued)

4. Internalizing Negations

   *a. $\sim(A \vee \sim B) \underset{Nor}{\Longleftrightarrow} \sim A . \sim \sim B \underset{N}{\Longleftrightarrow} \sim A . B$

   *b. $\sim((A.B) \supset C) \underset{Nif}{\Longleftrightarrow} (A.B).\sim C$

5. Reexpressing in $\sim$, ., v.

   *a. $(A.B) \supset C \underset{Mif}{\Longleftrightarrow} \sim(A.B) \vee C \underset{Nand}{\Longleftrightarrow} \sim A \vee \sim B \vee C$

   *b. $A \supset (B \equiv C) \underset{Mif}{\Longleftrightarrow} \sim A \vee (B \equiv C) \underset{Eqo}{\Longleftrightarrow} \sim A \vee (B.C) \vee (\sim B. \sim C)$

Answers to E III 4

1. *b.
A	$\sim$A
T	F
F	T

$(A \supset \sim A) \supset A$
T   T
F   F ← Neither tautology nor contradiction

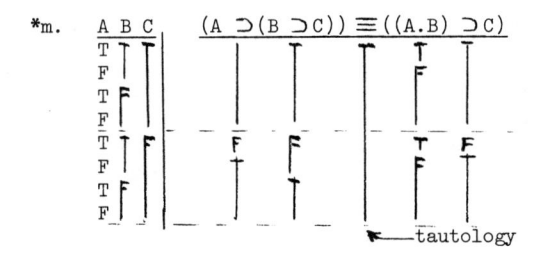

   *f.
A B	$(A.B) \supset B$
T T	T T T
F T	F T T
T F	F T F
F F	F T F

← tautology

   *m.
A B C $(A \supset (B \supset C)) \equiv ((A.B) \supset C)$

← tautology

Answers Section

Answers to E IV 1

1. *a. Arch will go but Bea won't. $A . \sim B$
   *e. Della will go, provided Arch does. $A \supset D$
   *m. Della will not be going, while Claude and $\sim D . ((C . B) \vee \sim A)$
        Bea will unless Arch does not go either.

*2. a. Modus Ponens.
       $R \supset O$ R: It rains today.
       $\underline{R \quad\quad}$ O: The party is off.
       O (Note that "because" signals reason, ie., a premiss.
                  Usually, "because" <u>follows</u> the conclusion.)

    b. Elimination.
       $S \vee M$ S: The case is a sinus infection.
       $\underline{\sim M}$ M: The case is malaria.
       S (Note: In presenting a deductive argument, premisses
                  are often given with an indication of the <u>inductive</u>
                  evidence supporting <u>them</u>. In this example, malaria
                  is ruled out on the strongly felt, but not especially
                  solid ground that it is "unthinkable".)

    c. (Compound) Dilemma.
       $N \vee C$ M: Jean misses the countryside.
       $N \supset M$ N: Jean goes to New York.
       $\underline{C \supset M}$ C: Jean goes to Chicago.
       M (Note: The conclusion (which comes first in this example)
                  may not be signalled by "therefore", "hence", or any
                  other special word, but must be recognized from context.
                  Note furthermore that tenses have all been converted to
                  a "neutral" present tense, for symbolizing. This is
                  wise practice for laying bare the <u>form</u> of an inference
                  (unless the inference <u>hinges</u> on the time relationships
                  involved).)

    d. Modus Ponens.
       $E \supset \sim J$ E: An earthquake occurs.
       $\underline{E \quad\quad}$ J: Jeff goes to school.
       $\sim J$ (Note: If J stood for Jeff does <u>not</u> go to school, the
                  form would be represented as:
                                                 $E \supset J$
                                                 $\underline{E \quad}$
                                                 J
       which more closely conforms to the simple pattern shown
       for Modus Ponens. But we have already noted that the
       simple forms given were <u>meant</u> to permit the sentences
       involved to be compounds, such as $\sim J$.)

Answers to E IV 1 (continued)

    e. Other. Invalid.
        $G \supset R$ G: Green's broker gives good advice.
        $\underline{R}$ R: Green's broker is rich.
        G   (This is an <u>invalid</u> inference form called "the fallacy of affirming the consequent" - in contrast to Modus Ponens, which "affirms" the antecedent.)

    f. Modus Tollens.
        $T \supset B$ B: A blip shows.
        $\underline{\sim B}$ T: Kappa tachyons are present.
        $\sim T$

    g. Link. (Not covered as a rule in II.)
        $\sim S \supset L$ S: A ship is sighted.
        $\underline{T \supset \sim S}$ T: The typhoon hits.
        $T \supset L$ L: We take the longboat.
        (Note: The word "mean" often signals the conclusion of an inference. The "would" suggests that the strength of the valid inference is being used, not to support the conclusion, but to suggest making the first premiss false by changing the agreement.)

    h. (Complex) Dilemma.
        $O \vee S$ O: Beamis escaped over the wall.
        $O \supset W$ S: Beamis escaped by swimming.
        $\underline{S \supset D}$ W: Beamis is in the woods.
        $W \vee D$ D: Beamis died in the ebbtide.
        (Note: "has to" often signals the conclusion of an inference.)

    i. Modus Ponens.
        $F \supset B$ B: You buy me a bottle of sack.
        $\underline{F}$ F: Fitzhugh bowls out Cowles.
        B   (Note: There is a connection between "said", "buy", and "owe", here, of course. But the basic inference form being appealed to is MP, as indicated.)

    j. Other. Invalid.
        $D \supset \sim L$ D: Rač plans to defect.
        V   L: Rač left his wife in Apheim.
        $\underline{(V \supset \sim L)}$ V: Rač sent his wife to Vienna.
        D   (This is an invalid form, even supplying the tacit premiss, shown in parentheses. It relies on the form $D \supset \sim L$, $\sim L$ /D, which is, again, the "fallacy of affirming the consequent".)

Answers to E IV 1 (continued)

   k. Modus Tollens.
       H ⊃ M   H: There is a life hereafter.
       ∼M   M: Myra is happy.
       ∼H   (Note: The context indicates an ongoing dispute and the existence of evidence for Myra's being unhappy, both of which can be ignored in identifying the deductive form.)

   l. Other. Valid.
       D ⊃ R   D: Interest rates drop.
       P ⊃ ∼R   R: The market rises.
       ∼(D.P)   P: The energy pinch continues.
       (Note: This is a valid form not yet covered.)

Answers to Exercises IV 2

*1. The contractor's policy: Make true
                                   Make false
                                   Ignore

	A	C	E
Make true		✓	
Make false	✓		
Ignore			✓

3. *a. The holder's policy: Make true
      for A C G   Make false
           T T F   Ignore

	B	D	E
Make true			✓
Make false		✓	
Ignore	✓		

Answers to Exercises IV 3

*2. $(B^F \supset A^F) \supset (C^T \vee B^F)$ Conc. Prem.
      $\overline{\sim A^F \supset B^F}$ A B   C   Loophole found.
                                 F F   T   INVALID

*4. $(A \vee B) \supset (A.B)$ Conc. Prem. 2 Prem. 1
      $\underline{A^F.B^F}$ A B   Forced   (Need   VALID
      $A^F \vee B^F$ F F   False   not be
                                                    inspected)

A 341

Answers Section

Answers to E IV 4

Simplify: Answers

1. A.(~B v A)   A
2. (A.B) v (A.~B)   A
3. A.(C v ~A)   A.C
4. (L.M) v (M.~L)   M
5. (A v B) v (~C v B)   A v B v ~C
6. (H v J v ~H).K   K
7. (A.B).(A v (A.B))   A.B
8. ((A ⊃ B) v A).B.C   B.C
9. (A.B) ≡ (A.~A)   ~A v ~B
10. A ≡ (A.B)   ~A v B
11. (A ⊃ B).(A v B)   B
12. ~(A ⊃ B) v (B.~B.C.A)   A.~B
13. (A.(~B v C)) v (C.A) v (A.~B)   A.(~B v C)
14. (A ⊃ B) ⊃ (((C.(~A ⊃ B)) v ((B.(~B ⊃ A)))   A v B
15. A.(B v ~C)   multiplies to (A.B) v (A.~C)
16. A v (~B.C)   (A v ~B).(A v C)
17. (A.B) v (C.~D)   (A v C).(A v ~D).(B v C).(B v ~D)
18. (~E v G).(H v E)   (~E.H) v (~E.E) v (G.H) v (G.E)
                                       (drops)

Answers to E V 1A

*3 If population grows indefinitely, essential resources will be exhausted
    If essential resources are exhausted population will not grow indefinitely
    Population will not grow indefinitely   (G,E)

```
     1│1   A ⊃ B
     2│2   B ⊃ ~A       /~A
   1,2│3   A ⊃ ~A       1,2 Link
   1,2│4   ~A v ~A      3 Mif
   1,2│5   ~A           4 Red
```

*4 Archer gets the loan or else Bates, Ltd., is bankrupt and Carla
        stays home
    Archer gets the loan or Carla stays home

```
     1│1   A v (B.C)    /A v C
     2│2   ~A           S
   1,2│3   B.C          1,2 Elim
   1,2│4   C            3 Drop
     1│5   ~A ⊃ C       2,4 SQ
     1│6   ~~A v C      5 Mif
     1│7   A v C        6 N
```

Note that this displays a useful additional suppositional strategy:
instead of responding to a A ⊃ B conclusion by supposing A, one
can respond to an A v B conclusion by supposing ~A.

*5 Either Ahmed's victory means Bultz gets the next match or the
        championship is vacated
    It was not the case that the championship was vacated unless
        Bultz got the next match
    Ahmed was not victorious   (A,B,C)

```
     1│1   (A ⊃ B) v C
     2│2   ~(C v B)     /~A            Recall the (gerund + "means")
     2│3   ~C.~B        2 Nor          construction.  Let A stand
     2│4   ~C           3 Drop         for Ahmed (is) victorious.
   1,2│5   A ⊃ B        1,4 Elim
     2│6   ~B           3 Drop
   1,2│7   ~A           5,6 MT
```

A 343

Answers to E V 1A (continued)

*8. If Akins takes archaeology he will have to master Benton's text
     and dig civilization
     If Akins masters Benton's text, he won't dig civilization
     Akins will not take archaeology   (A,B,C)

```
         Most natural deduction                Shorter way, using Mif, Nand

   1 |1   A ⊃ (B.C)        P                1 |1   A ⊃ (B.C)     P
   2 |2   B ⊃ ~ C          P  /~A           2 |2   B ⊃ ~ C       P  /~A
   3 |3   A                S                2 |3   ~B v ~C       2 Mif
 1,3 |4   B.C              1,3 MP           2 |4   ~(B.C)        3 Nand
 1,3 |5   B                4 Drop         1,2 |5   ~A            1,4 MT
1,2,3|6   ~C               2,5 MP
 1,3 |7   C                4 Drop
 1,2 |8   ~A               3,6,7 SA
```

*15. Prof. McFiend has taken over the rocket controls, but if he does
     not notice Alan's absence, he will be able to shut off the
     power before we reach position C
     Prof. McFiend can't both have taken over the controls and also
        notice Alan's absence
     We will fail to make Mars only if we are not able to shut off
        the power before we reach position C
     We will make Mars   (P,N,S,M)

```
         Indirect (Absurdity) Strategy

   1  |1    P.(~N ⊃ S)       P
   2  |2    ~(P.N)           P
   3  |3    ~M ⊃ ~S          /M
   4  |4    ~M               S
  3,4 |5    ~S               3,4 MP
   1  |6    ~N ⊃ S           1 Drop
 1,3,4|7    N                5,6 MT(N)
   1  |8    P                1 Drop
 1,3,4|9    P.N              7,8 Join
 1,2,3|10   M                4,2,9 SA(N)
```

Answers to E V 1B

*1. Simple Dilemma.

*2.
```
   1 |1  (A ⊃ B) v C v (D.E)    P
   2 |2  ~(D.E)                 P
   3 |3  ~C                     P  /A ⊃ B
 1,2 |4  (A ⊃ B) v C            1,2 Elim
1,2,3|5  A ⊃ B                  3,4 Elim
```

*3. Link

Answers to E VI 1

1. *a. Alex and Bea are juniors.   (a,b,J)   Ja.Jb

   *b. Alex and Bea are cousins.   (a,b,C)   Cab (or, Cab.Cba)

   *c. Alex likes Bette or Della.   (a,b,d,L) Lab v Lad

   *d. Alex gave Rover, but not
       Spot to Bea   Garb. ~Gasb

Answers to E VI 2

1. *a. Everything falls.   (F)   ∀xFx

   *e. There are no ogres. (O)   ~∃xOx or ∀x~Ox

   *g. Not all animals are herbivorous. (A,H)   ~∀x(Ax ⊃ Hx)

   *h. No lions are herbivorous. (L,H)   ∀x(Lx ⊃ ~Hx)

   *k. Nothing that is not sealed will
       be mailed.   (S,M)   ∀x(~Sx ⊃ ~Mx)

   (Logical equivalents are possible, of course.)

2. *a. All lions are carnivorous
       <u>Rex is a lion</u>
       Rex is carnivorous
```
   1 |1  ∀x(Lx ⊃ Cx)    P
   2 |2  Lr             P  /Cr
   1 |3  Lr ⊃ Cr        1 UI
 1,2 |4  Cr             2,3 MP
```

   *b. Rex is a lion
       <u>Rex does not howl</u>
       Some lions do not howl
```
   1 |1  Lr             P
   2 |2  ~Hr            P  /∃x(Lx.~Hx)
 1,2 |3  Lr.~Hr         1,2 Join
 1,2 |4  ∃x(Lx.~Hx)     3 EG
```

Answers to E VI 2 (continued)

2. *d. Wolves howl
        Fido howls
        <u>Fido is not a wolf</u>
        Not everything that
           howls is a wolf

        (or Not only wolves howl.
        Explain the "only" from
        the symbolization!)

```
1 |1  ∀x(Wx ⊃ Hx)      P
2 |2  Hf                P
3 |3  ~Wf               P        /~∀x(Hx ⊃ Wx)
4 |4  ∀x(Hx ⊃ Wx)       S
4 |5  Hf ⊃ Wf           4 UI
3,4|6  ~Hf              3,5 MT
2,3|7  ~∀x(Hx ⊃ Wx)     4,2,6 SA
```
Note: Premiss 1 was superfluous

*e. Every applicant who
       speaks Spanish will be
       considered
    <u>Jane speaks Spanish</u>
    If Jane applies, she
       will be considered

```
1 |1   ∀x((Ax.Sx) ⊃ Cx)   P
2 |2   Sj                  P    /Aj ⊃ Cj
1 |3   (Aj.Sj) ⊃ Cj        I UI
4 |4   Aj                  S
2,4|5  Aj.Sj               2,4 Join
1,2,3|6 Cj                 3,5 MP
1,2|7  Aj ⊃ Cj             4,6 SQ
```

Note: By reading Ax as <u>x applies</u>, "Every applicant who speaks Spanish" is symbolized as "Every x such that x applies and x speaks Spanish".

3. *a. ~∀x(Gx ⊃ Hx); neg: ∃x(Gx.~H). Some germs are not harmful.

   *b. ~∃x(Mx.~Hx); by either of the following sequences:

        ∀x~(Mx.~Hx)   QN ⟶

        ∀x(~Mx v ~~Hx)   Nand   ∀x(Mx ⊃ ~~Hx)   Mif

        ∀x(~Mx v Hx)   N   ∀x(Mx ⊃ Hx)   N

        ∀x(Mx ⊃ Hx)   Mif

        All members are honest.

Answers to E VI 2 (continued)

4.
*a. ∀x(Px ⊃ Cx)   *b. ∀x(Wx ⊃ ~Bx)   *c. ∃x(Lx.Ix)

*d. ~∀x(Px ⊃ Lx)   Note that abstract nouns such as "poverty and "laziness" may often be paraphrased by predications which use the corresponding predicate adjectives: Px: x is poor; Lx: x is lazy. Informal reading of the symbolized sentence: "It is not the case that everyone who is poor is lazy."

*e. ∀x(∀x ⊃ (Rx v Dx))

*f. "Horses and cows are mammals" is a factored English form for "Horses are mammals and cows are mammals". The symbolization for this is ∀x(Hx ⊃ Mx).∀x(Cx ⊃ Mx). This is logically equivalent to ∀x((Hx v Cx) ⊃ Mx); i.e., Everything which is a horse or a cow is a mammal. Note that ∀x((Hx.Cx) ⊃ Mx) means Everything that is both a horse and a cow is a mammal!

*g. ∀x(Px ⊃ Sx)   *h. ∀x(Cx ⊃ (Px v Tx))   *i. ∀x(Gx ⊃ (Jx v Hx))

*j. ∃x(Sx.Ox)   *k. ∀x(Sx ⊃ Rx)   Note that "A scout is outside" is gramatically similar to "A scout is reverent" but the first is understood as about some scout and the second as about all scouts. Only meaning and context indicate the difference.

*l. ∀x(Gx ⊃ (Ex.Ox))   *m. ∀x(Gx ⊃ (Sx.Px))   *n. ∃x(Gx.Sx.Tx)
Although 18 is clearly about some governor, 16 and 17 depend more heavily on context. 16 would be understood as universal in a textbook on political science, but as referring to a particular man in an explanation of his public relations.

*o. ∀x((~Ox.(Cx v Gx)) ⊃ Sx)   Note that the last qualification in the English belongs in the antecedent. ∀x(Px ⊃ (~Ox ⊃ ((Cx v Gx) ⊃ Sx))) (Logical equivalent are possible, of course.)

Answers to E VI 3

*1. 
S: Scholars
F: Those like footnotes
U: Those who are untidy   VALID

*2. 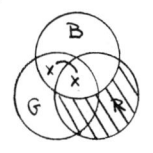 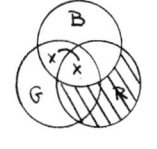
R: Robins
B: Layers of blue eggs
G: Birds in my garden

X could be outside R   INVALID

*3. 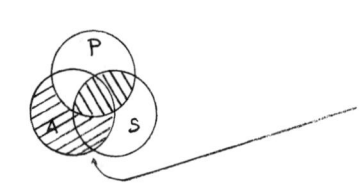
S: Spies
P: Publicity seekers
A: Actors

S-and-A region blacked out   VALID

*4. 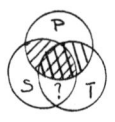
S and T region not
all blacked out   INVALID

*5.
$\forall x(Cx \supset Mx)$
$\underline{\forall x(Lx \supset Mx)}$
$\forall x(Cx \supset Lx)$

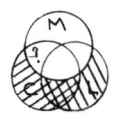

("Only" phrasing was
not used in traditional
syllogism, but same
method applies.)

C-region not confined
to L-region   INVALID

Answers to E VII 1

*1. a. ∃x∀y∃z ~Rxyz
    b. Pb.∃x~Hbx
    c. ∀x∃yRxy.~Hzb
    d. ∃x∀y(Hxy.~Rxb)
    e. ∃x(Px.∀y~Syx)
    f. ∃x(∃ySyx.~Px)

*2. a. Bruce smiles at someone. ∃xSbx
    b. Everyone smiles at Bruce. ∀xSxb
    c. Bruce envies no one. ∀x~Ebx
    d. If Bruce is glum, he smiles at no one. Gb ⊃ ∀x~Sbx
    e. If no one smiles at Bruce, he is glum. ∀x~Sxb ⊃ Gb
    f. Bruce is anxious unless someone smiles at him. Ab v ∃xSxb
    g. Not everyone envies someone. ~∀x∃yExy
    h. Every celebrity is envied by someone. ∀x(Cx ⊃ ∃yEyx)
    i. Everyone Bruce smiles at likes him. ∀x(Sbx ⊃ Lxb)
    j. Bruce smiles at every girl who is pretty. ∀x((Gx.Px) ⊃ Sbx)
    k. Whoever smiles at everyone is not liked by some. ∀x(∀ySxy ⊃ ∃y~Lyx)
    l. Mary has a lamb. m: Mary, Hxy: x has(owns) y, Lx: x is a lamb
       ∃x(Hmx.Lx)
    m. Mary has an uncle. m: Mary, Uxy: x is an uncle of y   ∃xUxm
    n. Everyone who has a pool has friends. Hxy: x has(owns) y, Px: x is a pool.
       Fxy: x is a friend of y   ∀x(∃y(Hxy.Py) ⊃ ∃yFxy)

*3. a.   1 | 1 ~Is   P
        2 | 2 ∀x(Emx ⊃ Ix)   P /~Ems
        1 | 3 Ems ⊃ Is   1 UI
      1,2 | 4 ~Ems   1,3 MT

    b.   1 | 1 Ck ⊃ ∀xCx   P
        2 | 2 ~(Cb.Cj)   P /~Ck
        3 | 3 Ck   S
      1,3 | 4 ∀xCx   1,3 MP
      1,3 | 5 Cb   4 UI
      1,3 | 6 Cj   4 UI
      1,3 | 7 Cb.Cj   5,6 Join
      1,2 | 8 ~Ck   3,2,7 SA

    c.   1 | 1 ∀x(Sx ⊃ Sj)   P   or   1 | 1 ∃xSx ⊃ Sj   P
        2 | 2 Sb   P   2 | 2 Sb   P
        1 | 3 Sb ⊃ Sj   1 UI   2 | 3 ∃xS   2 EG
      1,2 | 4 Sj   2,3 MP   1,2 | 4 Sj   1,3 MP

    d.   1 | 1 ∀x(Bx ⊃ Txd)   P
        2 | 2 ∃xTxd ⊃ Cd   P
        3 | 3 Bb   P /Cd
        1 | 4 Bb ⊃ Tbd   1 UI
      1,3 | 5 Tbd   3,4 MP
      1,3 | 6 ∃xTxd   5 EG
    1,2,3 | 7 Cd   2,6 MP

Answers to E VII 2

*1. ∃xRxb   C,S,   *2. ∀x(Px ⊃ Rgx)   X (g not in Lang)

*3. ∀xPx ⊃ Qx   C,O   *4. ∀x(Qxb ⊃ Ry)   X (wrong degrees)

*5. ∀x(Px ⊃ ∃y(Gayx v Pb))   C,S

*6. Rax ⊃ ∃x∀y(Rxy ⊃ ∀xGyzx)   C,O

*7. Pa v ∀xQx ⊃ Px   X (needed parens missing)

*8. ∀x(Px v (∀xSxx . ∃yGxyz))   C,O

Answers to E VII 3

1. *a. Pb v Qa v Qb   *b. (Pb v Qa) v (Pb v Qb) (equiv. to a)

   *e. (∀yRay v ∀yRby) v Pb   which expands to :

        ((Raa.Rab) v (Rba.Rbb)) v Pb

Answer Section

Answers to E VIII 1

*1.
```
   1  |1   ∀x(Px ⊃ Bx)
   2  |2   ∀x(Bx ⊃ Cx)    /∀x(Px ⊃ Cx)    or   1  |1   ∀x(Px ⊃ Bx)
   3  |3   Py             S                     2  |2   ∀x(Bx ⊃ Cx)
   1  |4   Py ⊃ By        1 UI                  1  |3   Py ⊃ By       1 UI
 1,3  |5   By             3,4 MP                2  |4   By ⊃ Cy       2 UI
   2  |6   By ⊃ Cy        2 UI                1,2  |5   Py ⊃ Cy       3,4 Link
1,2,3 |7   Cy             3,6 MP              1,2  |6   ∀x(Px ⊃ Cx)   5 UGy
 1,2  |8   Py ⊃ Cy        3,7 SQ
 1,2  |9   ∀x(Px ⊃ Cx)    8 UGy
```

*2.
```
   1  |1   ∃x(Px.∼Sx)
   2  |2   ∀x(∼Sx ⊃ Rx)   /∃x(Px.Rx)
   1  |3   Py.∼Sy         1 EIy
   1  |4   ∼Sy            3 Drop
   2  |5   ∼Sy ⊃ Ry       2 UI
 1,2  |6   Ry             4,5 MP
   1  |7   Py             3 Drop
 1,2  |8   Py.Ry          6,7 Join
 1,2  |9   ∃x(Px.Rx)      8 EG
```

*3.
```
   1  |1   ∀x(Px ⊃ ∼Mx)
   2  |2   ∀x(Sx ⊃ Mx)    /∀x(Sx ⊃ ∼Px)
   1  |3   Py ⊃ ∼My       1 UI
   2  |4   Sy ⊃ My        2 UI
   1  |5   My ⊃ ∼Py       3 Contra(N)
 1,2  |6   Sy ⊃ ∼Py       4,5 Link
 1,2  |7   ∀x(Sx ⊃ ∼Px)   6 UGy
```

*4.
```
   1  |1    ∀x(Ax ⊃ (Bx.Cx))
   2  |2    ∃y(Py.Ay)          /∃z(Pz.Cz)
   2  |3    Py.Ay              2 EIy
   2  |4    Ay                 3 Drop
   1  |5    Ay ⊃ (By.Cy)       1 UI
 1,2  |6    By.Cy              4,5 MP
 1,2  |7    Cy                 6 Drop
   2  |8    Py                 3 Drop
 1,2  |9    Py.Cy              7,8 Join
 1,2  |10   ∃z(Pz.Cz)          9 EG
```

Answers to E VIII 1 (continued)

*5.
```
   1  | 1   ∀x((Cx v ~Gx) ⊃ Tx)
   2  | 2   ∃z(Bx.~Gz)           /∃x(Tx.Bx)
   2  | 3   By.~Gy               2 EIy
   1  | 4   (Cy v ~Gy) ⊃ Ty      1 UI
   2  | 5   ~Gy                  3 Drop
   2  | 6   Cy v ~Gy             5 Add
  1,2 | 7   Ty                   4,6 MP
   2  | 8   By                   3 Drop
  1,2 | 9   Ty.By                7,8 Join
  1,2 |10   ∃x(Tx.Bx)            9 EG
```

*6.
```
   1   | 1   ∃xAx ⊃ ∀y(Cy ⊃ By)
   2   | 2   ∀x(Gx ⊃ (Ax.Cx))        /∀x(Gx ⊃ Bx)
   3   | 3   Gx                      S
   2   | 4   Gx ⊃ (Ax.Cx)            2 UI
  2,3  | 5   Ax.Cx                   3,4 MP
  2,3  | 6   Ax                      5 Drop
  2,3  | 7   ∃xAx                    6 EG
 1,2,3 | 8   ∀y(Cy ⊃ By)             1,7 MP
 1,2,3 | 9   Cx ⊃ Bx                 8 UI
  2,3  |10   Cx                      5 Drop
 1,2,3 |11   Bx                      9,10 MP
  1,2  |12   Gx ⊃ Bx                 3,11 SQ
  1,2  |13   ∀x(Gx ⊃ Bx)             12 UGx
```

*7.
```
   1  | 1   ∃x(Wx.Sx)
   2  | 2   ∃x(Ex.Sx)        /∃x(Wx.Ex.Sx)
   1  | 3   Wy.Sy            1 EI y
   1  | 4   Wy               3 Drop
   2  | 5   Ey.Sy            2 EI y     (y flagged twice!)
  1,2 | 6   Wy.Ey.Sy         4,5 Join   "Deduction" for invalid inference
  1,2 | 7   ∃x(Wx.Ex.Sx)     6 EG       disregarding safeguard rule
```

Note: Invalidity may be more apparent for the following readings:
Wx: x is western, Ex: x is eastern, Sx: x is a state

Answers to E VIII 2

*1. To prove: $(\forall xFx.P) \supset \forall x(Fx.P)$

      1∣1 $\forall xFx.P$ S
      1∣2   P   1 Drop
      1∣3 $\forall xFx$ 1 Drop
      1∣4   Fx   3 UI
      1∣5   Fx.P   2,4 Join
      1∣6 $\forall x(Fx.P)$ 5 UGx
       ∣7 $(\forall xFx.P) \supset \forall x(Fx.P)$ 1,6 SQ

*3. If anyone enters, Clyde is trapped.

    b. $\exists xEx \supset Tc$ A   Tc is blind to x, recall
    c. $\forall x(Ex \supset Tc)$ A* $\forall x(Ex \supset P) \Leftrightarrow \exists xEx \supset P$

*4. If anyone enters, he is a suspect.

    b. $\forall x(Ex \supset Sx)$ A*

*5. Everyone is safe unless Clyde has escaped.

    a. $\forall xSx \vee Ec$ A*
    b. $\forall x(Sx \vee Ec)$ A   (Extending scope over blind Ec, past $\vee$)
    e. $\forall x(\sim Ec \supset Sx)$ A   (Extending scope over blind $\sim$Ec, past $\supset$)

*6. If someone enters, Clyde hides.

    b. $\forall x(Ex \supset Hc)$ A
    c. $\exists xEx \supset Hc$ A*   (Better, because "someone" suggests "$\exists x$")

*9. If someone enters, he is in danger.

    d. $\forall x(Ex \supset Dx)$ A*   ("Someone" in antecedent, <u>without</u> blind
                                   consequent acts like "anyone"(≠"every") in English)

Answers for E VIII 3

*1. *b.
```
1|1   ∀x(Fx.Gx)                    S
1|2   Fx.Gx                        1 UI
1|3   Fx                           2 Drop
1|4   ∀xFx                         3 UG x
1|5   Fy.Gy                        1 UI        2nd UI provides different variable so
1|6   Gy                           5 Drop      that 2nd UG does not double flag
1|7   ∀xGx                         6 UG y
1|8   ∀xFx.∀xGx                    4,7 Join
 |9   ∀x(Fx.Gx) ⊃ (∀xFx.∀xGx)      1,8 SQ
```

*e.
```
1|1    ∃xFx v ∃xGx                    S
2|2    ∃xFx                           S
2|3    Fy                             2 EI y
2|4    Fy v Gy                        3 Add
2|5    ∃x(Fx v Gx)                    4 EG
 |6    ∃xFx ⊃ ∃x(Fx v Gx)             2,5 SQ
7|7    ∃xGx                           S
7|8    Gz                             7 EI z
7|9    Fz v Gz                        8 Add
7|10   ∃x(Fx v Gx)                    9 EG
 |11   ∃xGx ⊃ ∃x(Fx v Gx)             7,10 SQ
1|12   ∃x(Fx v Gx)                    1,6,12 Dcomp
 |13   (∃xFx v ∃xGx) ⊃ ∃x(Fx v Gx)    1,12 SQ
```

*f.
```
1|1    ∀x∀y(Fx v Gy)                   S
1|2    ∀y(Fx v Gy)                     1 UI
1|3    Fx v Gy                         2 UI
4|4    Fx                              S
4|5    ∀xFx                            4 UG x
5|6    Gy                              S
5|7    ∀xGx                            6 UG y
 |8    Fx ⊃ ∀xFx                       4,5 SQ
 |9    Gy ⊃ ∀xGx                       6,7 SQ
1|10   ∀xFx v ∀xGx                     3,8,9 Dplex
 |11   ∀x∀y(Fx v Gy) ⊃ (∀xFx v ∀xGx)   1,10 SQ
```

*2 a.
```
  1|1   ∀x(Fx ⊃ Gx)     P
  2|2   ∀xFx            P
  1|3   ∀xFx ⊃ ∀xGx     1 QF
1,2|4   ∀xGx            2,3 MP
```
(Usual deduction needs 6 lines)

b.
```
  1|1   ∃xFx v ∃xGx           P
  2|2   ∀x((Fx v Gx) ⊃ Pb)    P
  1|3   ∃x(Fx v Gx)           1 QF
  2|4   ∃x(Fx v Gx) ⊃ Pb      2 QP
1,2|5   Pb                    3,4 MP
```
(Usual deduction takes 16 lines)

Answers for E VIII 4

5. *g. ∃xFx ⊃ ∃xGx
       ~∃xFx v ∃xGx   Mif
       ∀x ~Fx v ∃xGx   QN
       ∀x ~Fx v ∃yGy   RBV
       ∀x(~Fx v ∃yGy)   Q Pas.
       ∀x∃y(~Fx v Gy)   Q Pas.
       ∀x∃y(Fx ⊃ Gy)   (optional)

   *h. ∀xFx ≡ ∀xGx
       (∀xFx.∀xGx) v (~∀xFx.~∀xGx)   Eqo
       (∀xFx.∀xGx) v (∃x~Fx.∃x~Gx)   QN
       (∀xFx.∀yGy) v (∃z~Fz.∃w~Gw)   RBV
       ∀x∀y∃z∃w((Fx.Gy) v (~Fz.~Gw))
                                       (second method)

Answers to E IX 1

1. *a. (Py.Ryay) v ∃xSxby
   *b. Unchanged. All occurrence of x are bound.
   *c. Unchanged. No occurrences of x.
   *d. (∀xRxy v ∀yRyy.∃zRyy)
          ↑   ↑
       bound   captured

2. *a. Rxyw   Distinct
   *b. Rxyx   Not distinct
   *c. ∃xHxx   Not distinct (and not clear; x captured)
   *d. ∃xKxx ⊃ Szx   Neither distinct nor clear

3. *a. Line 3 is not an instance of the scope in line 4.
       Hence 4 is not a correct EG.
   *b. EI may not be to a name.
   *c. w has not been substituted for every free occurrence of x
       in Pxy ⊃ Gxzx.
   *d. Not clear; y is captured.
   *e. Correct. Distinct instance.
   *f. Incorrect. Premiss is only an if-sentence with a universal
       antecedent. One may not apply UI to a proper component
       of a line.

A 355

Answers to E IX 2

*1. Some of the steps below are correct. Others violate safeguards. Mark
each correct or cite the specific violation.

C   a. | ∀x∃yRxyz | ∀xC
        | ∃yRzyz   UI | C(z/x)   Clear, but not distinct. OK for UI.

X   b. | ∃yRzyz | C(z/x) Not distinct, as needed for UG.
        | ∀x∃yRxyz UGz | ∀xC

C   c. | ∃yRzyz | C(z/x) Clear, but not distinct. OK for EG.
        | ∃x∃yRxyz EG | ∃xC

C   d. | ∃yRzyz | ∃yC   (Instantial vbl same as quantified vbl.)
        | Rzyz   EIyz | C(y/y)

X   e. | ∀x(Rxy ⊃ Hxbyz) | ∀xC
        | Ryy ⊃ Hybyx UI | No instance. Incomplete substitution.

X   f. | ∀x(∃y(Rzy v Rxz) ⊃ Px) | ∀xC
        | ∃y(Rzy v Ryz) ⊃ Py   UI | C(y/x) Not clear.
              ↖—captured

X   g. | Rxyz   Rxyz is not an instance of Rzyz - not obtainable by subst.
        | ∃zRzyz   EG

X   h. | ∀x∀yRxy ⊃ Ryx   Attempted UI from partial line, antecedent only.
        | ∀xRxy ⊃ Ryx   UI

C   i. | ∃yRxz   OK despite vacuous ∃y.
        | ∀x∃yRxz   UGxz
              ╭—— capt.
X   j. | ∀xRxyz   C(x/w) Not clear.
        | ∀w∀xRwyz UGxz ∀wC

X   k. | ∀x∀y(Rxy ⊃ Ryx)   Attempted partial line UI, dropping internal ∀y.
        | ∀x(Rxy ⊃ Ryx) UI

X   l. | ∃xRxb   Attempted UG from a name.
        | ∀y∃xRxy   UGb

X   m. | ∃yRzyz
        | Rzxz   EIyz Wrong variable flagged. The instantial vbl is x.

X   n. | Ryz
        | ∀xRxz   UGxz Wrong variable flagged. The instantial vbl is y.

Answers to E IX 2 (continued)

3. *a.

1	1	$\exists x(Px.\forall y(Dy \supset \sim Lxy))$	
2	2	$\exists x(Px.Dx)$	/$\exists x(Px.\sim\forall y(Py \supset Lyx))$
1	3	$Pw.\forall y(Dy \supset \sim Lwy)$	1 EIw
2	4	$Pz.Dz$	2 EIz
5	5	$\forall y(Py \supset Lyz)$	S
5	6	$Pw \supset Lwz$	5 UI
1	7	$\forall y(Dy \supset \sim Lwy)$	3 Drop
1	8	$Dz \supset \sim Lwz$	7 UI
2	9	Dz	4 Drop
1,2	10	$\sim Lwz$	8,9 MP
1	11	Pw	3 Drop
1,5	12	Lwz	6,11 MP
1,2	13	$\sim \forall y(Py \supset Lyz)$	5,10,12 SA
2	14	Pz	4 Drop
1,2	15	$Pz.\sim\forall y(Py \supset Lyz)$	13,14 Join
1,2	16	$\exists x(Px.\sim\forall y(Py \supset Lyx))$	15 EG

b.

1	1	$\forall x(Axx \supset Cx)$	
2	2	$\forall x\forall y(Cy \supset \sim Axy)$	/$\forall x\sim\forall y Ayx$
3	3	$\forall y Ayz$	S
3	4	Azz	3 UI
1	5	$Azz \supset Cz$	1 UI
1,3	6	Cz	4,5 MP
2	7	$\forall y(Cy \supset \sim Awy)$	2 UI
2	8	$Cz \supset \sim Awz$	7 UI
1,2,3	9	$\sim Awz$	6,8 MP
3	10	Awz	3 UI
1,2	11	$\sim \forall y Ayz$	3,9,10 SA
1,2	12	$\forall x\sim\forall y Ayx$	11 UGz

Answer Section

Answers to E X 1

*1. Proof (in H) of H1: $\forall x \forall y (Exy \equiv Eyx)$

```
H1 | 1  ∀x∀y(Exy ⊃ Eyx)        HI [Invoking]
   | 2  Euw ⊃ Ewu              1 UI (u/x)(w/y)
   | 3  Ewu ⊃ Euw              1 UI (w/x)(u/y)
   | 4  Euw ≡ Ewu              2,3 Ejoin
H1 | 5  ∀x∀y(Exy ≡ Eyx)        4 UG wu u
```

*2. Proof of H2: $\forall x \forall y (Hxy \supset \sim Hyx)$

```
HIV | 1  ∀x∀y(Hxy ≡ (∼Hyx.∼Exy))    HIV
    | 2  Hxy ≡ (∼Hyx.∼Exy)          1 UI (x/x)(y/y)
    | 3  Hxy ⊃ (∼Hyx.∼Exy)          2 Edrop
   4| 4  Hxy                        S
   4| 5  ∼Hyx.∼Exy                  3,4 MP
   4| 6  ∼Hyx                       5 Drop
    | 7  Hxy ⊃ ∼Hyx                 4,6 SQ
HIV | 8  ∀x∀y(Hxy ⊃ ∼Hyx)           7 UG yx x
```

Note that in the above, truth-functional steps were all explicit and uncombined. The following deduction summarizes them all as "T".

```
HIV | 1  ∀x∀y(Hxy ≡ (∼Hyx.∼Exy))    HIV
    | 2  Hxy ≡ (∼Hyx.∼Exy)          1 UI (x/x)(y/y)
    | 3  Hxy ⊃ ∼Hyx                 2 T
HIV | 4  ∀x∀y(Hxy ⊃ ∼Hyx)           3 UG yx x
```

A still shorter deduction results by writing line 2 above as obtained by applying UI to HIV, e.g.:

```
HIV | 1  Hxy ≡ (∼Hyx.∼Exy)          HIV UI [cited without invoking]
```

*3. Proof of H3: $\forall x \sim Hxx$

```
HIV | 1  ∀x∀y(Hxy ⊃ ∼Hyx)       H2 [previous result]
    | 2  Hxx ⊃ ∼Hxx             1 UI (x/x)(x/y)
    | 3  ∼Hxx v ∼Hxx            2 Mif  ⎫ combinable
    | 4  ∼Hxx                   3 Red  ⎭ as T
    | 5  ∀x ∼Hxx                4 UG x
```

Answers to E X 1 (continued)

*4. Proof of H4: $\forall x \forall y (Hxy \lor Exy \lor Hyx)$ (Weak Trichotomy)

```
HIV 1  Hxy ≡ (~Hyx.~Exy)         HIV UI (x/x)(y/y)
     2  (~Hyx.~Exy) ⊃ Hxy         1 Edrop    ⎫
     3  ~(~Hyx.~Exy) v Hxy        2 Mif      ⎬ combinable as T
     4  (Hyx v Exy) v Hyx         3 Nand(N)  ⎭
     5  (Exy v Hyx) v Hyx         4 Com
     6  Hxy v (Exy v Hyx)         5 Com
     7  ∀x∀y(Hxy v Exy v Hyx)     6 UG yx x
```

Hint: For H5 use H3 and H4.

Answers to EII 2

			Sym.	Trans.	Reflex
1.	*a.	parent of	-1	-1	-1
	*d.	outranks	-1	1	-1
	*e.	wife of	-1	1,-1	-1
	*g.	formally introduced	1	0	-1

		Sym.	Trans.	Reflex
2.	*a.	-1	1	-1
	*b.	1	-1	-1
	*g.	1,-1	1,-1	-1
	*h.	0	0	0

   Note that since someone who has a wife is never in turn a wife of anybody, the antecedent of the transitivity condition, (Wxy.Wyz) ⊃ Wxz, is always false. Therefore, the material if-then is always true. Wife-of is thus true, though <u>vacuously</u> so. Similarly, wife-of is vacuously intransitive. The idea is easily extended to informal talk about diagrams. Thus, if there are no tailgating pairs, the demand that every pair of tailgating arrows have a leapfrog arrow is said to be met vacuously also.
   Note that if a self-arrow represents Rbb, it would be pointless to draw a second self-arrow to represent Rbb.Rbb. Consequently, every self-arrow can be taken to represent a chain of tail-gating self-arrows, as long as desired. And since it can equally well represent a leapfrog arrow (from the "first" b to the "last"), a relation whose arrow diagram consists only of self-arrows counts as transitive. Similar reasons allow isolated self-arrows in the diagrams of other transitive relations, also (a hint for 2d).

Answers to E XI 1

*1. a. 1 ∀z(Pzw ⊃ ∃u(Fu.Ouz))
        2 ∀z(Pzw ⊃ ∃u(Fu.∃v(Pvu.Pvz)))   DfR O

    b. 1 ∀w∀z(∃y(Pyz.Pyw) ⊃ ∃x(Pxw.Pxz))
        2 ∀w∀z(Ozw ⊃ Owz)   DfR O (twice)

2. *a. Exy ≡ (~Hxy.~Hyx)   Df

    b. 1 ∀x∀y(Exy ⊃ Eyx)   I . H
        2 ∀x∀y((~Hxy.~Hyx) ⊃ Eyx)   2 DfR E
        3 ∀x∀y((~Hxy.~Hyx) ⊃ (~Hyx.~Hxy)) 3 DfR E

    Note 1. DfR steps may be combined. I.e., line 3 could be written
             as line 2.

    Note 2. Line 3 happens to be logically true (prove it to yourself)
             and hence need not be retained as an axiom of H-theory, as
             reformulated.

*4. Everyone is male or female; no one is both.

    (This axiom system may be investigated deductively, without
    deciding its biological truth.)

*5. D4 Dau(x,y) ≡ (Fe(x).Par(y,x))   Df
    D5 Son(x,y) ≡ (Ma(x).Par(y,x))   Df
    D6 Gpar(x,y) ≡ ∃z(Par(x,z).Par(z,y))   Df
    D7 Gmo(x,y) ≡ ∃z(Mo(x,z).Par(z,y))   Df
    D8 Gson(x,y) ≡ ∃z(Son(x,z).Ch(zy))   Df

*6. To prove: ∀x∀y(Par(x,y) ⊃ (Fa(x,y) v Mo(x,y)))

    1 | 1 Par(x,y)   S
       | 2 Ma(x) v Fe(x)   IK UI
    3 | 3 Ma(x)   S
    1,3| 4 Ma(x).Par(x,y)   1,3 Join
    1,3| 5 Fa(x,y)   4 DfR Fa
    6 | 6 Fe(x)   S
    1,6| 7 Fe(x).Par(x,y)   1,6 Join
    1,6| 8 Mo(x,y)   7 DfR Mo
    1 | 9 Ma(x) ⊃ Fa(x,y)   3,5 SQ
    1 |10 Fe(x) ⊃ Mo(x,y)   6,8 SQ
    1 |11 Fa(x,y) v Mo(x,y)   2,9,10 Dplex
       |12 Par(x,y) ⊃ (Fa(x,y) v Mo(x,y)) 1,11 SQ
       |13 [Theorem]   12 UG yx x (Twice)

Answers to E XII 1

*1. Brooks distrusts everyone but himself.
    $\forall x(x \neq b \supset Dbx)$

*2. Brooks admires only himself.
    $\forall x(Abx \supset x=b)$

*3. Trapp and someone else had the combination.
    $Ct . \exists x(x \neq t . Cx)$

*4. No one other than Fitch could have escaped.
    $\forall x(Ex \supset x=f)$, or $\forall x(x \neq f \supset {\sim} Ex)$

*5. Tully and Cicero were one and the same individual.
    $t=c$

*6. One's brother is never identical with oneself.
    $\forall x \forall y (Bxy \supset x \neq y)$

Answers to E XII 2

*1. | 1 | 1 | $t=c$ | /Btc |
     | 2 | 2 | $\forall x {\sim} Bxx$ | |
     | 2 | 3 | ${\sim} Btt$ | 2 UI |
     | 1,2 | 4 | ${\sim} Btc$ | 1,3 IR |

*6. | 1 | 1 | $x=y$ | S |
     | | 2 | $x=x$ | I |
     | 1 | 3 | $y=x$ | 1,2 IR (substituting y into 2nd line) |
     | | 4 | $x=y \supset y=x$ | 1,3 SQ |

*7. | 1 | 1 | $x=y . y=z$ | S |
     | 1 | 2 | $x=y$ | 1 Drop |
     | 1 | 3 | $y=z$ | 1 Drop |
     | 1 | 4 | $x=z$ | 2,3 IR |
     | | 5 | $(x=y . y=z) \supset x=z$ | 1,4 SQ |

*8. | 1 | 1 | $\exists x(Fx . x=y)$ | S |
     | 1 | 2 | $Fz . z=y$ | 1 EI z (x would do as well as z) |
     | 1 | 3 | Fz | 2 Drop |
     | 1 | 4 | $z=y$ | 2 Drop |
     | 1 | 5 | Fy | 3,4 IR |
     | | 6 | $\exists x(Fx . x=y) \supset Fy$ | 1,5 SQ |

Answers to E XII 2 (continued)

*9.
```
1|1  Fy                    S
 |2  y=y                   I
1|3  Fy.y=y                1,2 Join
1|4  ∃x(Fx.x=y)            3 EG
 |5  Fy ⊃ ∃x(Fx.x=y)       1,4 SQ
```

*10.
```
1|1  ∀x(x=y ⊃ Fy)          S
1|2  y=y ⊃ Fy              1 UI
 |3  y=y                   I
1|4  Fy                    2,3 MP
 |5  ∀x(x=y ⊃ Fy) ⊃ Fy     1,4 SQ
```

Answers to E XII 3

*1. Everybody has exactly two parents.

∀x∃2yPyx
∀x∃y∃z(Pyx.Pzx.y≠z.∀w(Pw ⊃ (w=y v w=z)))
∀x∃y∃z(y≠z.∀w(Pwx ⊃ (w=y v w=z)))

Answers to E XIII 1

*1 a. Sib(x,y) ≡ (x≠y.∃z∃w(Par(z,x).Par(z,y).Par(w,x).Par(w,y).z≠w)   Df

    b. Bro(x,y) ≡ (Ma(x).Sib(x,y))   Df

    c. Sis(x,y) ≡ (Fe(x).Sib(x,y))   Df

    d. Co(x,y) ≡ ∃z∃w (Par(z,x).Sib(z,w).Par(w,y))   Df

Answers to E XIII 2

1. One-One ⎧ *Transitive: =
           ⎩ *Intransitive: husband-of

Answers to E XIV 1   Answer Section

*1. a. $\forall x(Ex \supset E(sx))$ Squares of even numbers are even.

     b. $\forall x E(dx)$ The double of any number is even.

     c. $\forall x E(s(dx))$ The square of the double of any number is even.

*2.
```
1  | 1  ∀x(Ex ⊃ E(sx))
 2 | 2  ∀xE(dx)                /∀xE(s(dx))
 2 | 3  E(dx)                   2  UI
 1 | 4  E(dx) ⊃ E(s(dx))        1  UI (dx/x)
1,2| 5  E(s(dx))                3,4 MP
1,2| 6  ∀xE(s(dx))              5  UG x
```

*3.
```
| 1  fx=fx            I
| 2  ∃y(y=fx)         1 EG    (parens for visual grouping, only)
| 3  ∀x∃y(y=fx)       2 UG x
```

*4.
```
1 | 1  y=fx.z=fx                           S
1 | 2  y=fx                                1 Drop
1 | 3  z=fx                                1 Drop
1 | 4  y=z                                 2,3 IR
  | 5  (y=fx.z=fx) ⊃ y=z                   1,4 SQ
  | 6  ∀x∀y∀z((y=fx.z=fx) ⊃ y=z)           5 UG zyx yx x
```

*7.
```
1 | 1  x=3            /s(x)=s(3)
  | 2  s(x)=s(x)      I
1 | 3  s(x)=s(3)      1,2 IR
```

Note: Although a mathematics book would call this squaring both sides, its validity rests not on mathematics, but on QIF logic. One should beware, however, of stepping from fx=fy to x=y. It is not a QIF step. Notice that s(3)=s(-3) but 3≠-3.

*9. A sentence logically implies any disjunction of which it is the first member.

*10. A contradiction logically implies every sentence.

Answers to E XIV 1 (continued)

*11. The conjunction of a sentence, with an implication of which it is the antecedent, logically implies the consequent of the implication. (The principle of Modus Ponens)

*12. True sentences logically imply only true sentences.

*13. A disjunction whose first member is a conjunction of the negation of one sentence and a second sentence and the first sentence is logically equivalent to a disjunction of the second and first sentences. (One of the (3/2) absorption laws)

Answer Section

Answers to E XV 1

*1
	1	1	∀Z(V(Z) ⊃ Z(a))	
	2	2	V(H)	/H(a)
	1	3	V(H) ⊃ H(a)	1 UI H/Z
	1,2	4	H(a)	2,3 MP

*2.
	1	1	Sb	
	2	2	H(S)	/∃X(H(X).X(b))
	1,2	3	H(S).Sb	1,2 Join
	1,2	4	∃X(H(X).X(b))	3 EG

*3.
	1	1	∀Z((A(Z).Z(j)) ⊃ Z(b))	
	2	2	∀Y((A(Y).Y(c)) ⊃ Y(j))	/∀X((A(X).X(c)) ⊃ X(b))
	1	3	(A(Z).Z(j)) ⊃ Z(b)	1 UI
	2	4	(A(Z).Z(c)) ⊃ Z(j)	2 UI (Z/Y)
	5	5	A(Z).Z(c)	S
	2,5	6	Z(j)	4,S MP
	5	7	A(Z)	5 Drop
	2,5	9	A(Z).Z(j)	6,7 Join
	1,2,5	10	Z(b)	3,9 MP
	1,2	11	(A(Z).Z(c)) ⊃ Z(b)	5,10 SQ
	1,2	12	∀X((A(X).X(c)) ⊃ X(b))	11 UG Z

*4.
	1	1	∃Z(A(Z).∀x(Mx ⊃ Zx))	(omitting obvious parens)
	2	2	∃x(Px.∀Y(A(Y) ⊃ ~Yx))	/∃x(Px.~Mx)
	2	3	Px.∀Y(A(Y) ⊃ ~Yx)	2 EI x
	1	4	A(Z).∀x(Mx ⊃ Zx)	1 EI Z
	2	5	∀Y(A(Y) ⊃ ~Yx)	3 Drop
	2	6	A(Z) ⊃ ~Zx	5 UI (Z/Y)
	1	7	A(Z)	4 Drop
	1,2	8	~Zx	6,7 MP
	1	9	∀x(Mx ⊃ Zx)	4 Drop
	1	10	Mx ⊃ Zx	9 UI
	1,2	11	~Mx	8, 10 MT
	2	12	Px	3 Drop
	1,2	13	Px.~Mx	11, 12 Join
	1,2	14	∃x(Px.~Mx)	13 EG

*5.
	1	1	Gf.Gs	
	2	2	V(G)	
	3	3	∀x∀y(∃Z(V(Z).Zx.Zy) ⊃ Sxy)	/Sfs.Ssf
	3	4	∃Z(V(Z).Zf.Zs) ⊃ Sfs	3 UI(f/x(s/y)
	3	5	∃Z(V(Z).Zs.Zf) ⊃ Ssf	3 UI(s/x)(f/y)
	1,2	6	V(G).Gf.Gs	1,2 Join
	1,2	7	∃Z(V(Z).Zf.Zs)	6 EG
	1,2,3	8	Sfs	4,7 MP
	1,2	9	V(G).Gs.Gf	1,2 T (Com, Join)
	1,2	10	∃Z(V(Z).Zs.Zf)	9 EG
	1,2,3	11	Ssf	5,10 MP
	1,2,3	12	Sfs.Ssf	8,11 Join

Answers to E XV 1 (continued)

*6.

1	1	$\exists Y(\forall x(Yx \supset Lax).\exists z(Yz.\sim Az))$	/$\exists x \exists y\ (\sim Ax.Ryx)$
2	2	$\forall x \forall y(Lxy \supset Rxy)$	1 EI Y
1	3	$\forall x(Yx \supset Lax).\exists z(Yz.\sim Az)$	3 Drop
1	4	$\forall x(Yx \supset Lax)$	3 Drop
1	5	$\exists z(Yz.\sim Az)$	5 EI z Y
1	6	$Yz.\sim Az$	6 Drop
1	7	Yz	4 UI z/x
1	8	$Yz \supset Laz$	7,8 MP
1	9	Laz	2 UI (a/x)(z/y)
2	10	$Laz \supset Raz$	9,10 MP
1,2	11	Raz	6 Drop
1	12	$\sim Az$	11,12 Join
1,2	13	$\sim Az.Raz$	13 EG
1,2	14	$\exists y(\sim Az.Ryz)$	14 EG
1,2	15	$\exists x \exists y\ (\sim Ax.Ryx)$	

Answer Section

Answers to E XV 2

*1.
a. $\forall x(Rwx \supset Ryw)$
b. $\forall x(Ryx \supset Ryy)$ clear though not distinct
c. $\forall w(Rxw \supset Ryx)$ Here relettering (RBV) has been necessary to avoid capture of x.
d. Some of the LPA steps that would be possible:

$[\lambda z \forall x(Rzx \supset Ryx)] z$
$[\lambda w \forall x(Rwx \supset Ryx)] z$
$[\lambda w \forall x(Rzx \supset Rwx)] y$

e. $\forall x \exists w(Ryx \supset Rwz)$ Here the existential quantification must be relettered (RBV) to avoid capture of y.
f. Possible LPA steps:

$[\lambda z \exists x(Bxz.Rzyz)] c$
$[\lambda z \exists x(Bxz.Rcyz)] c$
$[\lambda z \exists x(Bxc.Rczc)] y$

*2a.
1	1	$D(\lambda x \exists y Fxy)$	
2	2	$\forall x(Wx \supset Fbx)$	
3	3	$\forall x \forall Z((D(Z).Zx) \supset Sx)$	
4	4	Wb	/Sb
2	5	$Wb \supset Fbb$	2 UI
2,4	6	Fbb	4,5 T
2,4	7	$\exists y Fby$	6 EG
2,4	8	$[\lambda x \exists y Fxy] b$	7 LPA
3	9	$\forall Z((D(Z).Zb) \supset Sb)$	3 UI
3	10	$(D(\lambda x \exists y Fxy).[\lambda x \exists y Fxy] b) \supset Sb$	9 UI
1,2,3,4	11	Sb	1,8,10 T

Note: Overgenerously stated premises may validly lead to silly conclusions, of course.

*2b.
1	1	$\forall x(Vx \supset Dxx)$	
2	2	$C(\lambda x(Gx.\exists y Dxy))$	/$\forall x((Gx.Vx) \supset \exists Y(C(Y).Yx))$
3	3	Gx.Vx	S
1	4	$Vx \supset Dxx$	1 UI
1,3	5	Dxx	3,4 T
1,3	6	$\exists y Dxy$	5 EG
1,3	7	$Gx.\exists y Dxy$	3,6 T
1,3	8	$[\lambda x(Gx.\exists y Dxy)] x$	7 LPA
1,2,3	9	$C(\lambda x(Gx.\exists y Dxy).[\lambda x(Gx.\exists y Dxy)] x$	2,8 T
1,2,3	10	$\exists Y(C(Y).Yx)$	9 EG
1,2	11	$(Gx.Vx) \supset \exists Y(C(Y).Yx)$	3,10 SQ
1,2	12	$\forall x((Gx.Vx) \supset \exists Y(C(Y).Yx))$	11 UG x

Note: This misleadingly rosy inference stems from the weakness of of the second premiss, which would be more plausible, and less generous, if 'else' were inserted after 'somebody'.

Answers to E XV 2 continued

*3. a. Everything has some property. $\forall x \exists F\, Fx$

   b. There is some property everything has. $\exists F \forall x\, Fx$

   c. Not all properties have instances. $\sim \forall F \exists x\, Fx$

   d. There is some property which nothing has. $\exists F \forall x \sim Fx$

   e. Every two things have a property in common.
        $\forall x \forall y \exists F(Fx.Fy)$.

   f. For every two distinct things there is a property which the first has but the second lacks.
        $\forall x \forall y (x \neq y \supset \exists F(Fx. \sim Fy))$

4. a.
   1 $x=x$ I
   2 $[\lambda y(y=y)]\, x$ 1 LPA
   3 $\exists F\, Fx$ 2 EG
   4 $\forall x \exists F\, Fx$ 3 UG x

   b.
   1 $x=x$ I
   2 $[\lambda y(y=y)]\, x$ 1 LPA   Note: $\lambda y(y=y)$ is an example of a
   3 $\forall x [\lambda y(y=y)]\, x$ 2 UG x   <u>universal property</u>.
   4 $\exists F \forall x\, Fx$ 3 EG

   c.
   1 | 1 $\forall F \exists x Fx$ S
   1 | 2 $\exists x [\lambda y\, y \neq y] x$ 1 UI
   1 | 3 $\exists x (x \neq x)$ 2 LPR
   1 | 4 $x \neq x$ 3 EI x
     | 5 $x = x$ I
     | 6 $\sim \forall F \exists x Fx$ 1,4,5 SA

   d.
   | 1 $x = x$ I
   | 2 $\sim x \neq x$ 1 T
   | 3 $\sim [\lambda y(y \neq y)]\, x$ 2 LPA   Note: $\lambda y(y \neq y)$ is an example of an
   | 4 $\forall x \sim [\lambda y(y \neq y)]\, x$ 3 UG x   uninstantiated, <u>empty</u>, or <u>null</u>
   | 5 $\exists F \forall x \sim Fx$ 4 EG   property.

Answers to E XV 2 continued

4. e.
    1 x=x   I
    2 y=y   I
    3 [λz(z=z)] x   1 LPA
    4 [λz(z=z)] y   2 LPA
    5 [λz(z=z)] x.[λz(z=z)] y   3,4 T
    6 ∃F(Fx.Fy)   5 EG
    7 ∀x∀y∃F(Fx.Fy)   6 UG yx x

   f. 1| 1 x≠y   S
       | 2 x=x   I
       | 3 [λz(x=z)] x   2 LPA
     4| 4 [λz(x=z)] y   S
     4| 5 x=y   4 LPR
     1| 6 ∼[λz(x=z)] y   4,1,5 SA
     1| 7 [λz(x=z)] x.∼[λz(x=z)] y 3,6 T
     1| 8 ∃F(Fx.∼Fy)   7 EG
      | 9 x≠y ⊃ ∃F(Fx.∼Fy)   1,8 SQ
      |10 ∀x∀y(x≠y ⊃ ∃F(Fx.∼Fy)) 9 UG yx x

Answer Section

Answers to E XVI 1

*1. Bigamy is the property of being married to more than one person
    All bigamists are married

```
1   | 1   B = λx∃y∃z (y≠x.Mxy.Mxz)       P
2   | 2   Bx                              S
1,2 | 3   [λx∃y∃z(y≠z.Mxy.Mxz)] x         1,2 IR
1,2 | 4   ∃y∃z(y≠z.Mxy.Mxz)               3 LPR
1,2 | 5   y≠z.Mxy.Mxz                     4EI yx zyx
1,2 | 6   Mxy                             5 T
1,2 | 7   ∃yMxy                           6 EG
1   | 8   Bx ⊃ ∃yMxy                     2,7 SQ
1   | 9   ∀x(Bx ⊃ ∃yMxy)                  8 UG x
```

*2. To prove: Thm. of logic: F=λxFx

```
|1  Fy ≡ Fy                T
|2  ∀x(Fx ≡ Fx)             1 UG y
|3  ∀x(Fx ≡ [λxFx]x)        2 LPA
|4  F=λxFx                  3 PX
```

*3. To prove: Thm. of logic: ∀x(Fx ≡ Gx) ≡ (F=λxGx)

```
1  | 1   ∀x(Fx ≡ Gx)                S
   | 2   F=G                         1 PX
   | 3   G=λxGx                      Result of 2 Invoked
   | 4   F=λxGx                      2,3 IR
   | 5   ∀x(Fx ≡ Gx) ⊃ (F=λxGx)      1,4 SQ
6  | 6   F=λxGx                      S
   | 7   Fx ≡ Fx                     T
6  | 8   Fx ≡ [λxGx]x                6, 7 IR
6  | 9   Fx ≡ Gx                     8 LPR
6  |10   ∀x(Fx ≡ Gx)                 9 UG x
   |11   (F=λxGx) ⊃ ∀x(Fx ≡ Gx)      6, 10 SQ
   |12   ∀x(Fx ≡ Gx) ≡ (F=λxGx)      5, 11 E Join
```

Note: This is an important theorem of higher logic, in that it permits one to use a highly explicit form of definition. Instead of displaying a definiendum predicate, e..g, Oxy, with its trailing argument variables, one may display the definiendum predicate alone, e.g., O=λxy∃z(Pzx.Pzy) Df.(to be sure, this example uses a lambda on two variables. But the principle is the same, as will be seen when PX and the lambda rules are suitably extended.)

*4. To prove: Thm of Logic: $x=y \equiv \forall F(Fx \supset Fy)$

	1	$x=y$	S
	2	Fx	S
1,2	3	Fy	1,2 IR
1	4	$Fx \supset Fy$	2,3 SQ
1	5	$\forall F(Fx \supset Fy)$	4 UG Fxy
	6	$x=y \supset \forall F(Fx \supset Fy)$	1,5 SQ
7	7	$\forall F(Fx \supset Fy)$	S
7	8	$[\lambda z(x=z)]x \supset [\lambda z(x=z)]y$	7 UI ($\lambda z(x=z) / F$)
7	9	$x=x \supset x=y$	8 LPR twice
	10	$x=x$	I
7	11	$x=y$	9,10 T
	12	$\forall F(Fx \supset Fy) \supset x=y$	7,11 SQ
	13	$x=y \equiv \forall F(Fx \supset Fy)$	6,12 EJoin

Note: The clause $x=y \equiv \forall F(Fx \supset Fy)$ could be taken as a definition of identity, in higher logic. It is so taken in some systems, in fact, since it 'purges' such systems of any 'subject-matter' sign which might be subject to the suspicion of being a non-logical sign. Nevertheless, identity will be retained as a basic sign, with its rules I and IR, in the present system because of its convenience. Its logical status may be thought of as vindicated by the above theorem.

Answers to E XVI 2

*1. a. $D = \Lambda$
    b. $A \cap R \neq \Lambda$
    c. $(R \cap A) \subset H$
    d. $(R \cap A) \subset -H$
    e. $M \subset (R \cup D)$
    f. $(H \cup C) \subset M$

Answers Section

Answers to E XVII 1

*1.
1		1	f=g	S
		2	fx=fx	I
1		3	fx=gx	1,2 IR
1		4	∀x(Fx=gx)	3 UG x
		5	f=g ⊃ ∀x(fx=gx)	1,4 SQ

*2. Since x,y,z is an argument of type 0,0,0, f and g must both be of some type (0,0,0:t)   since their values could be of any type t.

*3.
1		1	f=g	S
		2	fxyz=fxyz	I
1		3	fxyz=gxyz	1,2 IR
1		4	∀x∀y∀z(fxyz=gxyz)	UG zyx yx x
		5	f=g ⊃ ∀x∀y∀z(fxyz=gxyz)	1,4 SQ

Note that   analogues of this result can be shown similarly for functions of all function-types, for arguments of corresponding types. Also, analogues for the theorems proved in E VII 2,*4 and E VIII 1,*3 can be given proofs, similarly, for other compatible types.

*4.
	1	Fx ≡ Fx	T
	2	[λyFy]x ≡ Fx	1 LPA
	3	∀x([λyFy]x ≡ Fx)	2 UG x F
	4	∃G∀x(Gx ≡ Fx)	3 EG
	5	∀F∃G∀x(Gx ≡ Fx)	4 UG F

Note: the theorem proved on line 5, and its analogues for other types, are of central importance for higher logics. They have been called laws of __comprehension__ or of __class-formation__, and will be discussed in the following.

*5.
1		1	∀F∃y∀x(Rxy ≡ Fx)	S
1		2	∃y∀x(Rxy ≡ [λy ~Ryy] x)	1 UI
1		3	∃y∀x(Rxy ≡ ~Rxx)	2 LPR
1		4	∀x(Rxy ≡ ~Rxx)	3 EI y
1		5	Ryy ≡ ~Ryy	4 UI
1		6	Ryy ⊃ ~Ryy	5 E drop
1		7	~Ryy ⊃ Ryy	5 E drop
1		8	~Ryy v ~Ryy	6 Mif
1		9	Ryy v Ryy	7 Mif(N)
1		10	~Ryy	8 Red
1		11	Ryy	9 Red
		12	~∀F∃y∀x(Rxy ≡ Fx)	1,8,9 SA

Note: Line 5 is an important form of contradiction. Lines 6-11 are detailed for complete clarity.

Detailed Contents

I. <u>Preliminary Conceptions.</u>

    1. <u>Inference</u> (Premiss, Conclusion   1

    2. <u>Deduction and Induction</u>   2
        Deduction   2
        Induction   3
        Hypothetico-deductive method   4

    3. <u>Truth and Falsity</u>   5
        Evidence and Shades of Gray   5
        Negation (negative prefixes)   6

    4. <u>Relations Between Truth and Validity</u> (of Inference)   7
        Arguments   8

    Exercises I 1 (True-False)   11
    (Optional Further Reading)

    <u>Complete Sentences and Relative Truth</u>   12

    <u>Vagueness and Ambiguity</u>   13

    <u>Accuracy and Truth</u>   14

    <u>The Weight of Evidence and Rational Belief</u>   15

II. <u>Stepwise Deduction.</u>

    1. <u>Keeping Track</u>   18
        Step, Line, Citation, Premiss Numbers   19
    <u>Exercises II 1</u> (Step-tracing using premiss numbers)   21

    2. <u>Justifying Steps by Rules</u>   22
        <u>Elimination</u> (Elim)   22
        <u>Modus Ponens</u> (MP)   22
        <u>Modus Tollens</u> (MT)   23
        <u>Dougle Negation</u> (Equivalence Rule (N)   24
            Combined (N) Step
    <u>Exercises II 2</u> (Deductions)   26

	3. Reasoning from Suppositions	27
	Rule of Supposition (S)	
	Discharge as Qualification (SQ)	
	Discharge as Absurd (SA)	
	Dilemmas	
	Simple (Dsimp), Compound (Dcomp), Complex(Dplex)	32
	Exercises II 3 (Deductions using Suppositions)	33
	4. Compounds and Their Logic	
	Grouping, Parentheses	35
	Kinds of Rules Stipulation (P,S),	
	Implication (Elim, MP, MT, D-rules),	
	Equivalence (N), Discharge (SQ,SA)	36
	Drop	36
	Join	37
	Add	37
	Overview of Rules (Table)	38
	Exercises II 4 (Deductions (in Symbols))	39
III.	Basing Validity on Meaning	
	1. The Meanings of Connectives as Truth Functions	40
	Negation	40
	Conjunction	41
	Disjunction (material, logical, etc.)	43
	Equivalence (m aterial, logical, etc.)	44
	Summary of Truth Rules (Tables)	45
	Evaluating Method	46
	Exercises III 1 (Evaluating)	47
	2. Validity Based on Truth Table Relationships	48
	Method, Displaying Basic Truth-Value Combinations	49
	Construction of the Characteristic Truth Column	
	of a Sentence	50
	Exercises III 2 (Testing Validity by Truth Tables)	52
	3. Logical Equivalence	53
	Contraposition	54
	De Morgan Laws (Nor and Nand)	54
	Mif, Nif, Eqi, Ego	55
	Exercises III 3 (Testing, L-equivalence, Direction of	
	L-implication, Internalizing Negations, Expressing	
	in $\sim$, ., v)	57

4. Logically Determinate Sentences 59
    Tautology, Contradiction 59
    Logical Truth, Falsity 60
    Inferences and Their Principles 61
Exercises III-3 (Testing for Tautology, Contradiction, Neither) 63

Reference Table of Tautologies 64

(Optional Further Reading) 66

Other Connectives 66

All 16 Possible Binary Truth Functions (Table) 68

Interdefinabilities among Connectives 69

Defining Power of Sheffer Stroke, Pierce's Arrow 70

Optional Exercise III 5 (Reexpressing in other connectives) 72

Possible Ternary Connectives, (Truth) functional completeness, ... 73

"Exactly one of the following. . .," "otherwise" 74

IV. Using the Logic of Connectives.

1. Connectives in English Usage 77
Exercises IV 1 (Symbolizing sentences and arguments) 86

2. Partial Evaluation, Laws, and Contracts 87
Exercises IV 2 (Contract clause problems) 89

3. Testing Validity by the Loophole Method 92
    Summary in the Loophole Method 94
Exercises IV 3 (Loophole Problems) 95

4. Simplification 96
    Summary of Simplification Procedures (Table) 101
Exercises IV 4 (Simplification Problems) 102

V. A Deductive System for Connective Logic.

    1. Deductive Systems (Syntactical, Semantical concepts for $\Rightarrow$)   103

    2. Rules of this System   104
           Implication Rules (Table)   106
           Equivalence Rules (Table)   107

    3. Discussion of the Rules   108

    Exercises V 1 (Deductions for inferences given in words, sumbols)   110

    (Optional Further Reading)
        Derived Rules of Inference (rule extensions)   115
        Axiomatics (soundness, completeness)   117
        Optional Exercises V 2 (Derived rules for a sparer system   119
        Model Theory Concepts (for connective logic)   120

VI. Predication and Quantification.

    1. Predication   122
        Names, predicates of various degrees   124

    Exercises VI 1 (symbolizing 'factored' English)   126

    2. Quantification   127
        Variables, open and closed clauses, quantifiers   128
        Readings, Universe of Discourse   129
        Universal Instantiation (like Drop);
           Existential Generalization (like Add)   130
        Quantifier Negations like Nand, Nor   131

    3. Quantifying Compounds   132
        A,E,I,O sentences, the Square of Opposition   136
        Summary of Quantifier Rules So Far (Table)   139
    Exercises VI 2 (Symbolization, Deductions, Internalizing Negations)   140

    4. Diagrams and Classes   143
        Categorical Syllogisms   145
    Exercises VI 3 (Syllogisms by Venn Diagram)   149

    (Optional Further Reading)
        Quantifiers and Inductive Inference   150

VII. More Complex Quantification.

    1. Relational Quantifications   152

    2. Combining Quantifiers and Connectives   152

    Exercises VII 1 (Internalizing Negations of Multiple
       Quantifications, Symbolizations, Deductions)   155

    3. Syntax for Quantificational Symbolism   157
         Examples and Discussion of the Definitions   159
    Exercises VII 2 (Questions on clause, scope, open,
       closed)   161

    (Optional Further Reading)
       Finite Expansions   162
         Finite Expansions for [a,b] (Table)   163
       Optional Exercises VII 3 (Finite Expansions)   164

VIII. Further Methods.

    1. New Quantifier Rules: Hypothetical Individuals   166
       Existential Instantiation (EI)   167
       Universal Generalization (UG)   169
       Universal Instantiation (UI, and Existential
         Generalization (EG)   170
       Preliminary Safeguards   172
         Instances, Flagging Instantial Variables   173
           Preliminary Safeguard Rules: (No flagged
           variable reflagged, or free in last
           line or its premisses)   174
    Exercises VIII 1 (Deductions with New Rules, Safeguards)   176

    2. Quantifier Shifting (Past "Blind" Components,
       Proofs)   178
    Exercises VIII 2 (Proofs, Symbolizations with
       Shifted Quantifiers)   182

    3. Fission and Fusion of Quantifiers   183
       Logically True Forms (Table)   185
    Exercises VIII 3 (Proofs of Shift Laws,
       Proofs Using Shifts   186

4. Prenex Form 187
   Relettering Bound Variables (RBV) 188
   Rules for Transforming to Prenex Form 188
Exercises VIII 4 (Optional) Prenexing 189

Optional Further Reading
   Semantics for Q-Languages (Defining ⊨) 190

IX. Final Safeguards.

1. Variable Capture, Kinds of Instances 196
   Clear Instances, Distinct Instances, Capture 197
Exercises IX 1 (Drill on Instances) 199

2. Quantifier Order and Dependencies Among
   Hypothetical Individuals 200
   Semiflagged Variables 202
   Flag Test (Cross-Out) 203
   Summary of Safeguards for Q-Deductions 206
Exercises IX 2 (Spotting Safeguard Violations,
   Deductions, Proof 207

3. Transitional Steps 209
   The Rationale for Transitional UG
      and Crossout Test

X. Theories.

1. Deductive Development from Axioms 219

2. Broadening Deductive Methods 223
   Adding Rules (RBV) Combining Steps 224

Exercises X 1 (Heaviness Theory 227

3. Some Common Relational Properties 228
   Symmetry, Transitivity, Reflexivity,
      Arrow Diagrams 229

Exercises X 2 (Relational property problems) 230

XI. Definitions

    1. Definitions in Theory Development   233
          Rule for Definition (Df)   234
          Definitional Replacement (DfR)   236
    Exercises XI 1 (Kinship Theory)   239

XII. Identity and Number.

    1. Identity   241
          Rule of Identity (I) and Identity
              Replacement (IR)   242
    Exercises XII 1 (Symbolizations)   247

    2. QI Deduction   248
    Exercises XII 2 (Symbolizations, proofs)   250

    3. Number   251
          Numerical Quantifiers (At least, At most,
              Exactly)   252
    Exercises XII 3 (Symbolizations, deductions,
      Kinship Theory)   255

XIII. QI Theories

    1. QI Axioms on Relations   256
          One-Many, One-One, Antisymmetric,
              Aliotransitive Relations   257
    Exercises XIII 1 (Defining relations for Kinship
      Theory)   258

    2. Order   259
          Connexity, strict-, simple-linear Order   260
          Sequence   262
          Rank Order   264
          Equivalence Relations   267

    3. Partial Order.   268
    Exercises XIII 2 (Questions on order, Kinship   271
      deductions)

XIV. Functions.

    1. Functions and Functional Relations   272
    2. QIF Logic (Changes Needed from QI Logic)   274

	3. Defining Function Symbols	276
	4. The Problem of Partial Functions	279
	Exercises XIV 1 (Symbolizations, deductions, proofs)	280
XV.	Toward Higher Logic	
	1. Quantifying Predicate Variables	282
	Exercises XV 1 (Deductions)	288
	2. Abstraction	289
	Lambda Predicate Abstraction (LPA) and Reduction (LPR)	291
	Lambda step examples	293
	Exercises XV 2 (Lambda steps, deductions, symbolizations, proofs	295
XVI.	Extensionality	
	1. Extensions	297
	Rule of (1-Place) Predicate Extensionality (PX^1)	299
	Exercises XVI 1 (Deduction, Proofs)	300
	2. The Theory of Classes	301
	Union, Intersection, Complement	302
	Boolean Algebra	303
	Exercises XVI 2 (Symbolizations)	304
XVII.	A System of Higher Logic	
	1. The System	305
	Presentation with metalinguistic notation	306
	Types (Explaining foregoing)	311
	Levels	312
	Lambda Rules	316
	Exercises XVII 1 (Proofs, Types)	318
XVIII.	Logic and Set Theory	
	1. Logic and Mathematics	319
	2. Russell's Paradox	320
	3. Set Theory	324

INDEX

A
Absorption, 65, 100
Abstraction, 289, Chapter XV
Absurdity, 30
Accuracy, 14
Add, 37, 64
Aliotransitive, 257
Ambiguity, 13
Antecedent, 23
Antisymmetric, 257
Argument (inference with asserted premisses), 8
Argument (to a predicate or function), 122
Arrowdiagrams, 228, Chap. X
Assignment, 121, 167
Axiom, 117
Axiomatic Theory, 117

B
Belief, Degree of, 15-17
Boolean Algebra, 303
Bound, 158
Blind component, 178

C
Categorical Forms, 145
Categorical Syllogism, 145-148
Church, Alonzo, 69
Citation, 19
Citation Number, 19
Clauses, (open and closed), 128, 158-59
Clear Instance, 196
Commutation (of antecedents, 69
Commutativity, 64
Complement, 302
Complete Sentence, 12
Completeness (of a system of logic), 119

Conclusion, 1
Conditional, 44
Conjunction, 41
Consequent, 23
Contradiction, 59
Contraposition, 54, 64
Contrary, 136-138
Correspondence Theory of Truth, 192
Crossout Test, 203

D
Definiens, definiendum, 235
Definition, Chapter XI
Definitional extension, 235
Definitional replacement (DFR) 236
Degree, 124
De Morgan's Laws (Nor and Nand), 54-55
Destructive Dilemma, 64
Determiner, 135
Dilemmas, Simple (Dsimp), Compound (Dcomp, 31, Complex (Dplex), 32
Disjunction (inclusive v, exclusive); 42
Distinct instance, 197
Distributivity, 64
Dominance, 65, 100
Double Negation (N), 24, 64
Drop, 36, 64

E
Elimination (Elim), 22, 64
Eqi, 56, 64
Ego, 56, 64
Equivalence relation, 267
Equivalence Rule, 24
Exportation, 65
Extension of a Predicate, 192, Chapter XVI
Evidence, 5, 15

F
Factor Law, 65
Fif, 45
First Order, 282
Flag Test, 203
Fission-Fusion of Quanti-
  fiers, 182-185
Flagged variable, 173
Function, 273
Functional completeness, 73
Functional relation, 274

H
Hypothetico-Deductive
  Method, 4

I
Identity, Chapter XII
Importation, 65
Induction, 2
Inference, 1
Instance, 173, 196
Internalizing Negations,
  57, 97
Intersection, 302

J
Join, 37

L
Lambda operator, 289,
  Chapter XV 2.
Line Number, 19
Link, 64
Logically determinate
  sentences, 59-60
Logical Truth, Falsity, 60
Loophole, 48, 60, 92-94
Loophole Method, 92-94

M
Material (implication, conditional, equivalence, bicon-
  ditional), 44-45

Metatheory, 220
Middle Term, 146
Mif, 55
Model, 121
Modus Ponens (MP), 22, 64
Modus Tollens (MT), 23, 64

N
Name, 122
Nand, 55, 64
Negation, 6, 40
Nif, 55
Nor, 55, 64
Null class, 302
Numerical Quantifier, 252

O
One-many, one-one, 256
Open clause (in inferences,
  principles), 128
Orderings, 256, 259, Chapter XIII

P
Partial order, Chapter XIII, 3
Particular Affirmative (I),
  Negative (o) Sentence, 135-136
Passage, rules or laws of, 181
Peirce's Arrow (Charles Peirce),
  69
Peirce's law, 65
Portation, 65
Predicate, 122, 146
Predicate variable, 282, Chapter XV
Premiss, I
Premiss Number, 19-20
Prenex Form, 187
Principle (of inference), 61-63
Probability, degree of, 4
Proof, 181

Q
Quantifier shifting, 178
Quine, Willard Van Orman, 173
Q-languages and logic, 157,
  chapters VI-X
QI languages and logic, 248, Chapt. XII

Q (cont.)
QIF languages, 274, Chapter XIV

R
Rank order, 264
Redundancy, 64
Reflexivity, 229
Relettering Bound Variables
   (RBV), 188, 223

S
Scope, 158
Self distribution (of   ), 65
Semantical (concept of)
   logical implication, 103-104
Semiflagged Variable, 202
Sequence, 262
Sheffer Stroke (Henry Sheffer),
   69
Simplification, 96-101
Soundness (of a system of
   logic), 119
Square of Opposition, 136
Step, 18, 22
Stepwise valid, 210
Subject, 146
Sum law, 65
Supposition, 28-31
Suppositions, Rule of (S), 28
Supposition Discharged as
   Qualification (SQ), 28;
   as Absurd (SA), 30
Sweet, H., 285
Symmetry, 228
Syntactical (Proof-Theoretic)
   derivability, 103-104
Syntax (for a Q-language), 157

T
Tautology, 59
Term, 158, 274
Three-two rules, 99, 100
Transitional UG, 174
Transitivity, 228
Truth, falsity, 5, 192

Truth function, 40
Truth table, 48
Truth value, 40
Type, 305, 311, Chapter XVII

U
Union, 302
Universal Affirmative (A),
   Negative (E), Sentences,
   135-137
Universal Class, 302
Universe of Discourse, 129

V
Vacuous quantification, 179
Vagueness, 13
Valid, 2, 7, 48-51
Venn diagrams, 143-148
Venn, John, 145

SYMBOLS (of more than passing interest): First appearance

∕	2	⟺	53	λ	289
⇒	8	↓	69	∩	302
∼	22	∣	69	∪	302
∨	22	⊢	104	−	302
⊃	23	⊬	104	⊂	302
·	34	⋁	128	⋎	302
≡	34	∃	128	∧	302
≢	42	⇌	242	∈	325

ABOUT THE AUTHOR

Herbert Gaylord Bohnert learned logic from Rudolf Carnap while a graduate student in physics at the University of Chicago. He completed his doctorate in philosophy under Nelson Goodman at the University of Pennsylvania. After teaching at Queens College (NY) and Swarthmore, he became engaged in various aspects of the use and design of computers and computer languages (Litton Industries, Planning Research Corporation), eventually spending seven years with IBM (Research Center). In 1968, he returned to teaching at Michigan State University where he has been a professor of philosophy since 1969. His career includes stints at the RAND Corporation and, as Fulbright lecturer, at the National University of Argentina (Cuyo). He is the author of articles on the logic of commands, utility, analyticity, logicism, Ramsey sentences, and the mind-body problem.